FEAR CASE

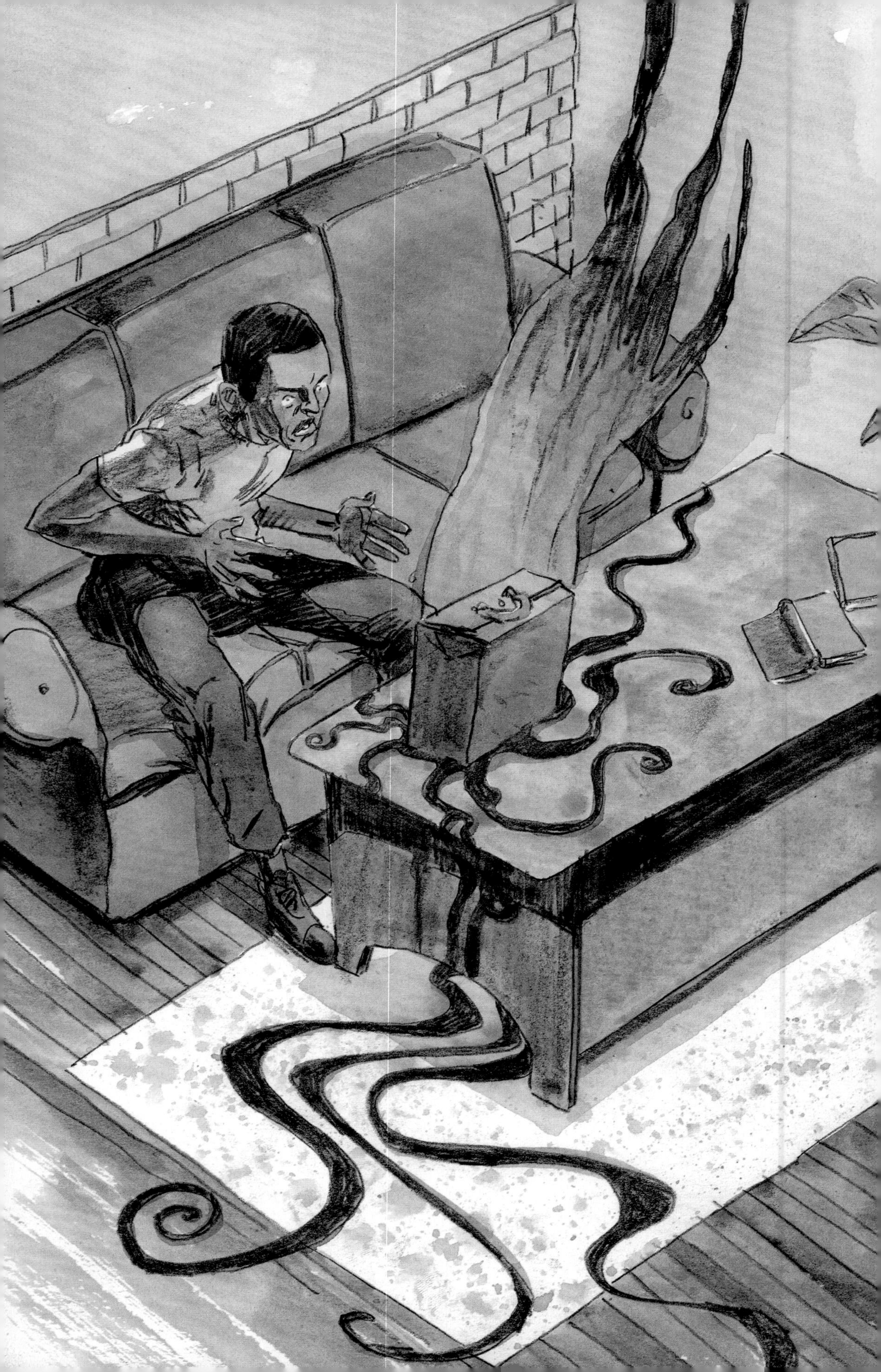

FEAR CASE

Writer
MATT KINDT
Art
TYLER JENKINS
Color Art
HILARY JENKINS
Letters
JIM CAMPBELL
Cover Artist
TYLER JENKINS
with **HILARY JENKINS**

FEAR CASE created by
MATT KINDT
and **TYLER JENKINS**

DARK HORSE BOOKS

President & Publisher
MIKE RICHARDSON

Editor
DANIEL CHABON

Assistant Editors
CHUCK HOWITT and **KONNER KNUDSEN**

Designer
PATRICK SATTERFIELD

Digital Art Technician
JOSIE CHRISTENSEN

FEAR CASE

Collects *Fear Case* #1–#4.

Library of Congress Cataloging-in-Publication Data

Names: Kindt, Matt, writer. | Jenkins, Tyler, artist. | Jenkins, Hilary
   (Colorist), colourist.
Title: Fear case / writer, Matt Kindt ; art, Tyler Jenkins ; color art,
   Hilary Jenkins.
Description: First edition. | Milwaukie, OR : Dark Horse Books, 2021. |
   "Fear Case created by Matt Kindt and Tyler Jenkins"
Identifiers: LCCN 2021009705 (print) | LCCN 2021009706 (ebook) | ISBN
   9781506721231 (trade paperback) | ISBN 9781506721248 (ebook)
Subjects: LCSH: Comic books, strips, etc.
Classification: LCC PN6728.F424 K56 2021 (print) | LCC PN6728.F424
   (ebook) | DDC 741.5/973--dc23
LC record available at https://lccn.loc.gov/2021009705
LC ebook record available at https://lccn.loc.gov/2021009706

Published by
DARK HORSE BOOKS
A division of Dark Horse Comics LLC
10956 SE Main Street
Milwaukie, OR 97222

DarkHorse.com

To find a comics shop in your area, visit comicshoplocator.com

First edition: September 2021
Ebook ISBN 978-1-50672-124-8
Trade paperback ISBN 978-1-50672-123-1

10 9 8 7 6 5 4 3 2 1
Printed in China

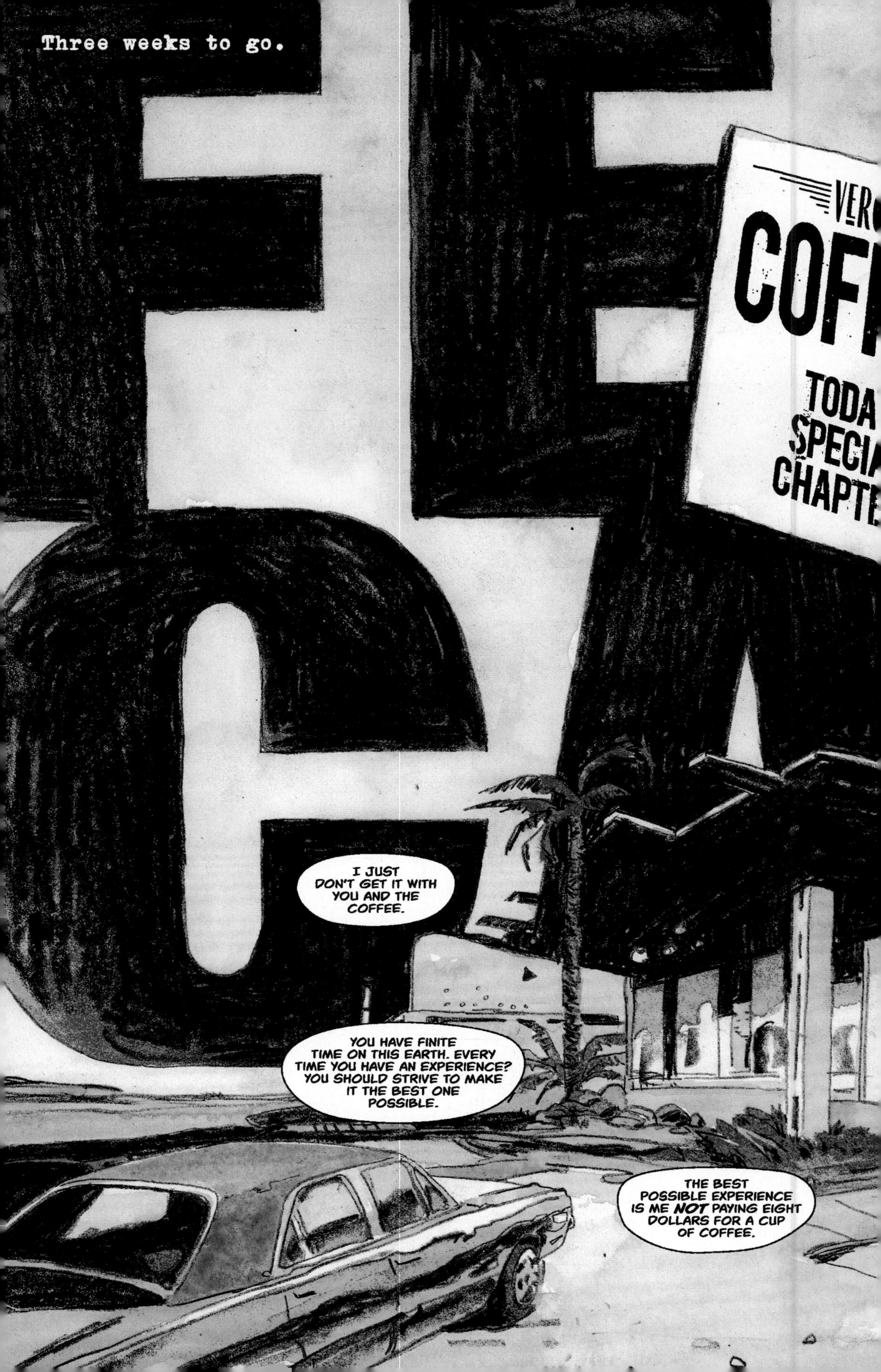
Three weeks to go.
I JUST DON'T GET IT WITH YOU AND THE COFFEE.
YOU HAVE FINITE TIME ON THIS EARTH. EVERY TIME YOU HAVE AN EXPERIENCE? YOU SHOULD STRIVE TO MAKE IT THE BEST ONE POSSIBLE.
THE BEST POSSIBLE EXPERIENCE IS ME *NOT* PAYING EIGHT DOLLARS FOR A CUP OF COFFEE.

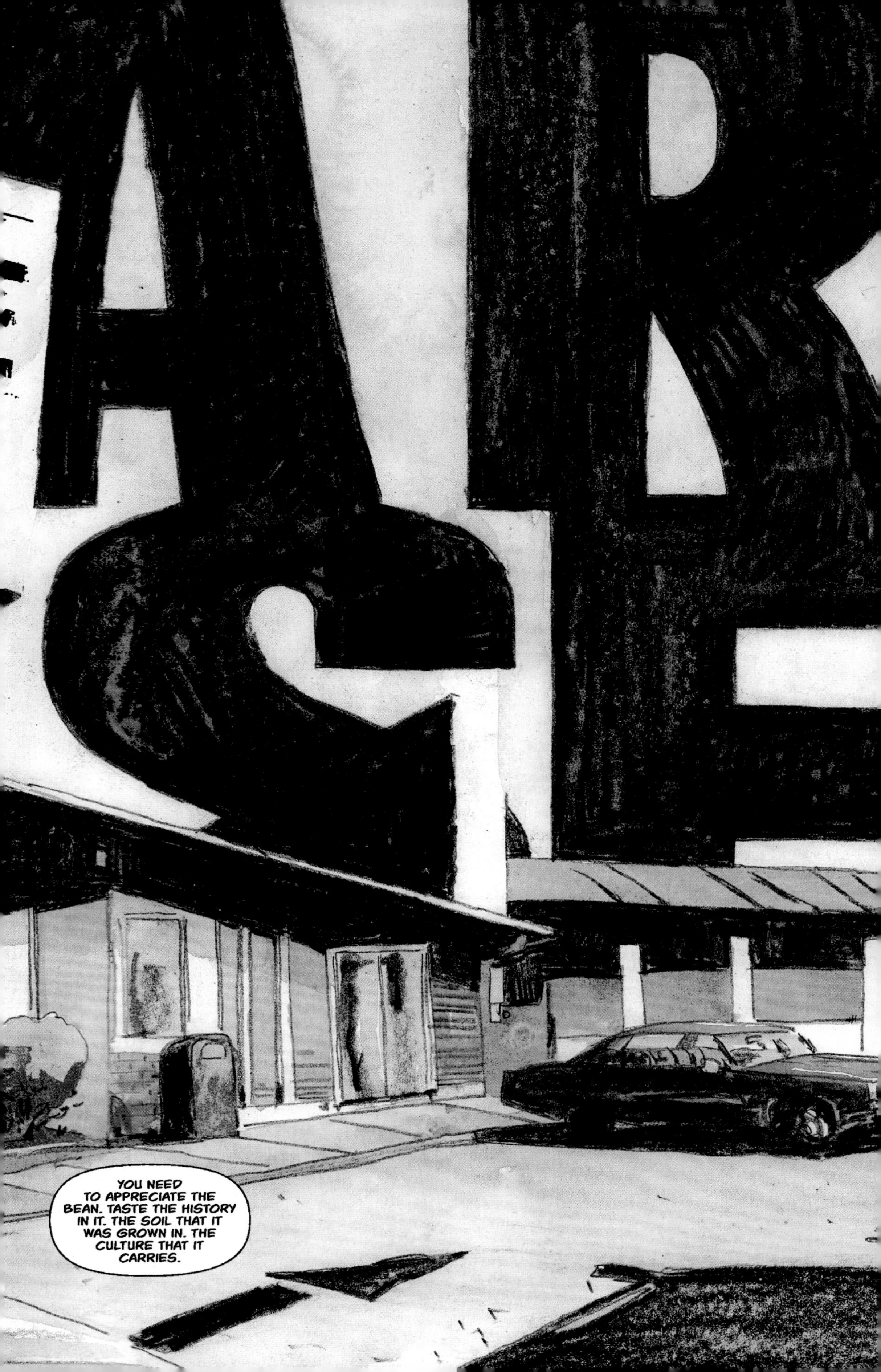
YOU NEED TO APPRECIATE THE BEAN. TASTE THE HISTORY IN IT. THE SOIL THAT IT WAS GROWN IN. THE CULTURE THAT IT CARRIES.

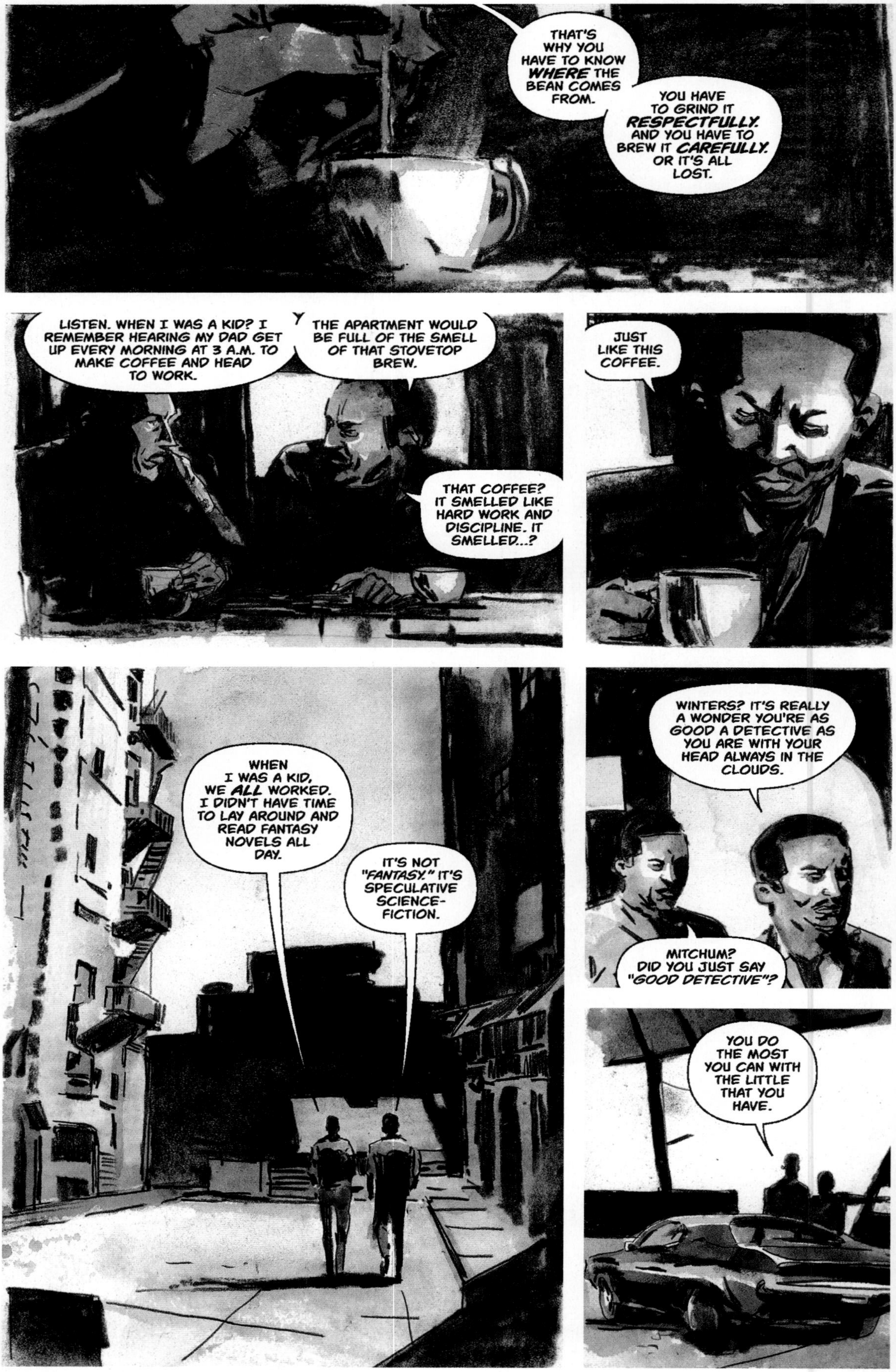
THAT'S WHY YOU HAVE TO KNOW *WHERE* THE BEAN COMES FROM.
YOU HAVE TO GRIND IT *RESPECTFULLY.* AND YOU HAVE TO BREW IT *CAREFULLY.* OR IT'S ALL LOST.
LISTEN. WHEN I WAS A KID? I REMEMBER HEARING MY DAD GET UP EVERY MORNING AT 3 A.M. TO MAKE COFFEE AND HEAD TO WORK.
THE APARTMENT WOULD BE FULL OF THE SMELL OF THAT STOVETOP BREW.
THAT COFFEE? IT SMELLED LIKE HARD WORK AND DISCIPLINE. IT SMELLED...?
JUST LIKE THIS COFFEE.
WHEN I WAS A KID, WE *ALL* WORKED. I DIDN'T HAVE TIME TO LAY AROUND AND READ FANTASY NOVELS ALL DAY.
IT'S NOT *"FANTASY."* IT'S SPECULATIVE SCIENCE-FICTION.
WINTERS? IT'S REALLY A WONDER YOU'RE AS GOOD A DETECTIVE AS YOU ARE WITH YOUR HEAD ALWAYS IN THE CLOUDS.
MITCHUM? DID YOU JUST SAY *"GOOD DETECTIVE"*?
YOU DO THE MOST YOU CAN WITH THE LITTLE THAT YOU HAVE.

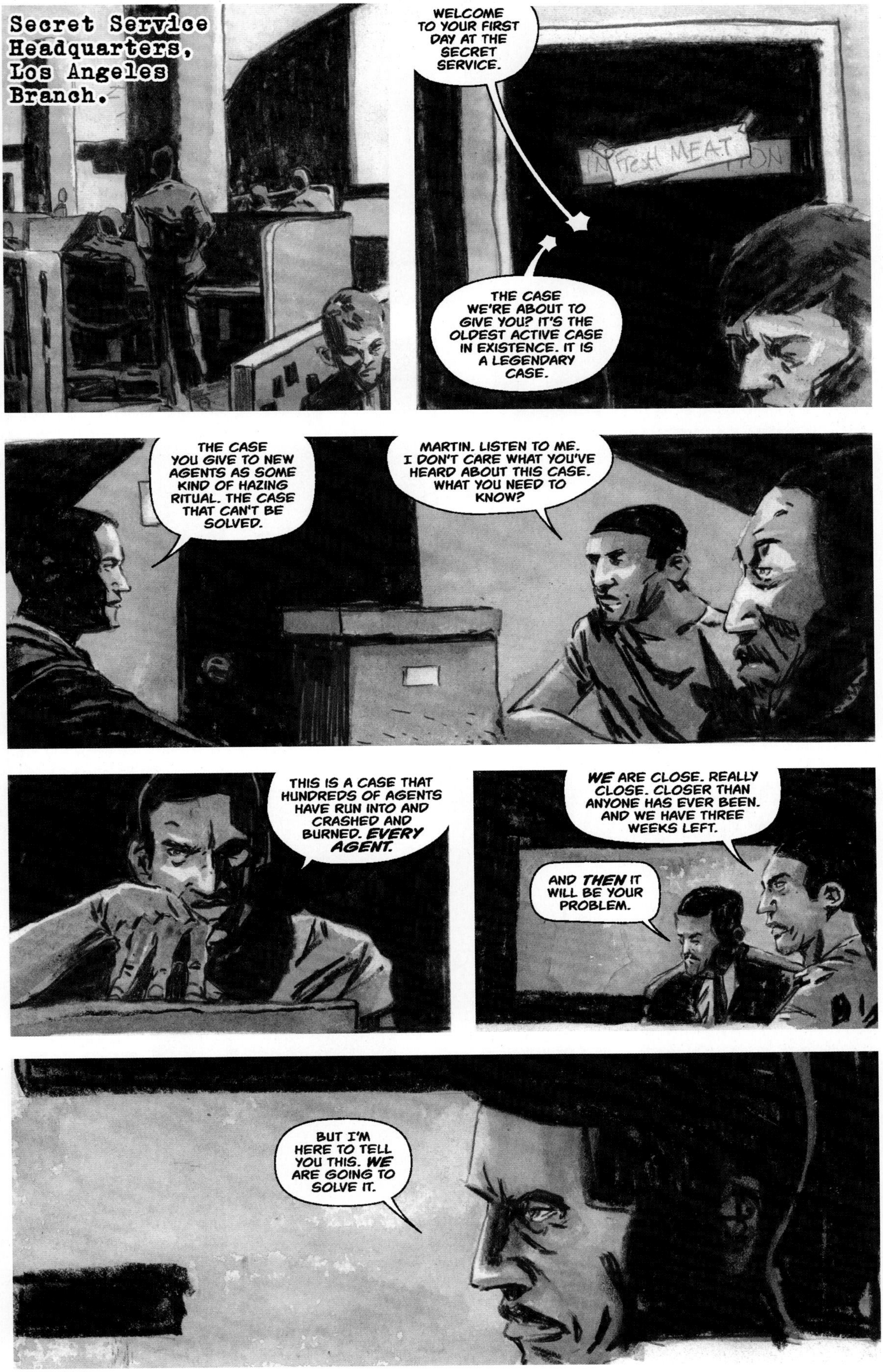
Secret Service Headquarters, Los Angeles Branch.
WELCOME TO YOUR FIRST DAY AT THE SECRET SERVICE.
Fresh MEAT
THE CASE WE'RE ABOUT TO GIVE YOU? IT'S THE OLDEST ACTIVE CASE IN EXISTENCE. IT IS A LEGENDARY CASE.
THE CASE YOU GIVE TO NEW AGENTS AS SOME KIND OF HAZING RITUAL. THE CASE THAT CAN'T BE SOLVED.
MARTIN. LISTEN TO ME. I DON'T CARE WHAT YOU'VE HEARD ABOUT THIS CASE. WHAT YOU NEED TO KNOW?
THIS IS A CASE THAT HUNDREDS OF AGENTS HAVE RUN INTO AND CRASHED AND BURNED. *EVERY AGENT.*
WE ARE CLOSE. REALLY CLOSE. CLOSER THAN ANYONE HAS EVER BEEN. AND WE HAVE THREE WEEKS LEFT.
AND *THEN* IT WILL BE YOUR PROBLEM.
BUT I'M HERE TO TELL YOU THIS. *WE* ARE GOING TO SOLVE IT.

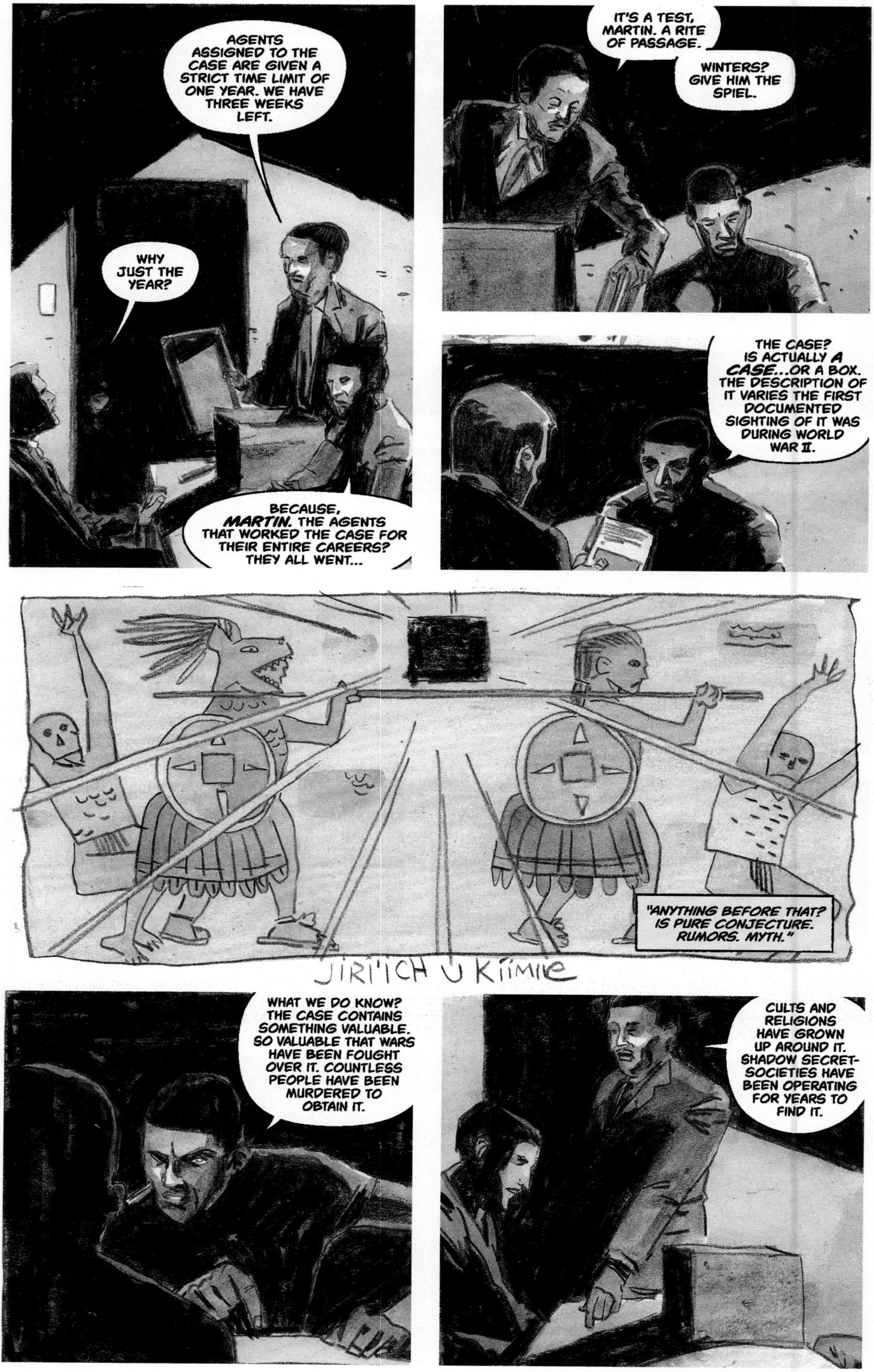
AGENTS ASSIGNED TO THE CASE ARE GIVEN A STRICT TIME LIMIT OF ONE YEAR. WE HAVE THREE WEEKS LEFT.
WHY JUST THE YEAR?
BECAUSE, MARTIN. THE AGENTS THAT WORKED THE CASE FOR THEIR ENTIRE CAREERS? THEY ALL WENT...
IT'S A TEST, MARTIN. A RITE OF PASSAGE.
WINTERS? GIVE HIM THE SPIEL.
THE CASE? IS ACTUALLY A CASE...OR A BOX. THE DESCRIPTION OF IT VARIES THE FIRST DOCUMENTED SIGHTING OF IT WAS DURING WORLD WAR II.
"ANYTHING BEFORE THAT? IS PURE CONJECTURE. RUMORS. MYTH."
JIRI'ICH U KIIMIE
WHAT WE DO KNOW? THE CASE CONTAINS SOMETHING VALUABLE. SO VALUABLE THAT WARS HAVE BEEN FOUGHT OVER IT. COUNTLESS PEOPLE HAVE BEEN MURDERED TO OBTAIN IT.
CULTS AND RELIGIONS HAVE GROWN UP AROUND IT. SHADOW SECRET-SOCIETIES HAVE BEEN OPERATING FOR YEARS TO FIND IT.

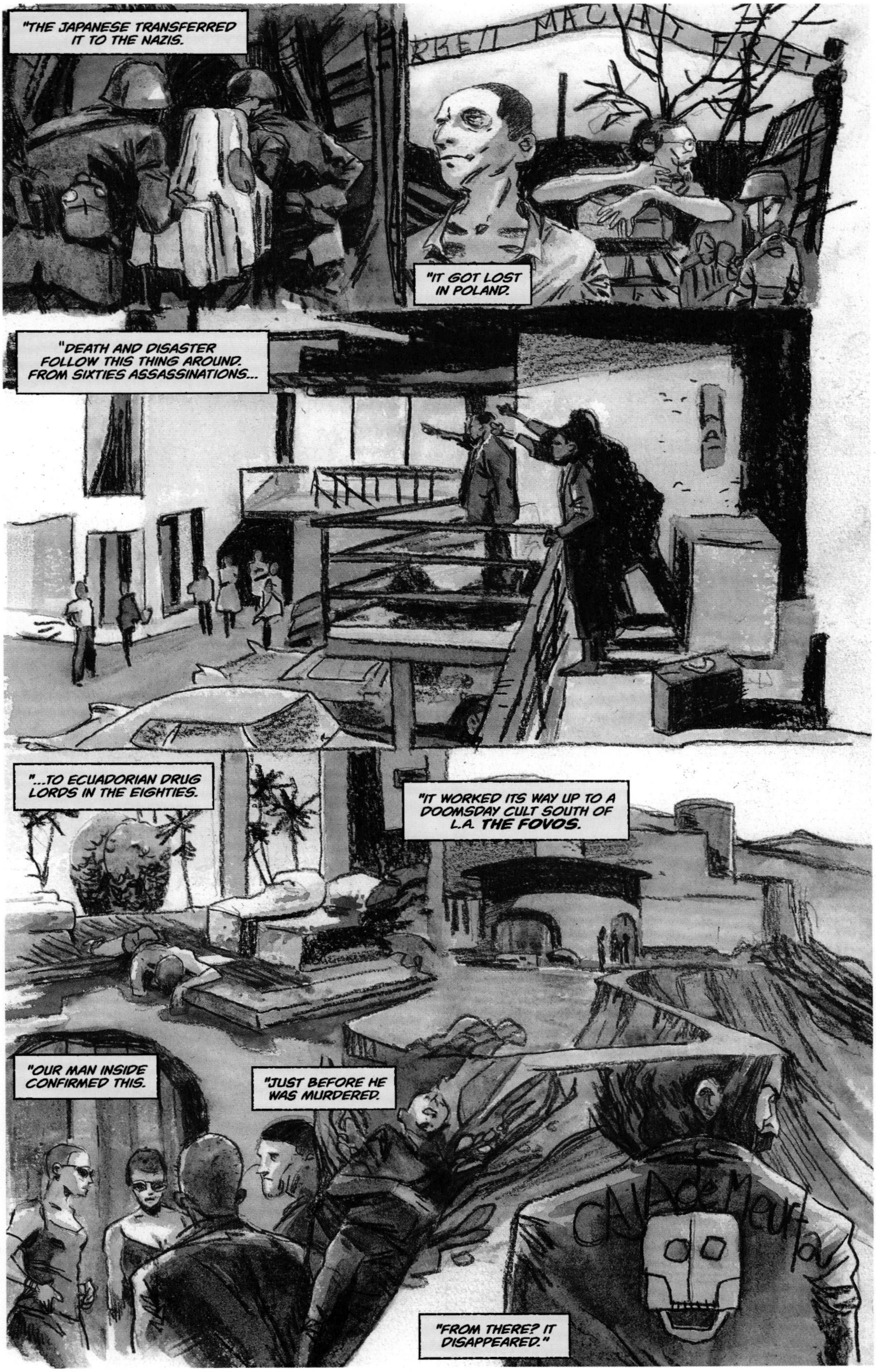
"THE JAPANESE TRANSFERRED IT TO THE NAZIS.
"IT GOT LOST IN POLAND.
"DEATH AND DISASTER FOLLOW THIS THING AROUND. FROM SIXTIES ASSASSINATIONS...
"...TO ECUADORIAN DRUG LORDS IN THE EIGHTIES.
"IT WORKED ITS WAY UP TO A DOOMSDAY CULT SOUTH OF L.A. THE FOVOS.
"OUR MAN INSIDE CONFIRMED THIS.
"JUST BEFORE HE WAS MURDERED.
"FROM THERE? IT DISAPPEARED."

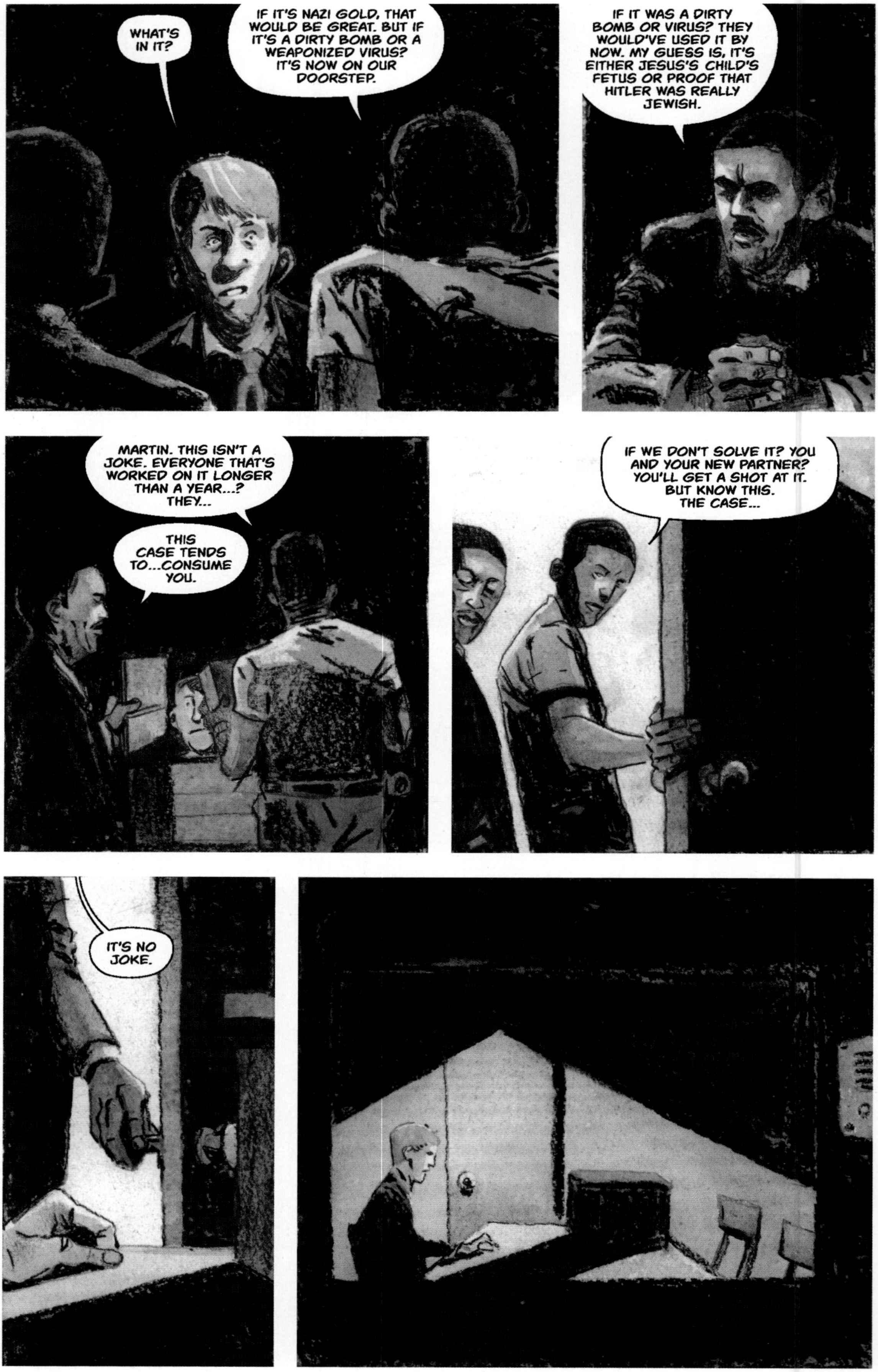
WHAT'S IN IT?
IF IT'S NAZI GOLD, THAT WOULD BE GREAT. BUT IF IT'S A DIRTY BOMB OR A WEAPONIZED VIRUS? IT'S NOW ON OUR DOORSTEP.
IF IT WAS A DIRTY BOMB OR VIRUS? THEY WOULD'VE USED IT BY NOW. MY GUESS IS, IT'S EITHER JESUS'S CHILD'S FETUS OR PROOF THAT HITLER WAS REALLY JEWISH.
MARTIN. THIS ISN'T A JOKE. EVERYONE THAT'S WORKED ON IT LONGER THAN A YEAR...? THEY...
THIS CASE TENDS TO...CONSUME YOU.
IF WE DON'T SOLVE IT? YOU AND YOUR NEW PARTNER? YOU'LL GET A SHOT AT IT. BUT KNOW THIS. THE CASE...
IT'S NO JOKE.

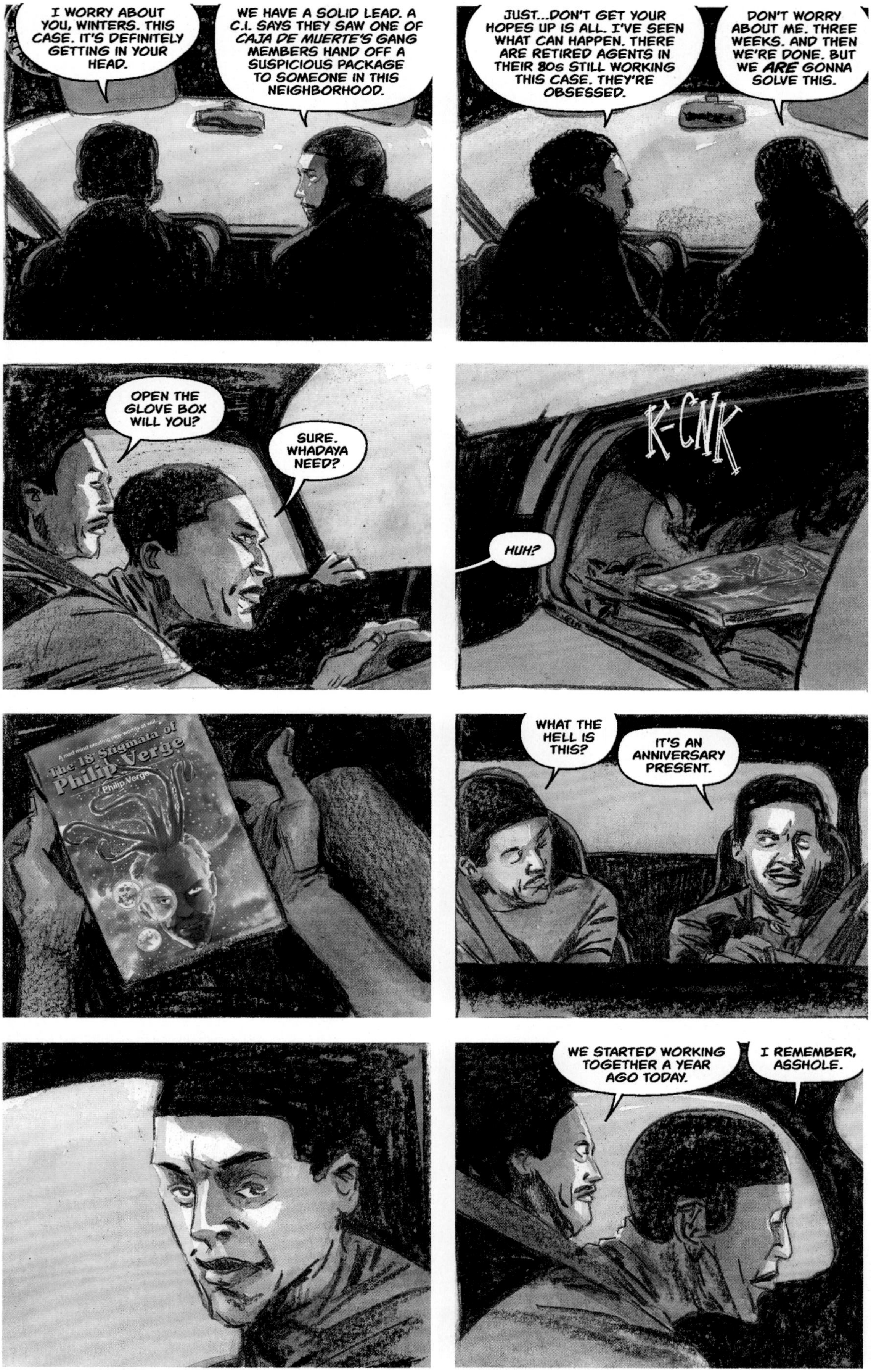
I WORRY ABOUT YOU, WINTERS. THIS CASE. IT'S DEFINITELY GETTING IN YOUR HEAD.
WE HAVE A SOLID LEAD. A C.I. SAYS THEY SAW ONE OF *CAJA DE MUERTE'S* GANG MEMBERS HAND OFF A SUSPICIOUS PACKAGE TO SOMEONE IN THIS NEIGHBORHOOD.
JUST...DON'T GET YOUR HOPES UP IS ALL. I'VE SEEN WHAT CAN HAPPEN. THERE ARE RETIRED AGENTS IN THEIR 80s STILL WORKING THIS CASE. THEY'RE OBSESSED.
DON'T WORRY ABOUT ME. THREE WEEKS. AND THEN WE'RE DONE. BUT WE ***ARE*** GONNA SOLVE THIS.
OPEN THE GLOVE BOX WILL YOU?
SURE. WHADAYA NEED?
K-CNK
HUH?
The 18 Stigmata of Philip Verge
Philip Verge
WHAT THE HELL IS THIS?
IT'S AN ANNIVERSARY PRESENT.
WE STARTED WORKING TOGETHER A YEAR AGO TODAY.
I REMEMBER, ASSHOLE.

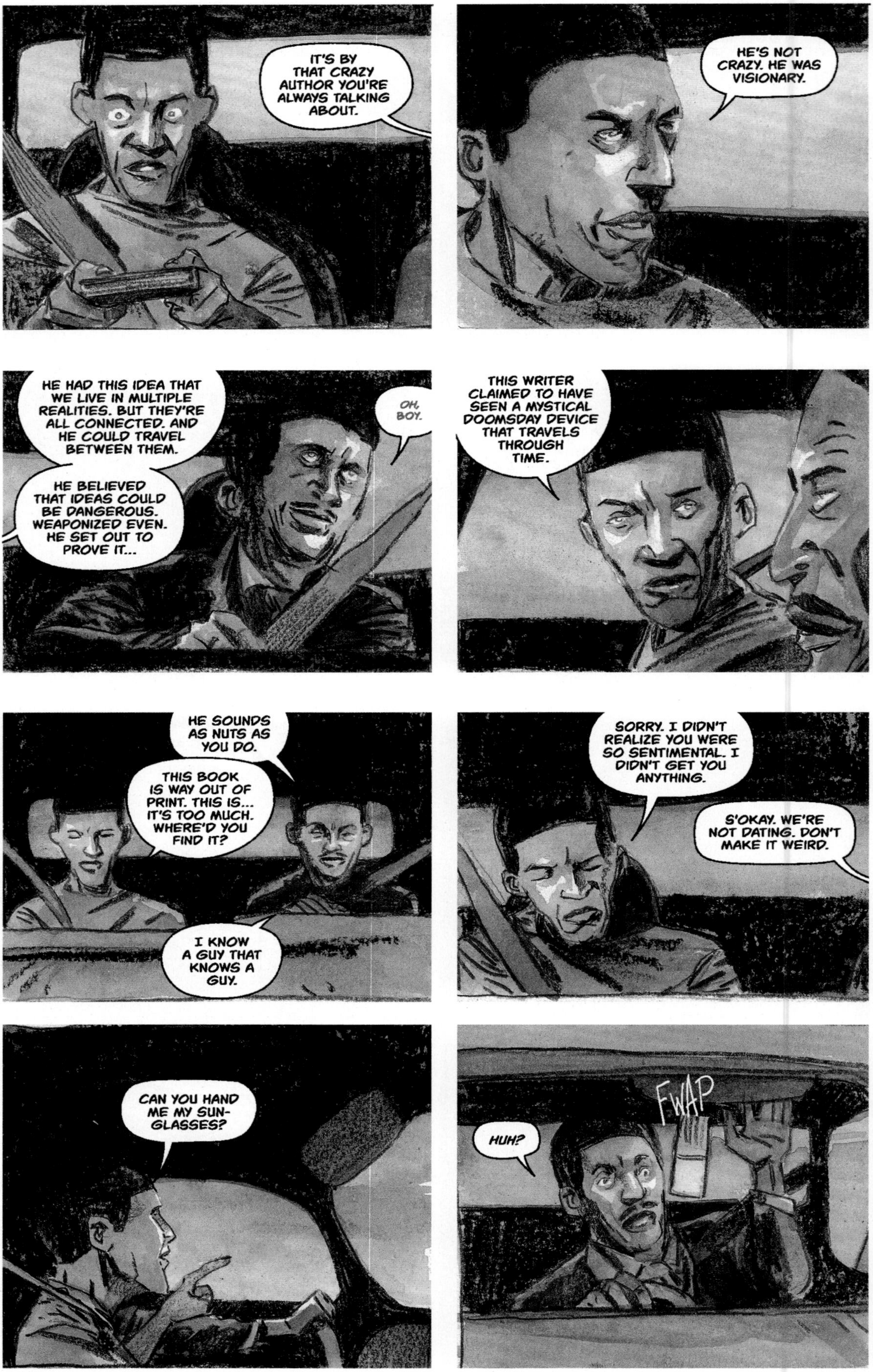
IT'S BY THAT CRAZY AUTHOR YOU'RE ALWAYS TALKING ABOUT.
HE'S NOT CRAZY. HE WAS VISIONARY.
HE HAD THIS IDEA THAT WE LIVE IN MULTIPLE REALITIES. BUT THEY'RE ALL CONNECTED. AND HE COULD TRAVEL BETWEEN THEM.
HE BELIEVED THAT IDEAS COULD BE DANGEROUS. WEAPONIZED EVEN. HE SET OUT TO PROVE IT...
OH, BOY.
THIS WRITER CLAIMED TO HAVE SEEN A MYSTICAL DOOMSDAY DEVICE THAT TRAVELS THROUGH TIME.
HE SOUNDS AS NUTS AS YOU DO.
THIS BOOK IS WAY OUT OF PRINT. THIS IS... IT'S TOO MUCH. WHERE'D YOU FIND IT?
I KNOW A GUY THAT KNOWS A GUY.
SORRY. I DIDN'T REALIZE YOU WERE SO SENTIMENTAL. I DIDN'T GET YOU ANYTHING.
S'OKAY. WE'RE NOT DATING. DON'T MAKE IT WEIRD.
CAN YOU HAND ME MY SUN-GLASSES?
FWAP
HUH?

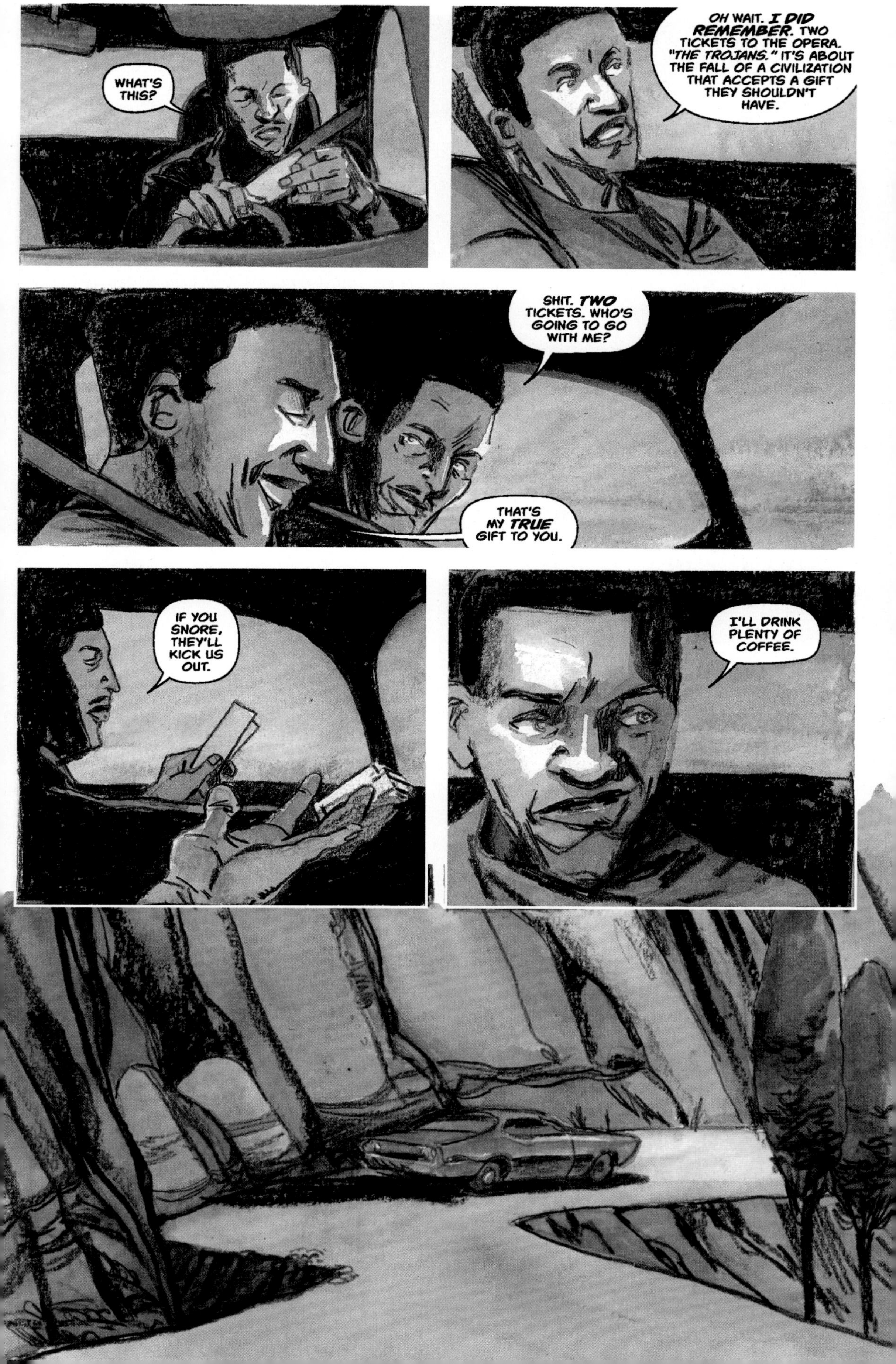
WHAT'S THIS?
OH WAIT. I DID REMEMBER. TWO TICKETS TO THE OPERA. "THE TROJANS." IT'S ABOUT THE FALL OF A CIVILIZATION THAT ACCEPTS A GIFT THEY SHOULDN'T HAVE.
SHIT. TWO TICKETS. WHO'S GOING TO GO WITH ME?
THAT'S MY TRUE GIFT TO YOU.
IF YOU SNORE, THEY'LL KICK US OUT.
I'LL DRINK PLENTY OF COFFEE.

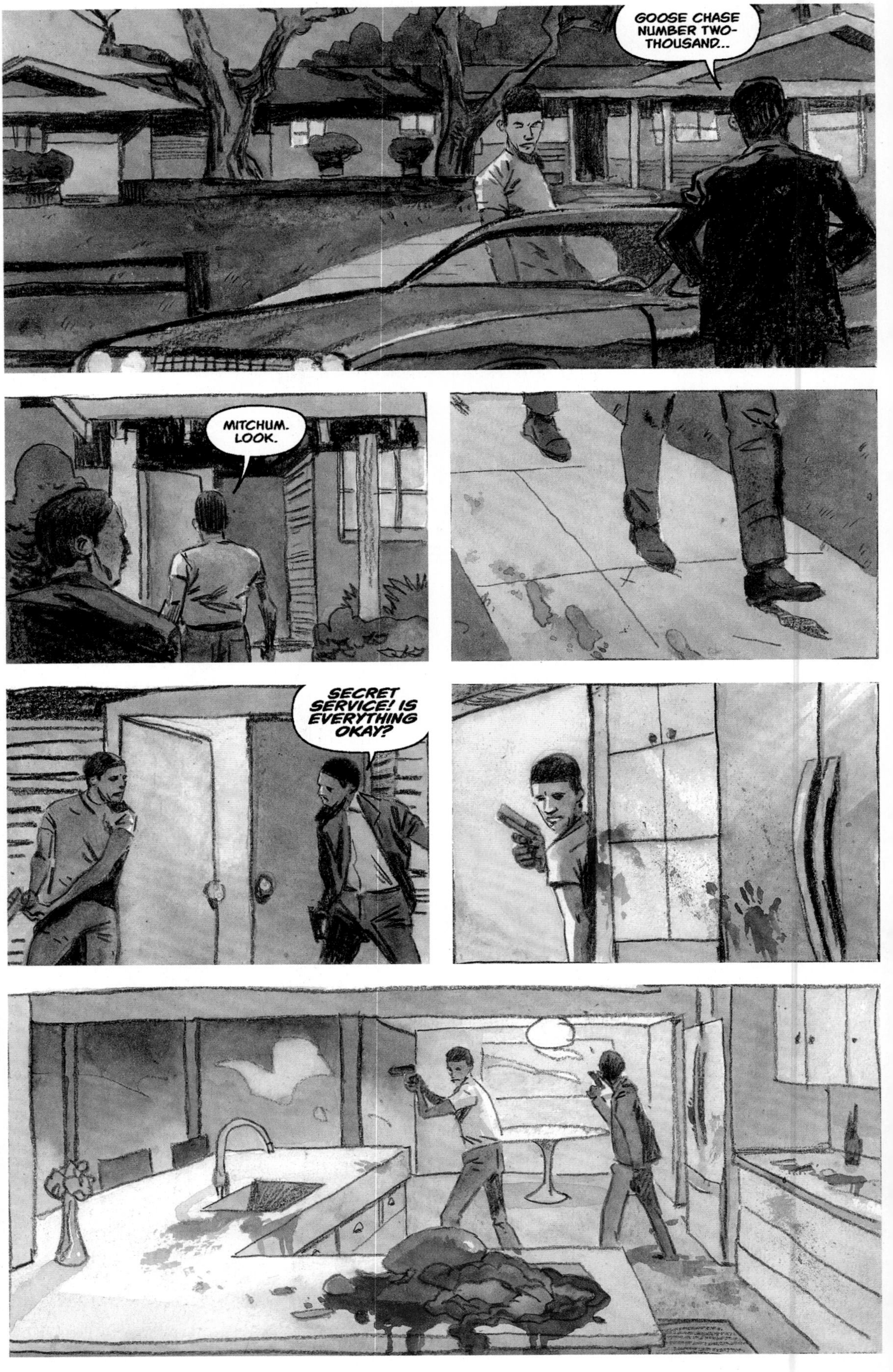
GOOSE CHASE NUMBER TWO-THOUSAND...
MITCHUM. LOOK.
SECRET SERVICE! IS EVERYTHING OKAY?

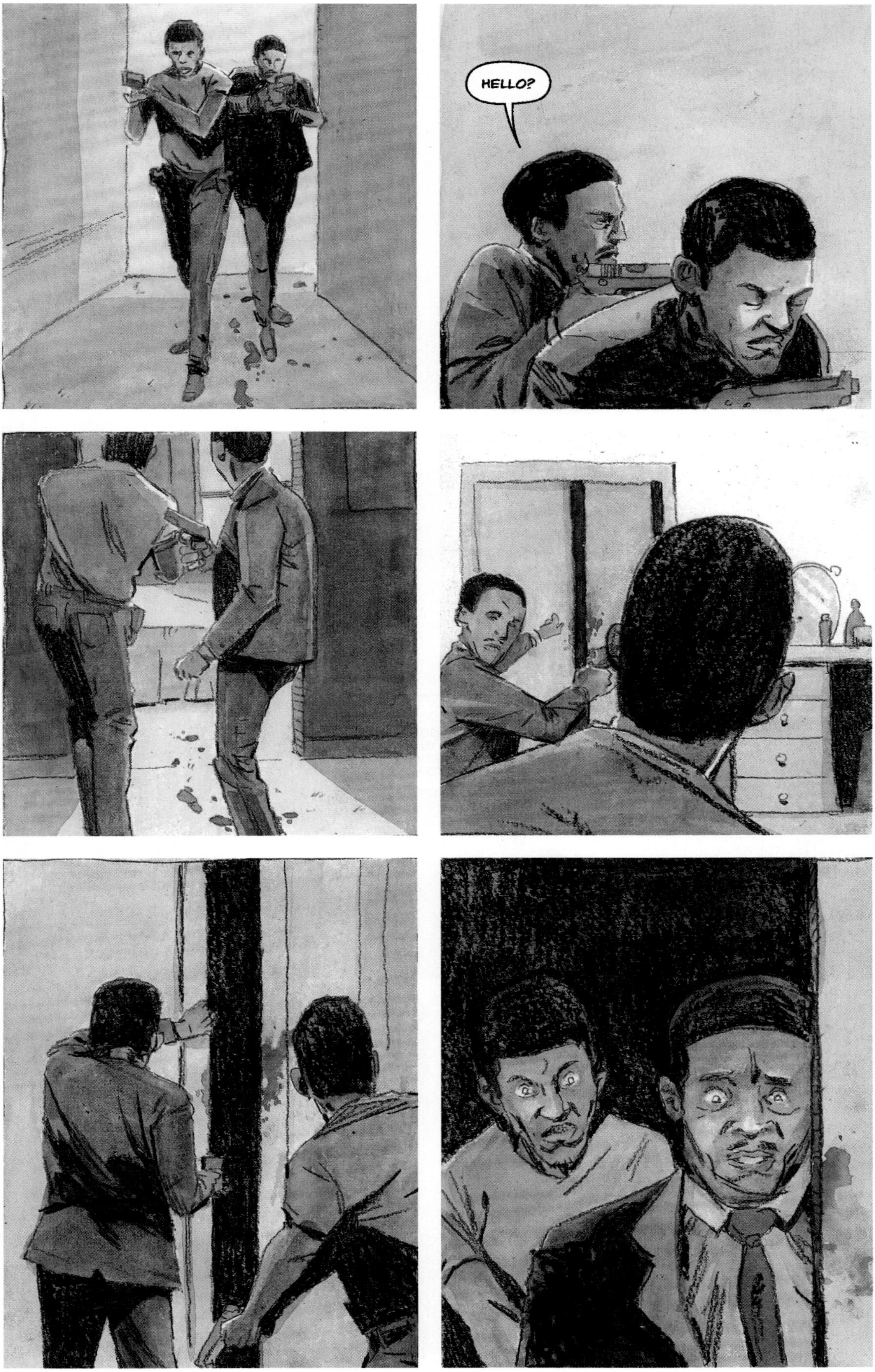
HELLO?

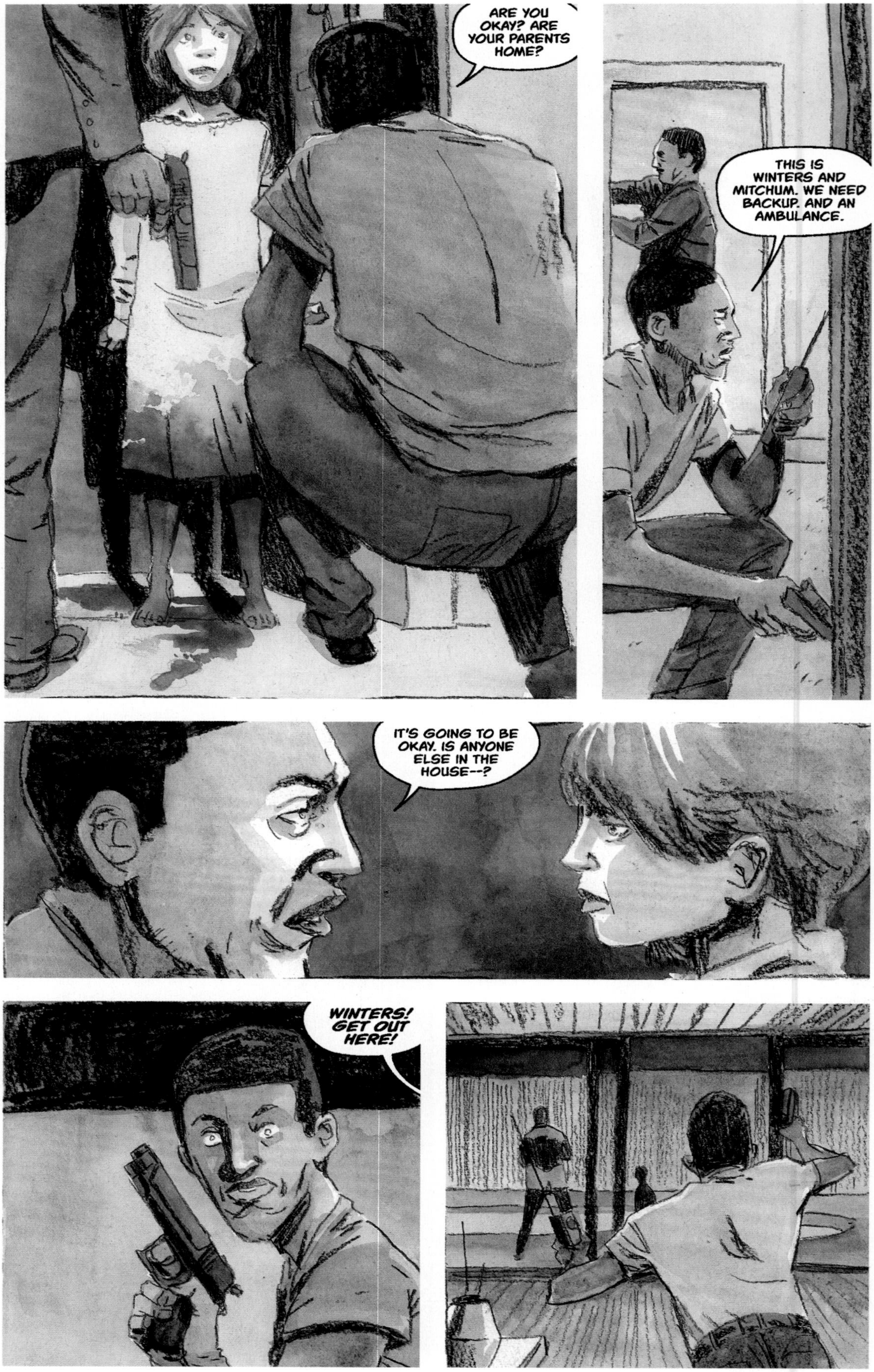
ARE YOU OKAY? ARE YOUR PARENTS HOME?
THIS IS WINTERS AND MITCHUM. WE NEED BACKUP. AND AN AMBULANCE.
IT'S GOING TO BE OKAY. IS ANYONE ELSE IN THE HOUSE--?
WINTERS! GET OUT HERE!

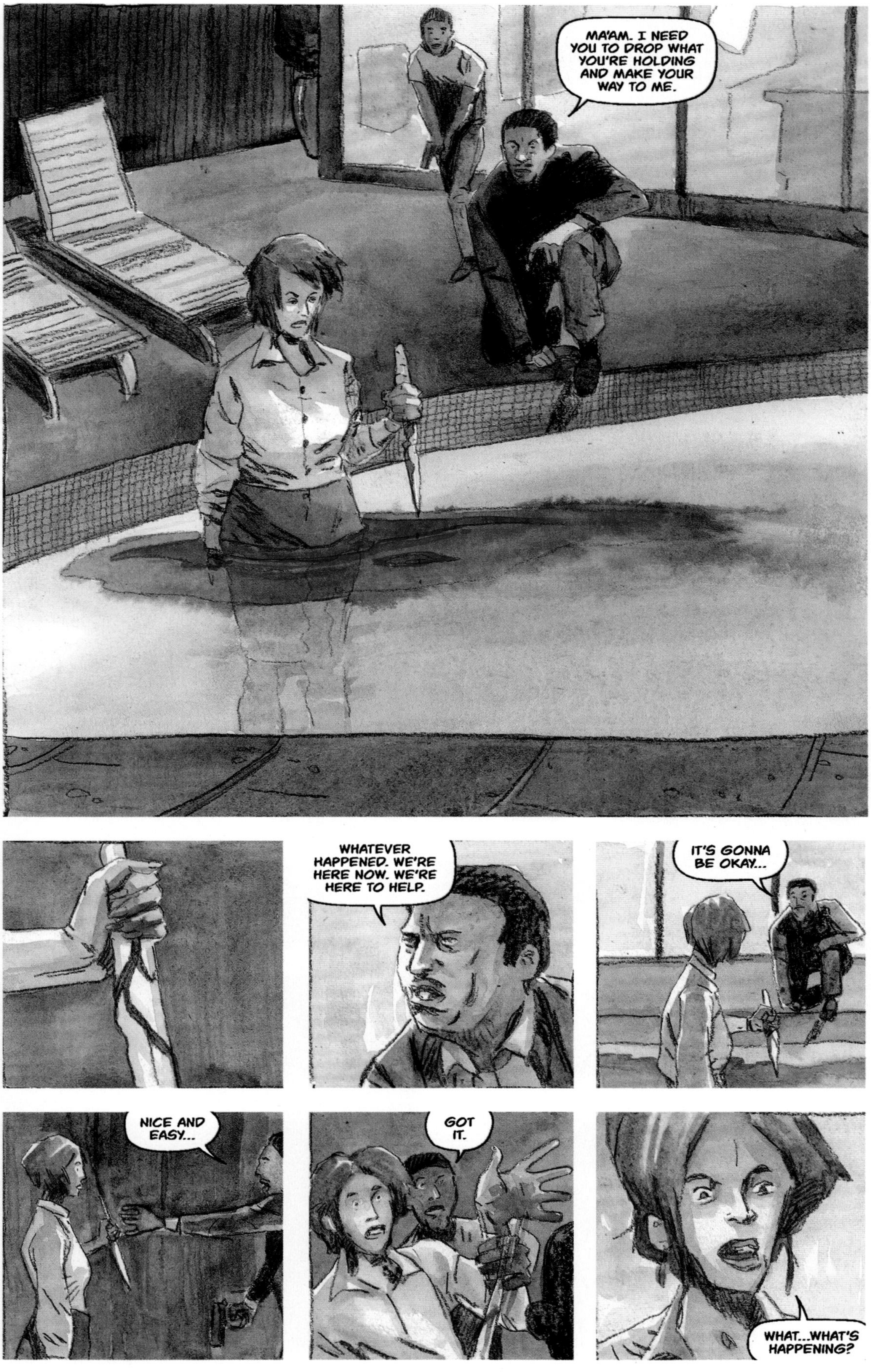
MA'AM. I NEED YOU TO DROP WHAT YOU'RE HOLDING AND MAKE YOUR WAY TO ME.
WHATEVER HAPPENED. WE'RE HERE NOW. WE'RE HERE TO HELP.
IT'S GONNA BE OKAY...
NICE AND EASY...
GOT IT.
WHAT...WHAT'S HAPPENING?

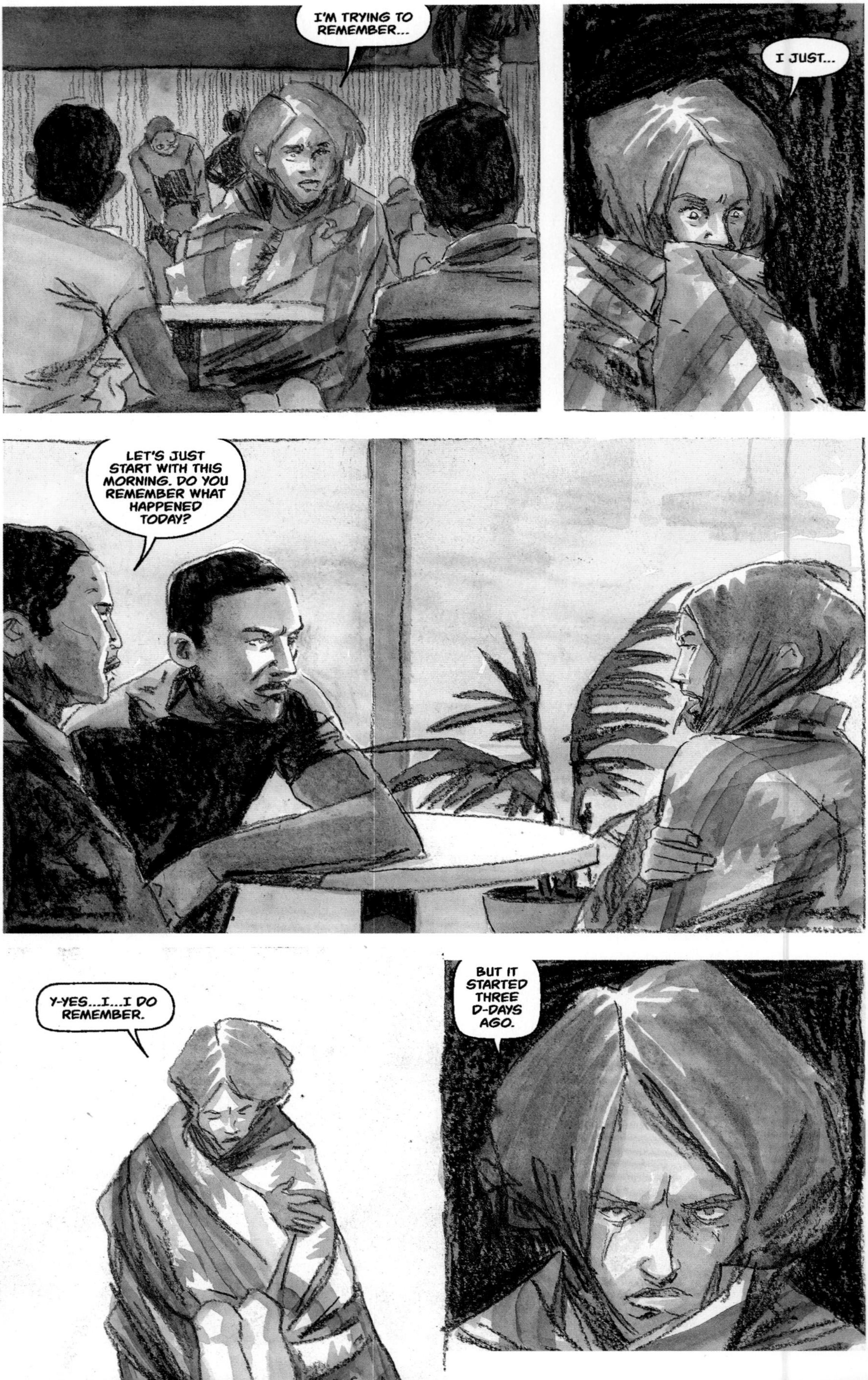
I'M TRYING TO REMEMBER...
I JUST...
LET'S JUST START WITH THIS MORNING. DO YOU REMEMBER WHAT HAPPENED TODAY?
Y-YES...I...I DO REMEMBER.
BUT IT STARTED THREE D-DAYS AGO.

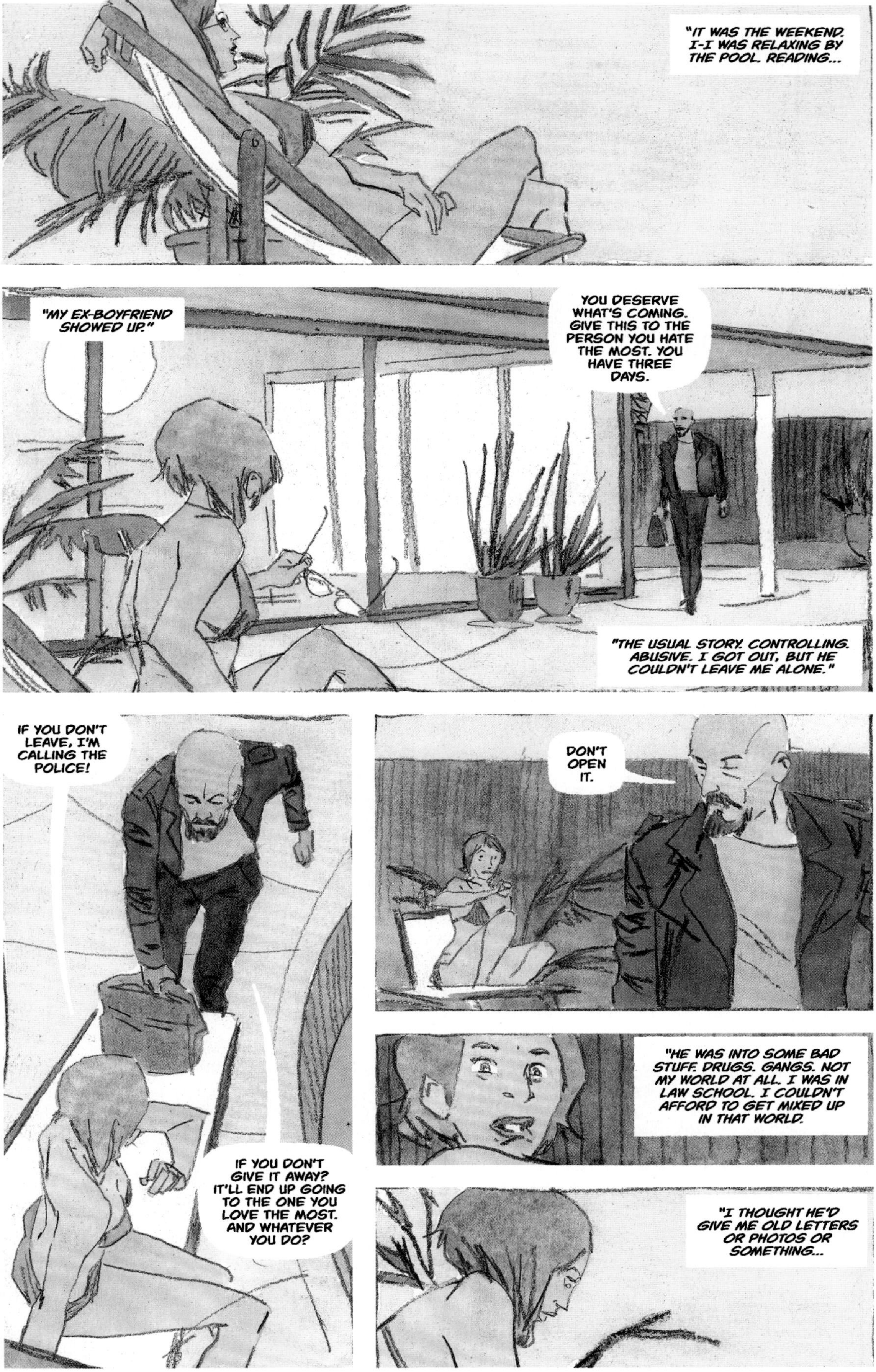
"IT WAS THE WEEKEND. I-I WAS RELAXING BY THE POOL. READING...
"MY EX-BOYFRIEND SHOWED UP."
YOU DESERVE WHAT'S COMING. GIVE THIS TO THE PERSON YOU HATE THE MOST. YOU HAVE THREE DAYS.
"THE USUAL STORY. CONTROLLING. ABUSIVE. I GOT OUT, BUT HE COULDN'T LEAVE ME ALONE."
IF YOU DON'T LEAVE, I'M CALLING THE POLICE!
IF YOU DON'T GIVE IT AWAY? IT'LL END UP GOING TO THE ONE YOU LOVE THE MOST. AND WHATEVER YOU DO?
DON'T OPEN IT.
"HE WAS INTO SOME BAD STUFF. DRUGS. GANGS. NOT MY WORLD AT ALL. I WAS IN LAW SCHOOL. I COULDN'T AFFORD TO GET MIXED UP IN THAT WORLD.
"I THOUGHT HE'D GIVE ME OLD LETTERS OR PHOTOS OR SOMETHING...

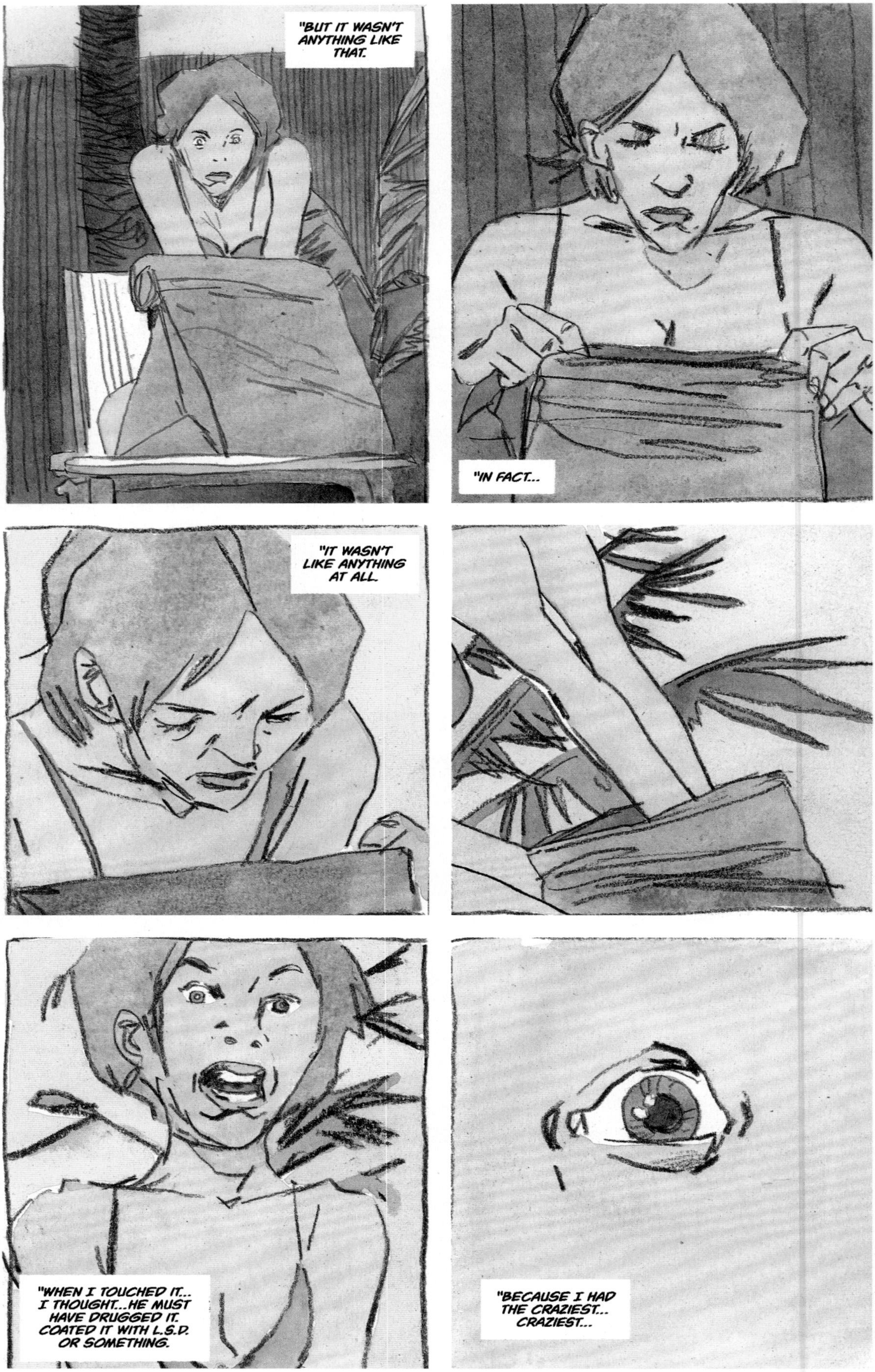
"BUT IT WASN'T ANYTHING LIKE THAT.
"IN FACT...
"IT WASN'T LIKE ANYTHING AT ALL.
"WHEN I TOUCHED IT... I THOUGHT...HE MUST HAVE DRUGGED IT. COATED IT WITH L.S.D. OR SOMETHING.
"BECAUSE I HAD THE CRAZIEST... CRAZIEST...

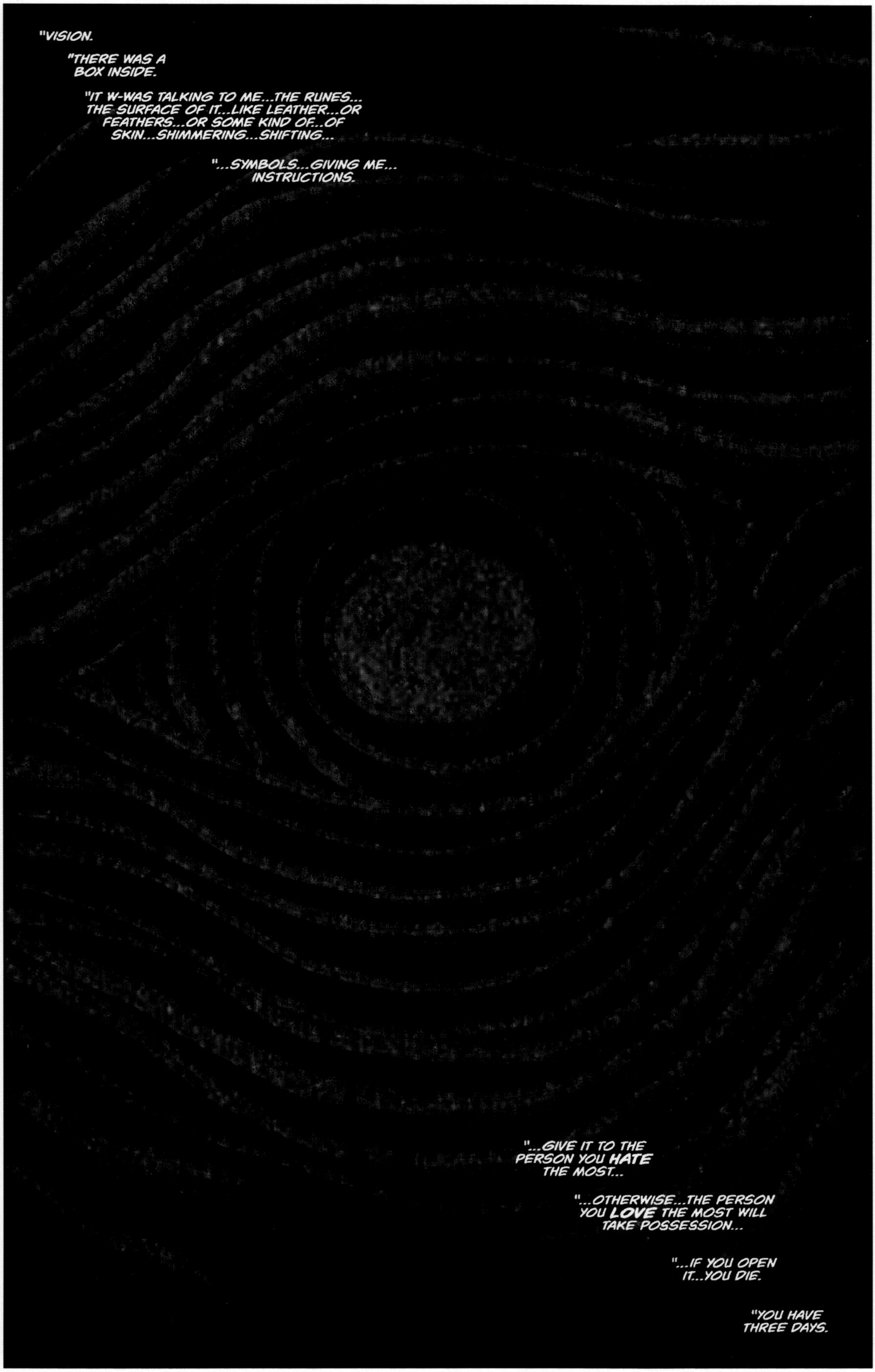
"VISION.
"THERE WAS A BOX INSIDE.
"IT W-WAS TALKING TO ME...THE RUNES... THE SURFACE OF IT...LIKE LEATHER...OR FEATHERS...OR SOME KIND OF...OF SKIN...SHIMMERING...SHIFTING...
"...SYMBOLS...GIVING ME... INSTRUCTIONS.
"...GIVE IT TO THE PERSON YOU **HATE** THE MOST...
"...OTHERWISE...THE PERSON YOU **LOVE** THE MOST WILL TAKE POSSESSION...
"...IF YOU OPEN IT...YOU DIE.
"YOU HAVE THREE DAYS.

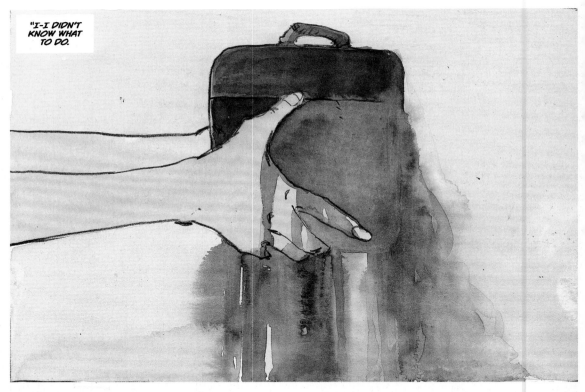

"I-I DIDN'T KNOW WHAT TO DO.

"I-I WAS SCARED. I TRIED TO LAUGH IT OFF.

"I STUCK IT IN THE CLOSET. AFRAID TO TOUCH IT AGAIN. I INTENDED TO CALL THE POLICE.

"B-BUT WORK WAS BUSY. LIFE WAS HECTIC. I JUST HADN'T GOTTEN AROUND TO IT.

"AND THINGS WERE BAD AT HOME.

"MY HUSBAND AND I HAD BEEN FIGHTING FOR MONTHS.

"HE HAD STARTED COMING HOME SMELLING...OF SOMEONE ELSE.

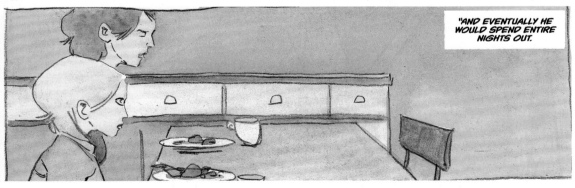

"AND EVENTUALLY HE WOULD SPEND ENTIRE NIGHTS OUT.

"WE HADN'T JUST GROWN APART. HE'D FOUND SOMEONE ELSE. AND HE WAS BEING OBVIOUS ABOUT IT.

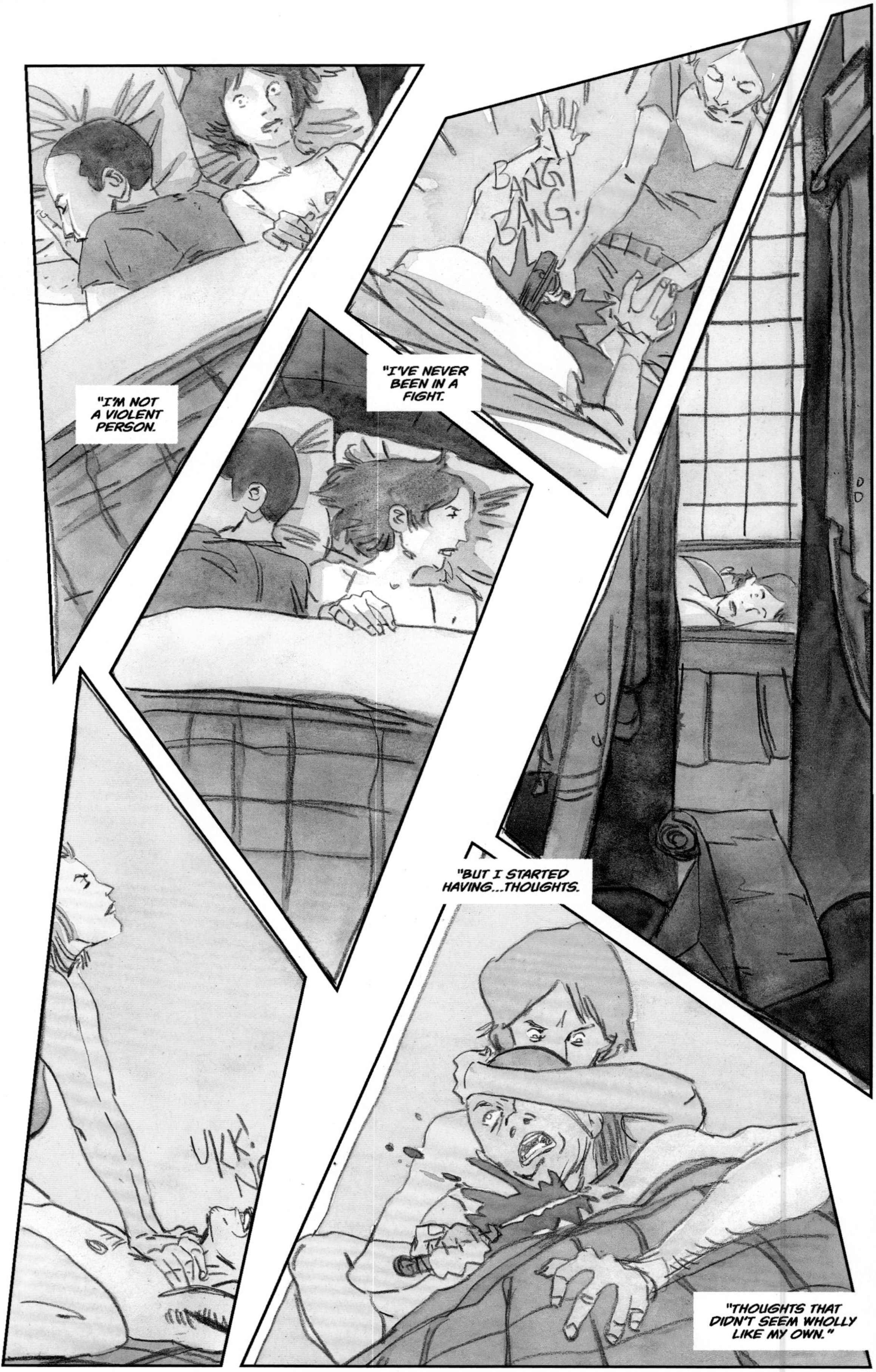
"I'M NOT A VIOLENT PERSON.
"I'VE NEVER BEEN IN A FIGHT.
BANG! BANG.
"BUT I STARTED HAVING...THOUGHTS.
UKK!
"THOUGHTS THAT DIDN'T SEEM WHOLLY LIKE MY OWN."

SORRY FOR THE LATE NIGHTS. OFFICE IS SWAMPED RIGHT NOW.

I'VE GOT SOMETHING FOR YOU.

WHAT IS THIS?

I KNOW WHY YOU COME HOME LATE. I'M NOT AN IDIOT.

LOOK. I'M SORRY. I SHOULD HAVE COME TO YOU SOONER. BUT LET'S MAKE THIS AMICABLE. FOR OUR DAUGHTER.

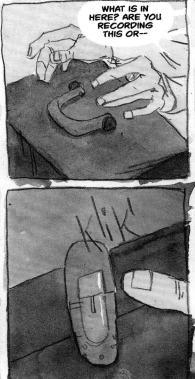

WHAT IS IN HERE? ARE YOU RECORDING THIS OR--

KLIK!

SHOULD WE SEE WHAT'S INSIDE?

"THE SOUND OF GLASS BREAKING..."

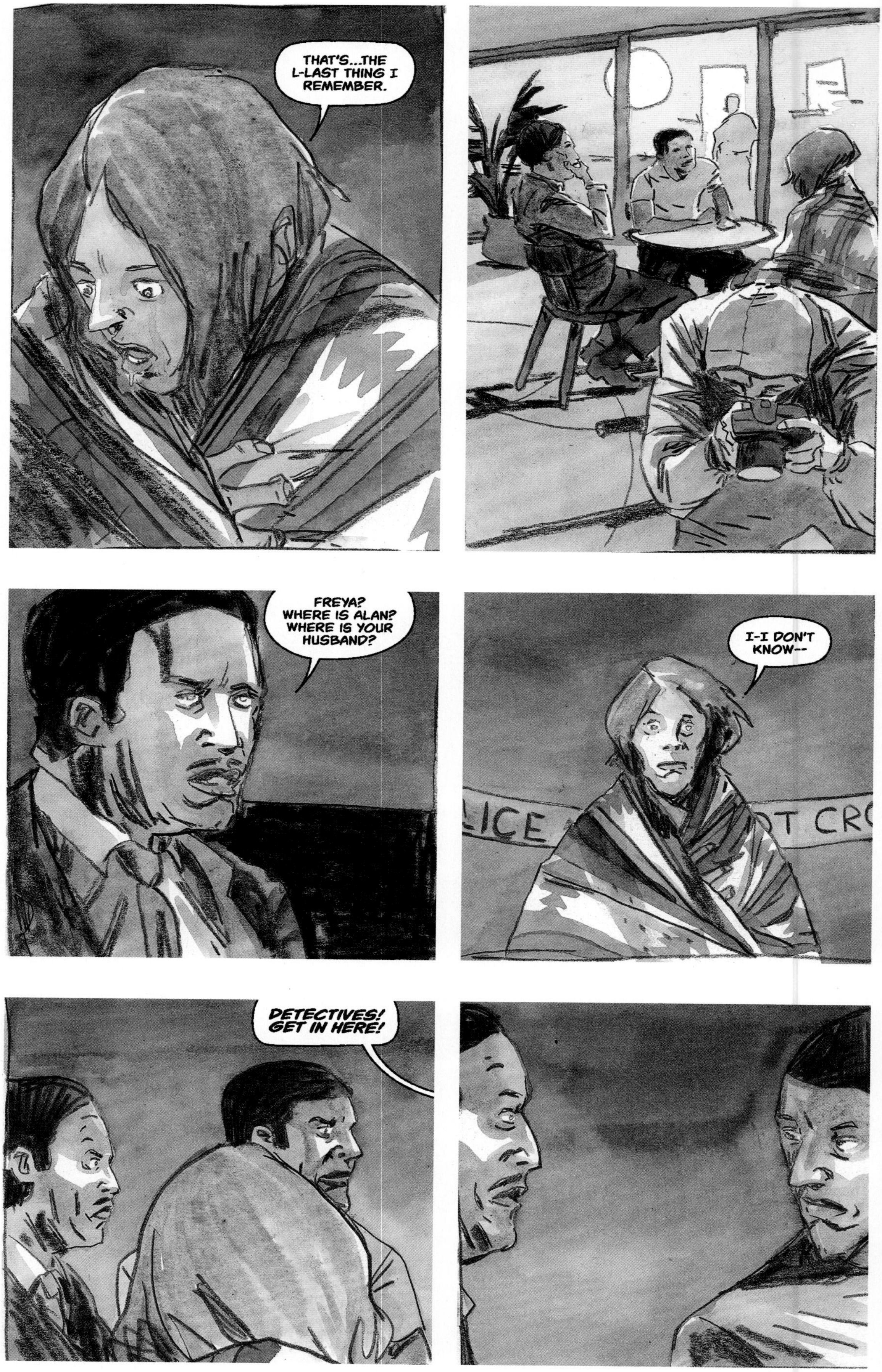
THAT'S...THE L-LAST THING I REMEMBER.
FREYA? WHERE IS ALAN? WHERE IS YOUR HUSBAND?
I-I DON'T KNOW--
DETECTIVES! GET IN HERE!

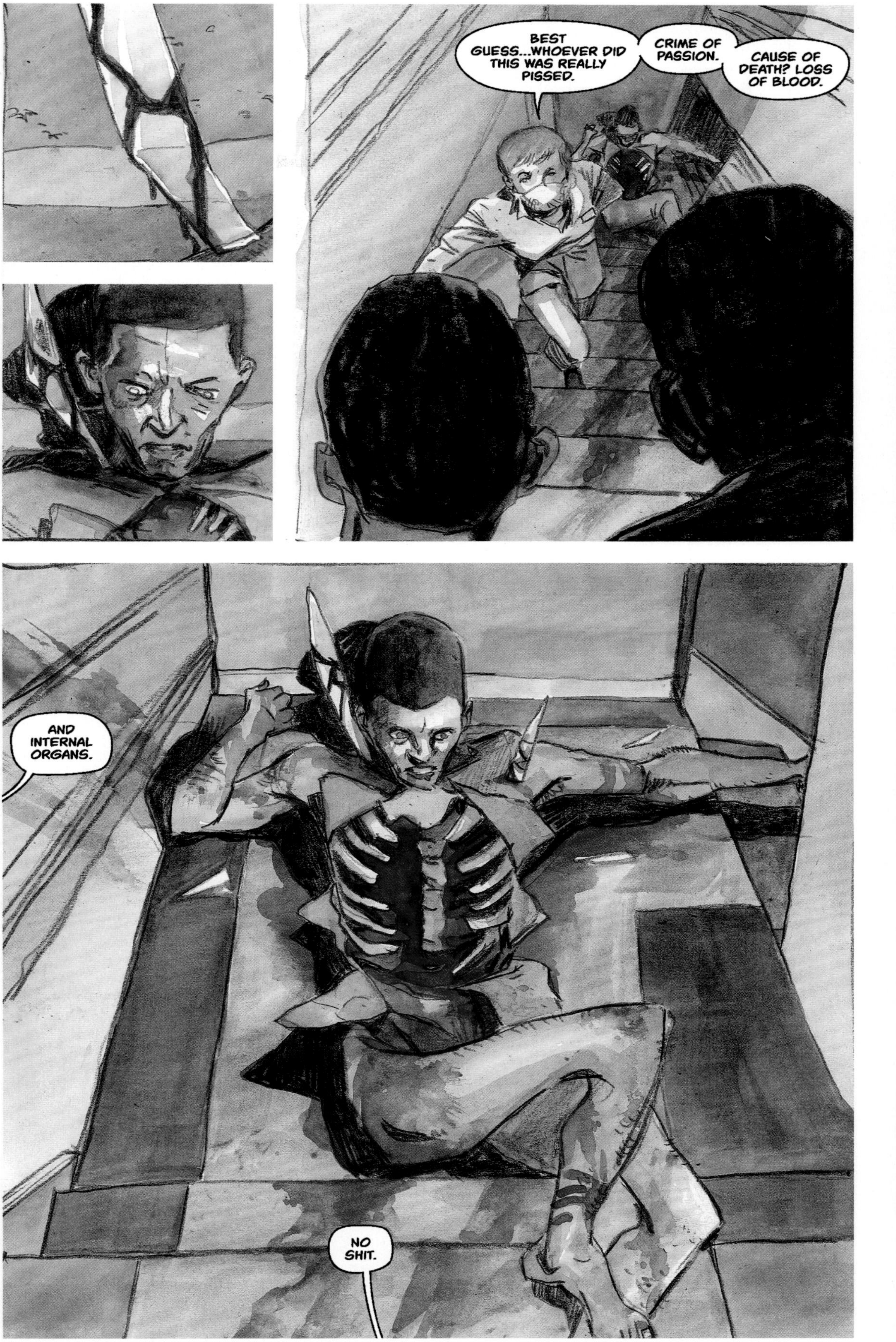
BEST GUESS...WHOEVER DID THIS WAS REALLY PISSED.
CRIME OF PASSION.
CAUSE OF DEATH? LOSS OF BLOOD.
AND INTERNAL ORGANS.
NO SHIT.

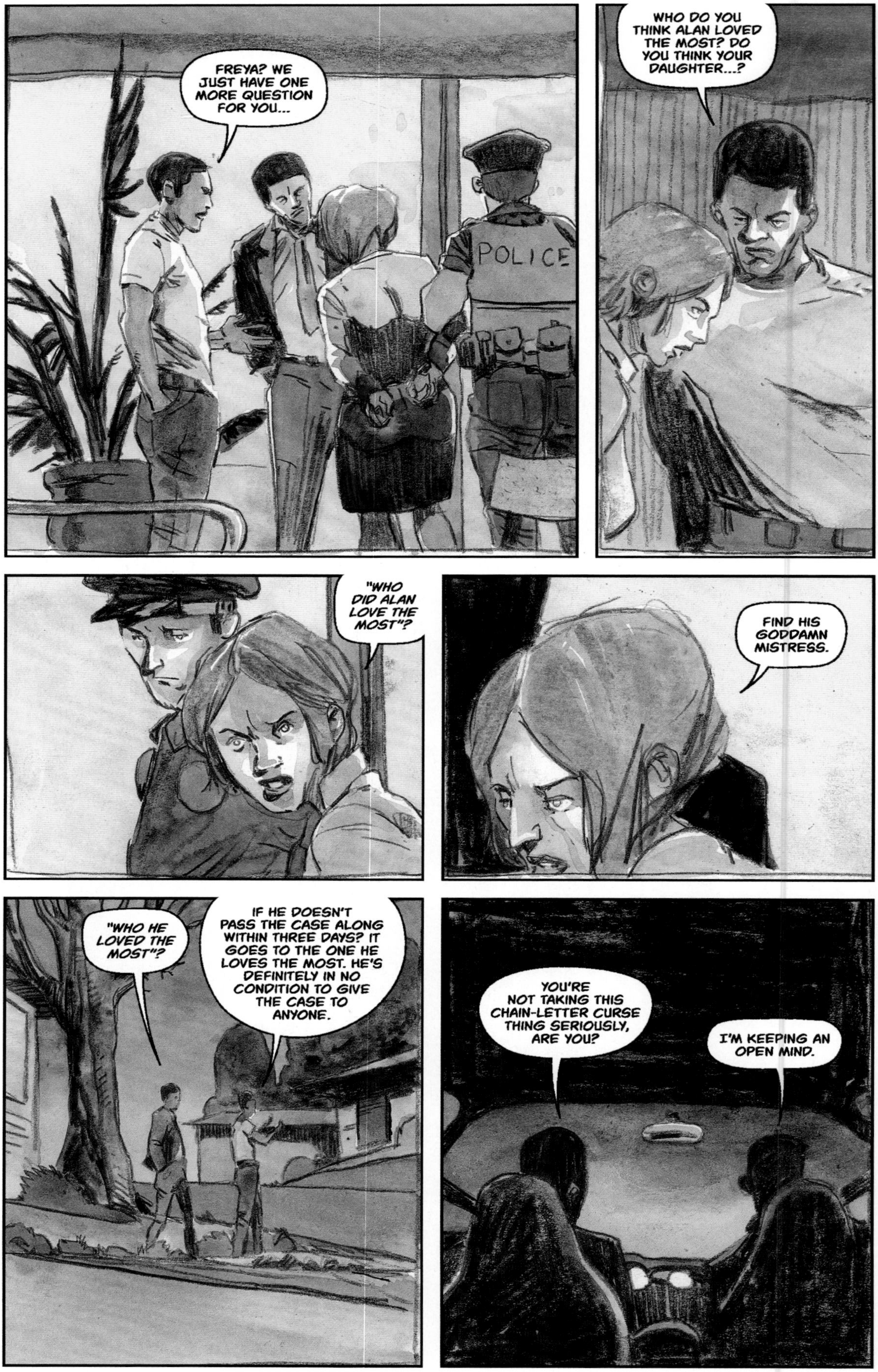
FREYA? WE JUST HAVE ONE MORE QUESTION FOR YOU...
WHO DO YOU THINK ALAN LOVED THE MOST? DO YOU THINK YOUR DAUGHTER...?
"WHO DID ALAN LOVE THE MOST"?
FIND HIS GODDAMN MISTRESS.
"WHO HE LOVED THE MOST"?
IF HE DOESN'T PASS THE CASE ALONG WITHIN THREE DAYS? IT GOES TO THE ONE HE LOVES THE MOST. HE'S DEFINITELY IN NO CONDITION TO GIVE THE CASE TO ANYONE.
YOU'RE NOT TAKING THIS CHAIN-LETTER CURSE THING SERIOUSLY, ARE YOU?
I'M KEEPING AN OPEN MIND.

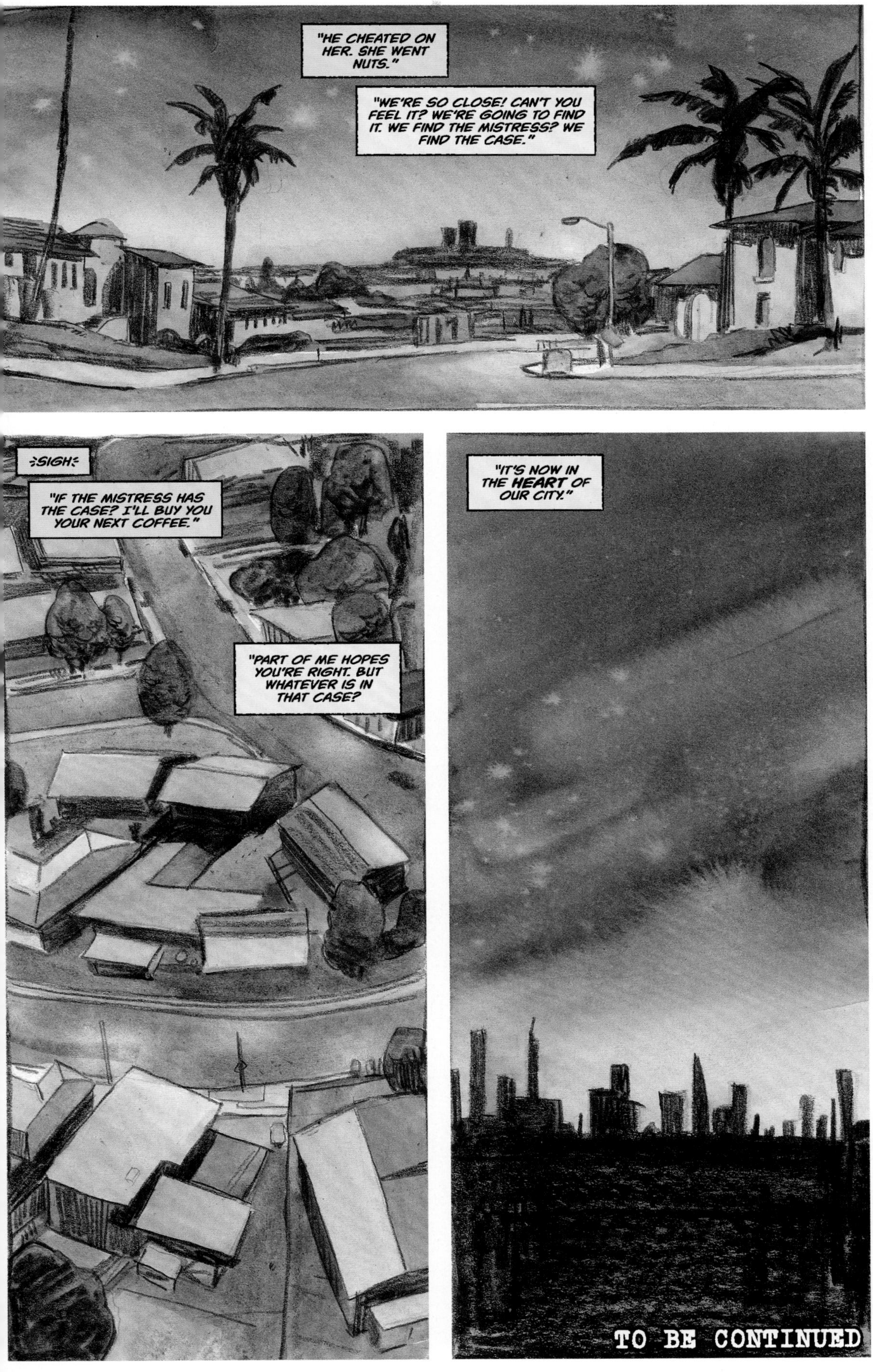
"HE CHEATED ON HER. SHE WENT NUTS."
"WE'RE SO CLOSE! CAN'T YOU FEEL IT? WE'RE GOING TO FIND IT. WE FIND THE MISTRESS? WE FIND THE CASE."
SIGH
"IF THE MISTRESS HAS THE CASE? I'LL BUY YOU YOUR NEXT COFFEE."
"PART OF ME HOPES YOU'RE RIGHT. BUT WHATEVER IS IN THAT CASE?
"IT'S NOW IN THE HEART OF OUR CITY."
TO BE CONTINUED

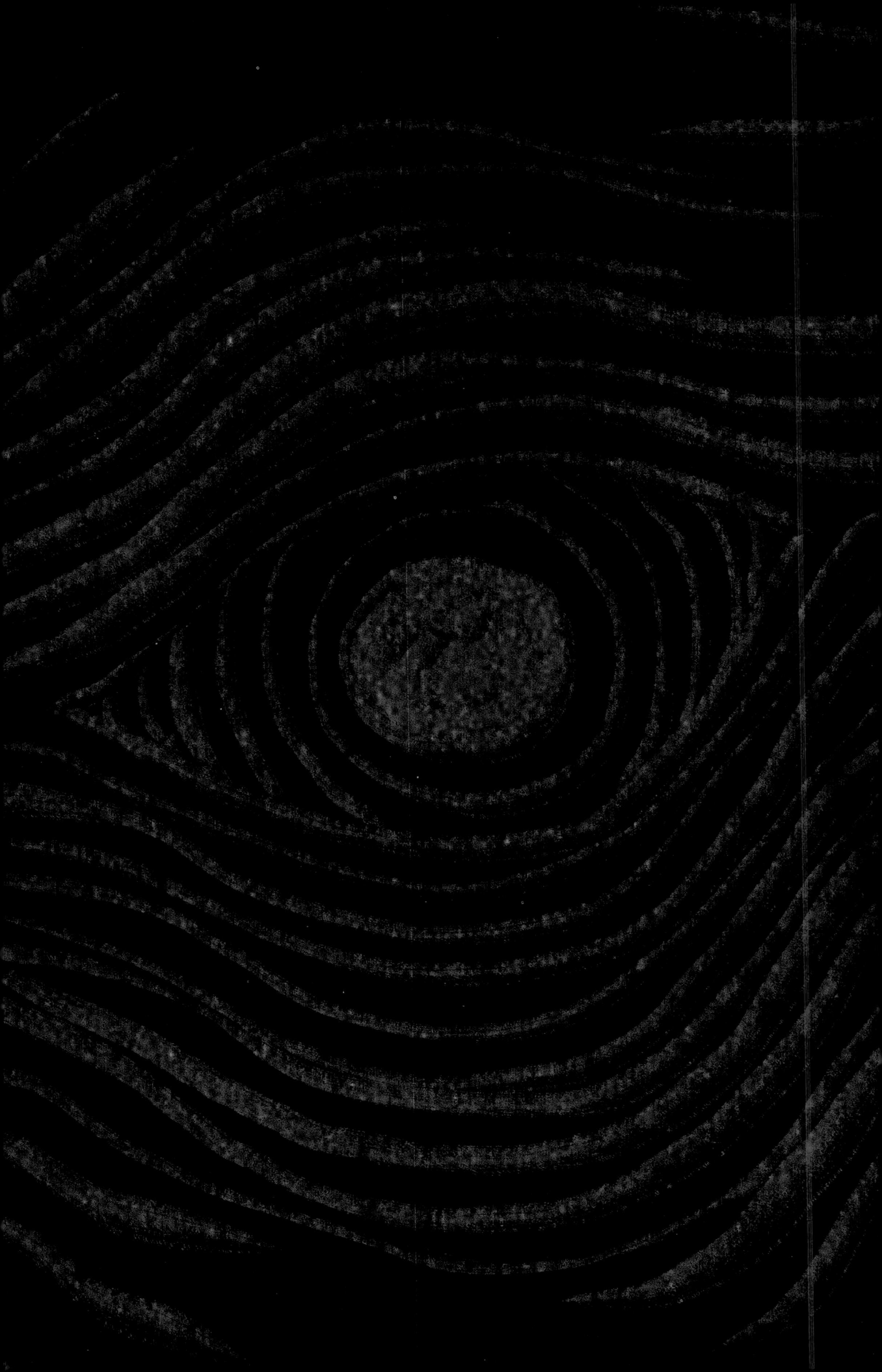

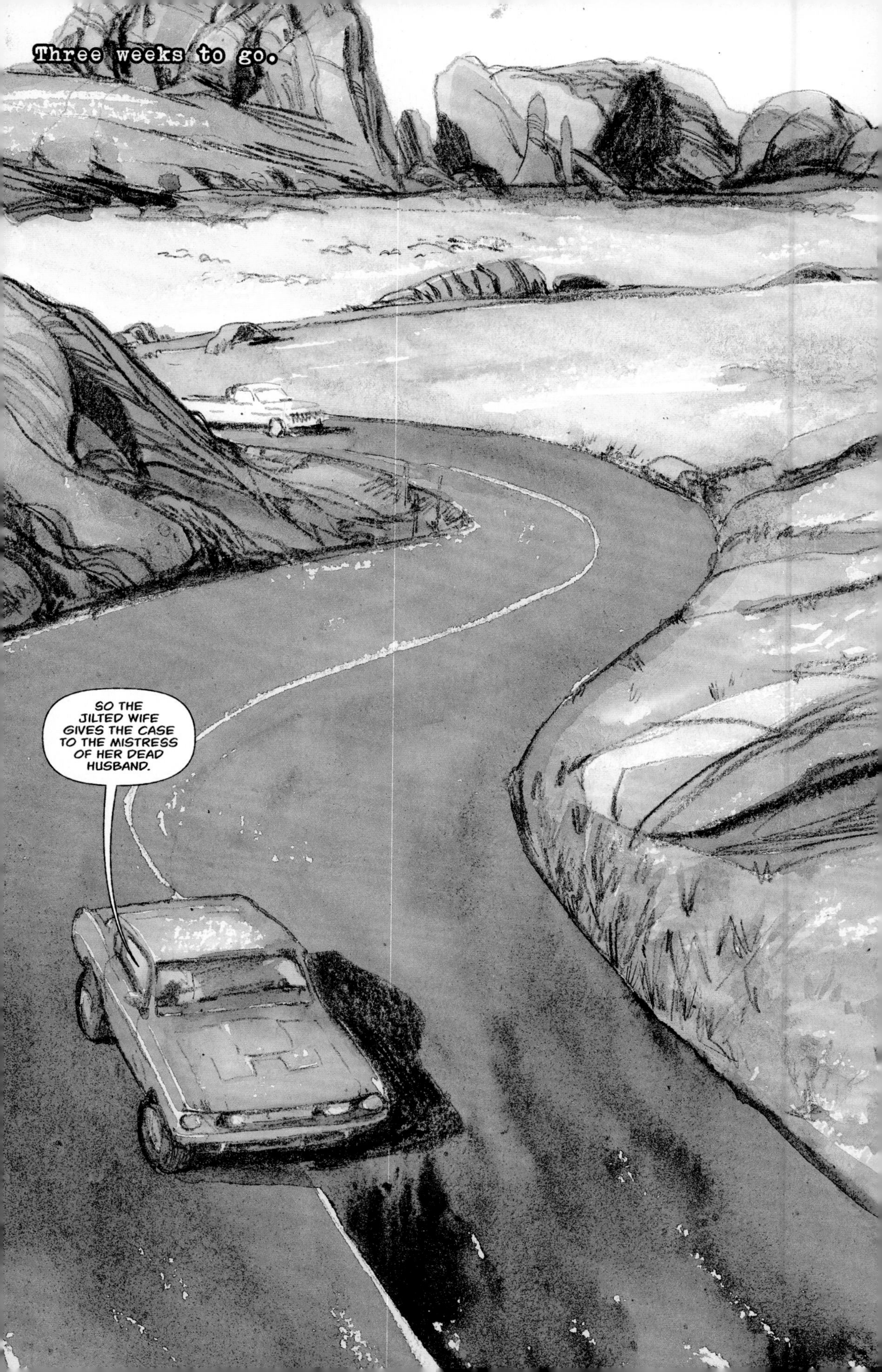
Three weeks to go.
SO THE JILTED WIFE GIVES THE CASE TO THE MISTRESS OF HER DEAD HUSBAND.

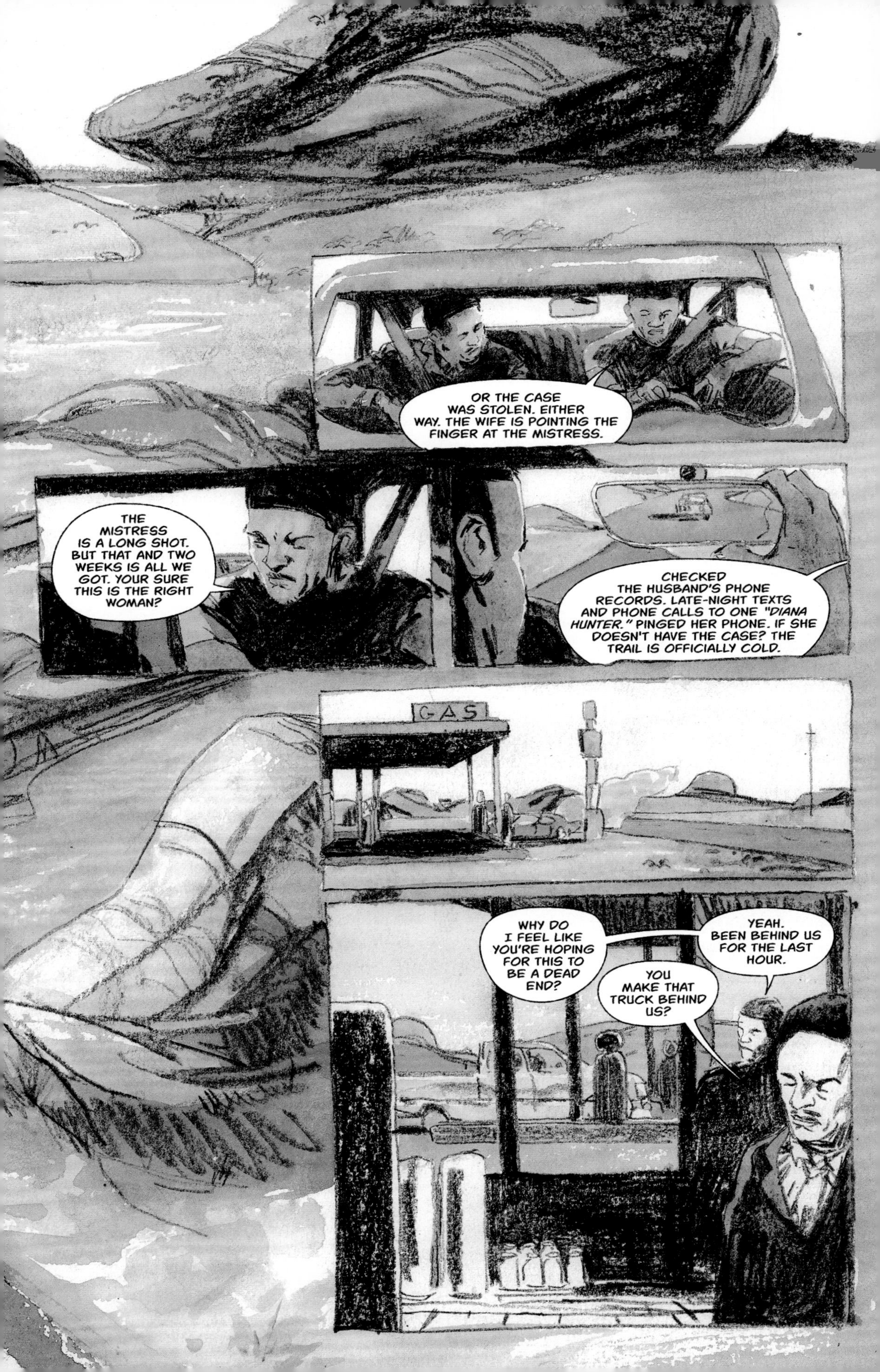
OR THE CASE WAS STOLEN. EITHER WAY. THE WIFE IS POINTING THE FINGER AT THE MISTRESS.
THE MISTRESS IS A LONG SHOT. BUT THAT AND TWO WEEKS IS ALL WE GOT. YOUR SURE THIS IS THE RIGHT WOMAN?
CHECKED THE HUSBAND'S PHONE RECORDS. LATE-NIGHT TEXTS AND PHONE CALLS TO ONE "DIANA HUNTER." PINGED HER PHONE. IF SHE DOESN'T HAVE THE CASE? THE TRAIL IS OFFICIALLY COLD.
GAS
WHY DO I FEEL LIKE YOU'RE HOPING FOR THIS TO BE A DEAD END?
YOU MAKE THAT TRUCK BEHIND US?
YEAH. BEEN BEHIND US FOR THE LAST HOUR.

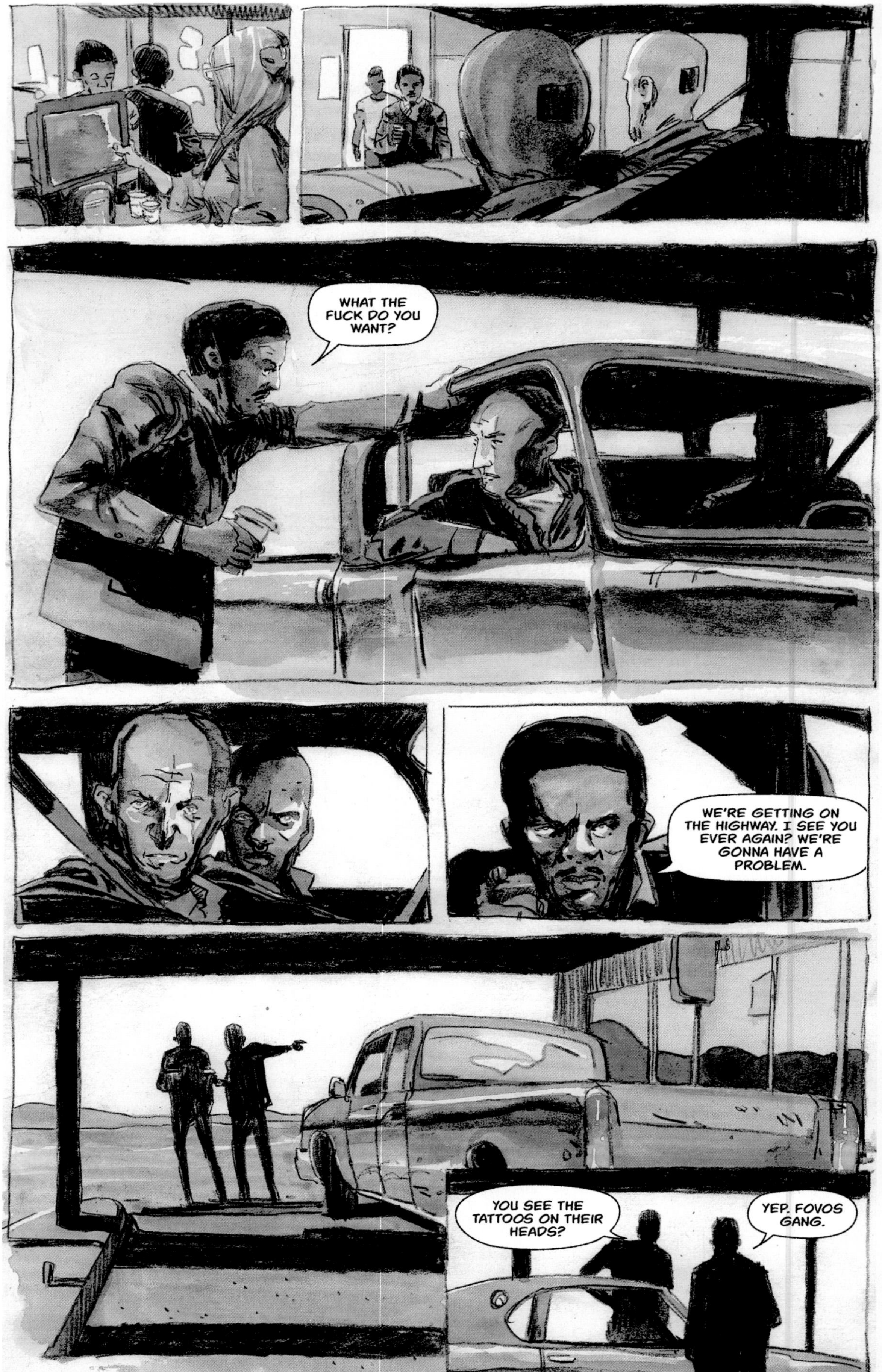
WHAT THE FUCK DO YOU WANT?
WE'RE GETTING ON THE HIGHWAY. I SEE YOU EVER AGAIN? WE'RE GONNA HAVE A PROBLEM.
YOU SEE THE TATTOOS ON THEIR HEADS?
YEP. FOVOS GANG.

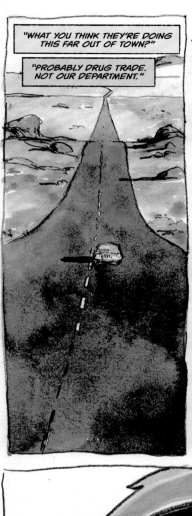

"WHAT YOU THINK THEY'RE DOING THIS FAR OUT OF TOWN?"

"PROBABLY DRUG TRADE. NOT OUR DEPARTMENT."

YEAH? WELL. THEY WERE DEFINITELY FOLLOWING US.

MAYBE. IT'S A LONG, LONELY ROAD. NOT A LOT OF TURNS. COULD BE COINCIDENCE.

I DON'T BELIEVE IN COINCIDENCE.

I BELIEVE YOU'VE BEEN ON THIS CASE TOO LONG. THIS IS WHY THEY LIMIT OUR TIME. STARTS TO MAKE YOU...

...PARANOID...

...

I DIDN'T SAY ANYTHING.

YOU'RE THINKING IT.

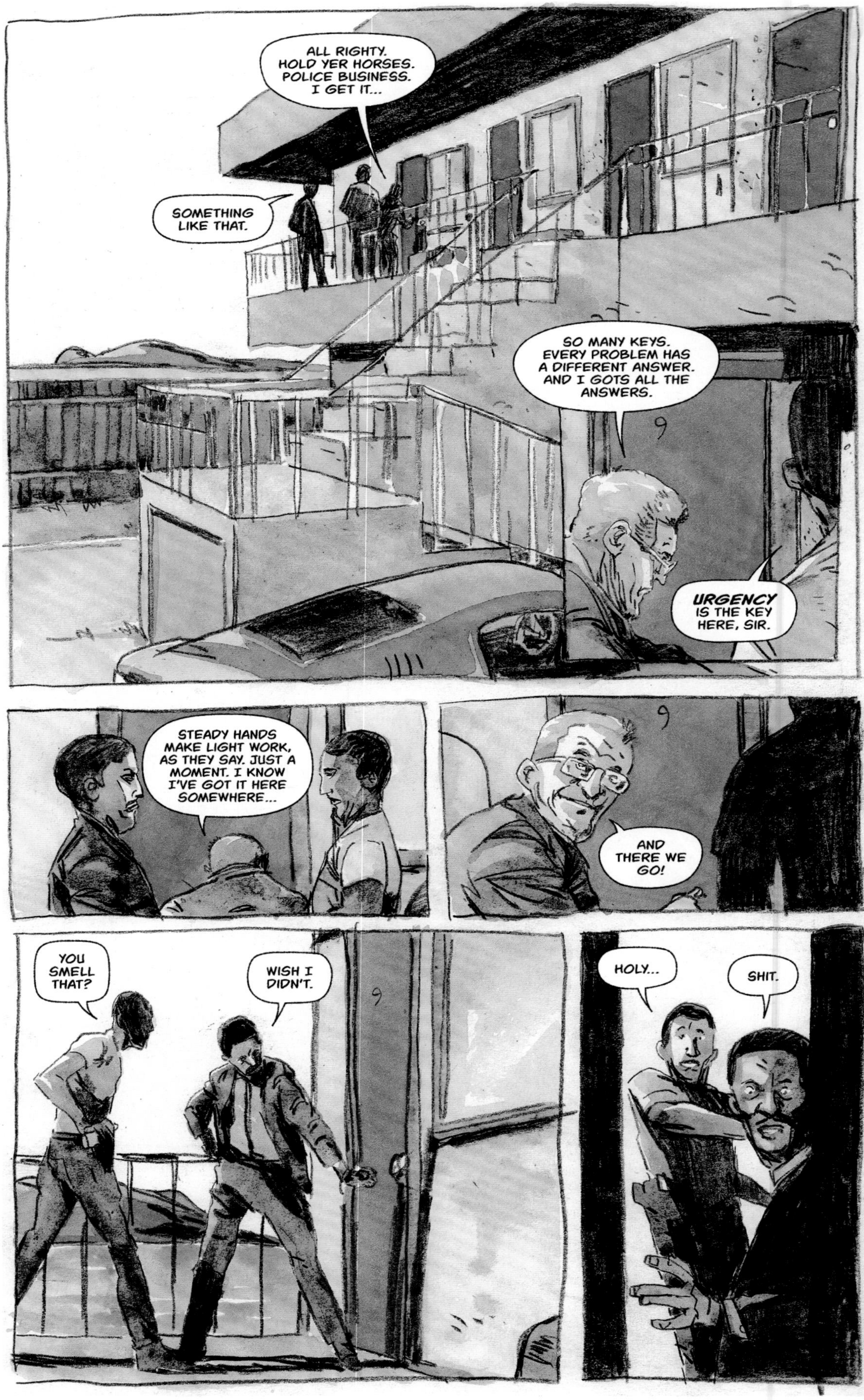
ALL RIGHTY. HOLD YER HORSES. POLICE BUSINESS. I GET IT...
SOMETHING LIKE THAT.
SO MANY KEYS. EVERY PROBLEM HAS A DIFFERENT ANSWER. AND I GOTS ALL THE ANSWERS.
URGENCY IS THE KEY HERE, SIR.
STEADY HANDS MAKE LIGHT WORK, AS THEY SAY. JUST A MOMENT. I KNOW I'VE GOT IT HERE SOMEWHERE...
AND THERE WE GO!
YOU SMELL THAT?
WISH I DIDN'T.
HOLY...
SHIT.

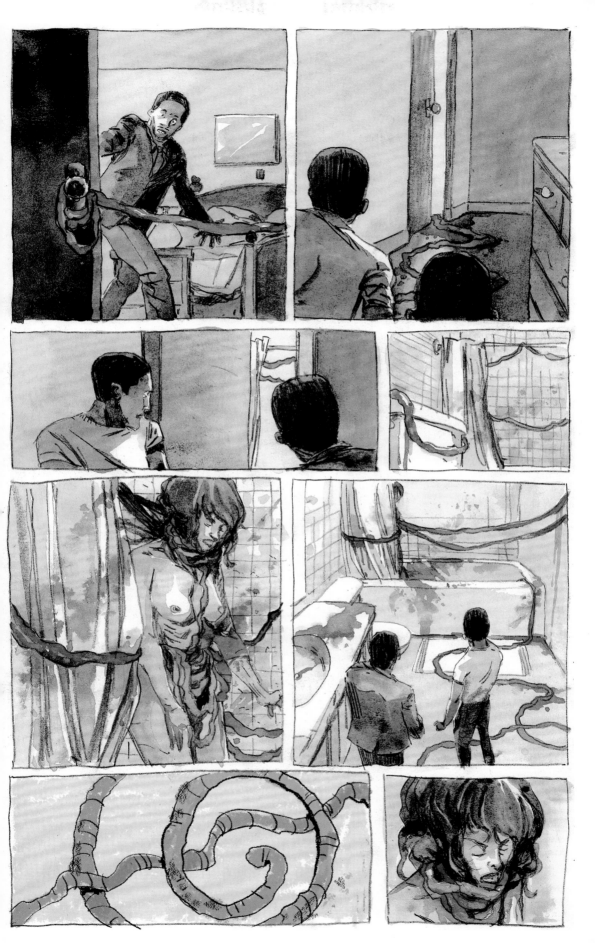

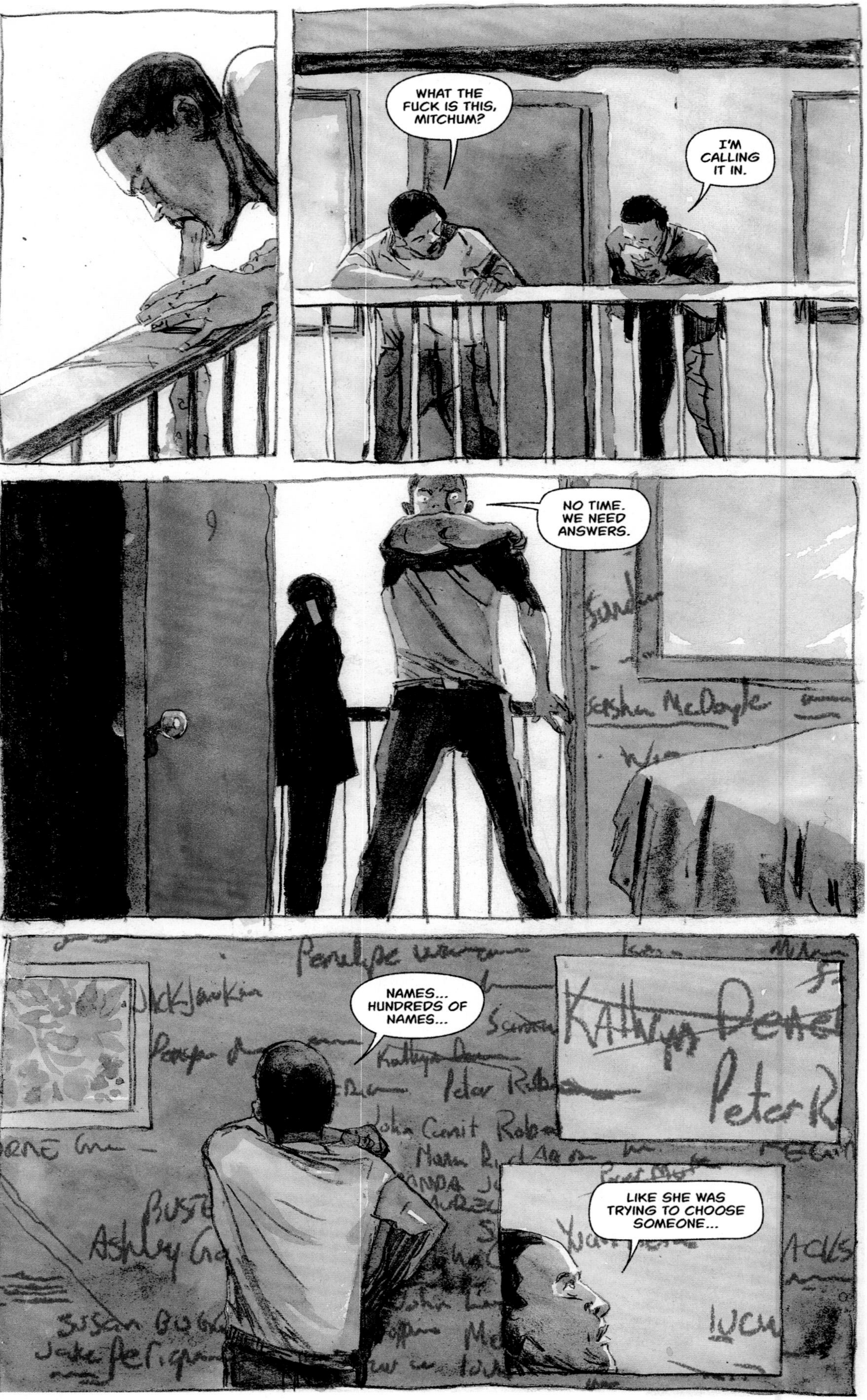
WHAT THE FUCK IS THIS, MITCHUM?
I'M CALLING IT IN.
NO TIME. WE NEED ANSWERS.
NAMES... HUNDREDS OF NAMES...
LIKE SHE WAS TRYING TO CHOOSE SOMEONE...

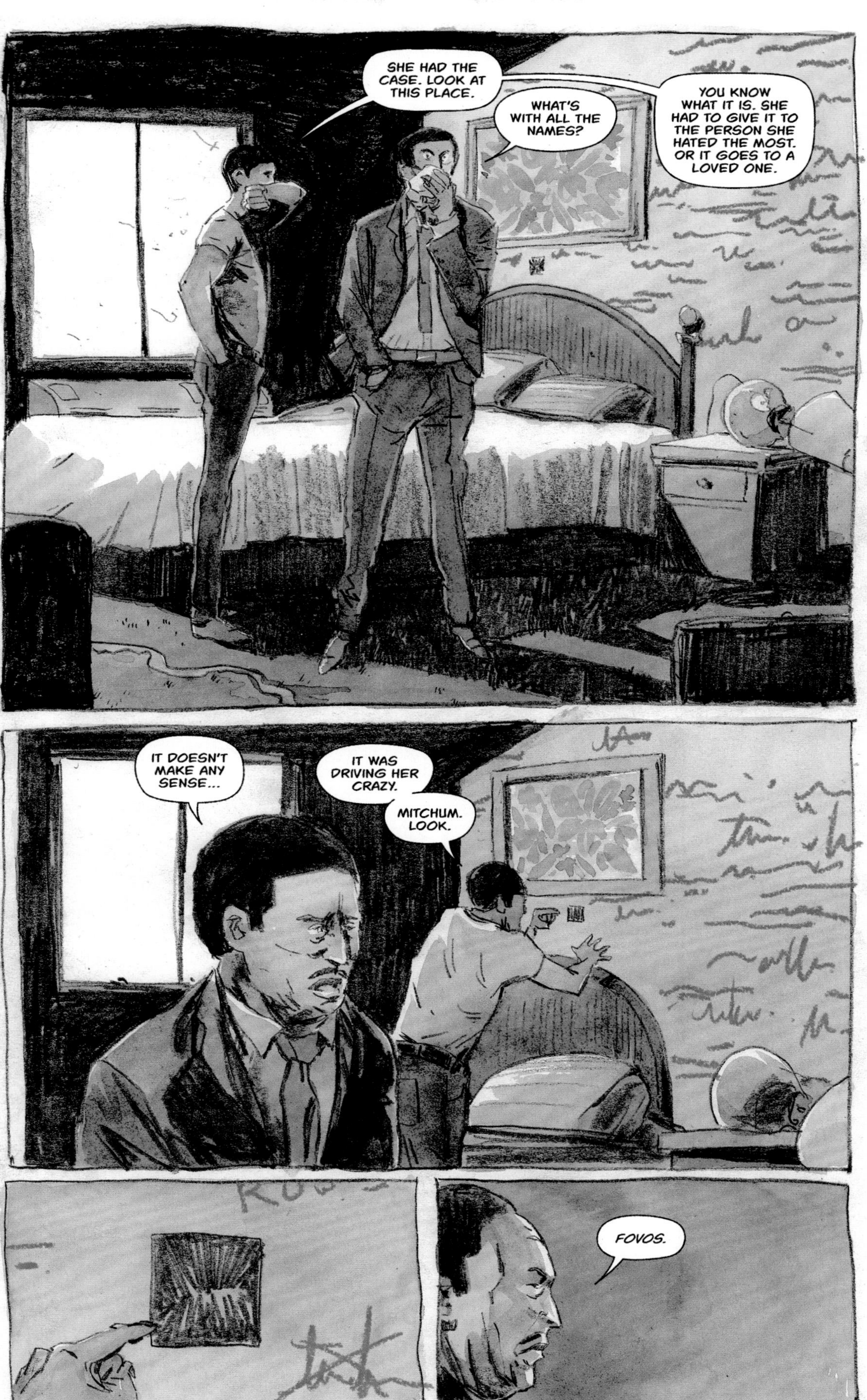
SHE HAD THE CASE. LOOK AT THIS PLACE.
WHAT'S WITH ALL THE NAMES?
YOU KNOW WHAT IT IS. SHE HAD TO GIVE IT TO THE PERSON SHE HATED THE MOST. OR IT GOES TO A LOVED ONE.
IT DOESN'T MAKE ANY SENSE...
IT WAS DRIVING HER CRAZY.
MITCHUM. LOOK.
FOVOS.

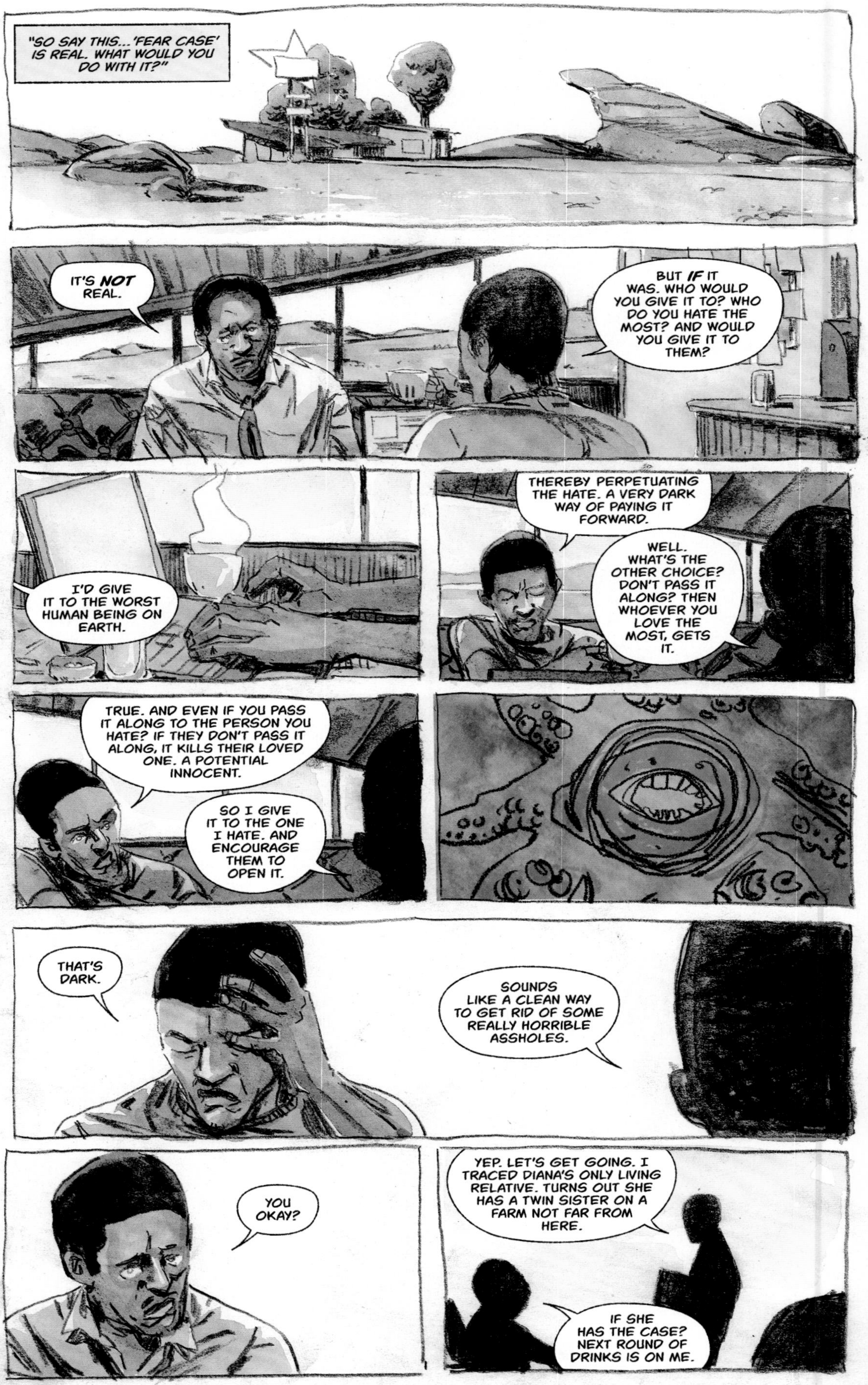
"SO SAY THIS...'FEAR CASE' IS REAL. WHAT WOULD YOU DO WITH IT?"
IT'S **NOT** REAL.
BUT **IF** IT WAS. WHO WOULD YOU GIVE IT TO? WHO DO YOU HATE THE MOST? AND WOULD YOU GIVE IT TO THEM?
I'D GIVE IT TO THE WORST HUMAN BEING ON EARTH.
THEREBY PERPETUATING THE HATE. A VERY DARK WAY OF PAYING IT FORWARD.
WELL. WHAT'S THE OTHER CHOICE? DON'T PASS IT ALONG? THEN WHOEVER YOU LOVE THE MOST, GETS IT.
TRUE. AND EVEN IF YOU PASS IT ALONG TO THE PERSON YOU HATE? IF THEY DON'T PASS IT ALONG, IT KILLS THEIR LOVED ONE. A POTENTIAL INNOCENT.
SO I GIVE IT TO THE ONE I HATE. AND ENCOURAGE THEM TO OPEN IT.
THAT'S DARK.
SOUNDS LIKE A CLEAN WAY TO GET RID OF SOME REALLY HORRIBLE ASSHOLES.
YOU OKAY?
YEP. LET'S GET GOING. I TRACED DIANA'S ONLY LIVING RELATIVE. TURNS OUT SHE HAS A TWIN SISTER ON A FARM NOT FAR FROM HERE.
IF SHE HAS THE CASE? NEXT ROUND OF DRINKS IS ON ME.

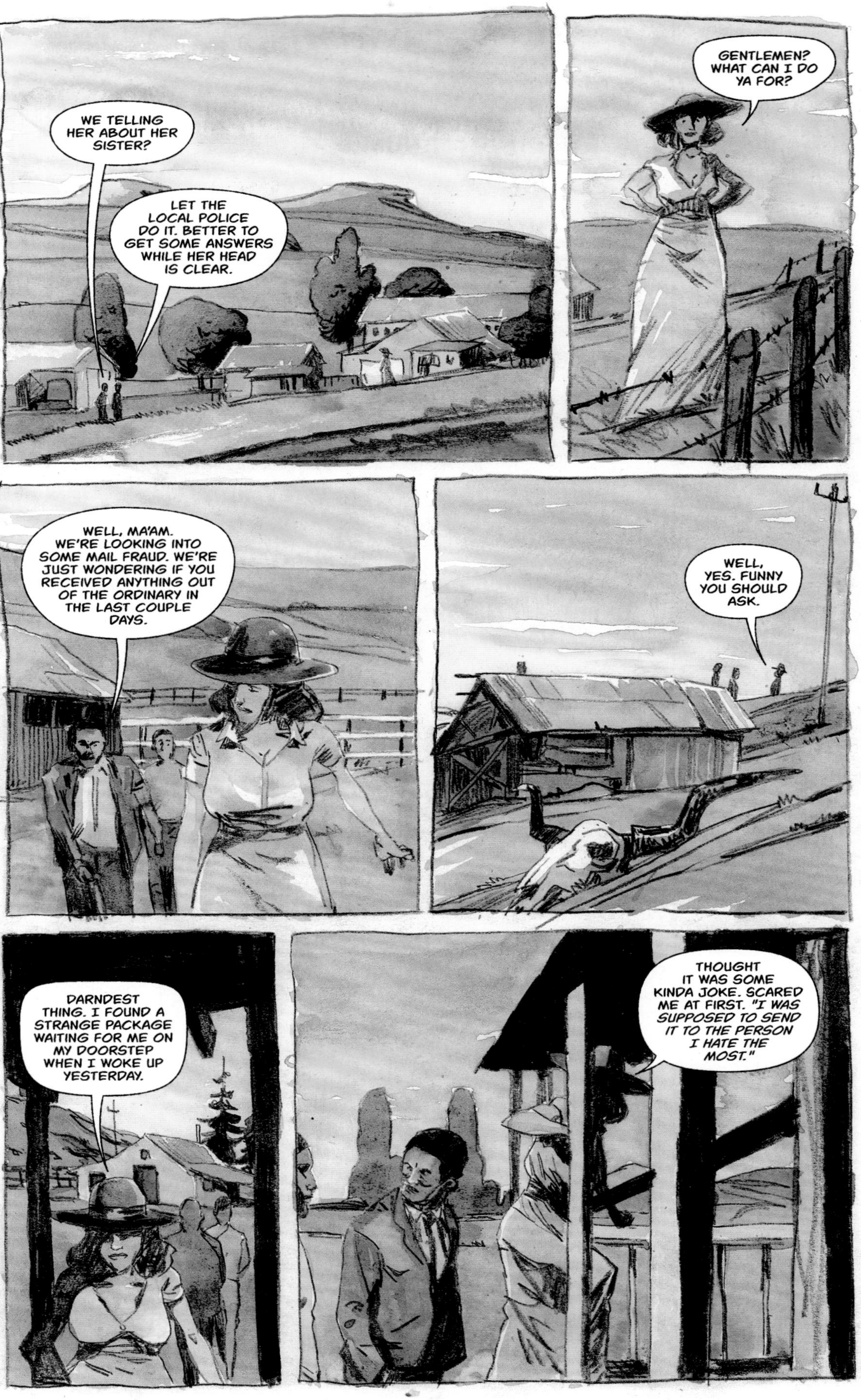
WE TELLING HER ABOUT HER SISTER?
LET THE LOCAL POLICE DO IT. BETTER TO GET SOME ANSWERS WHILE HER HEAD IS CLEAR.
GENTLEMEN? WHAT CAN I DO YA FOR?
WELL, MA'AM. WE'RE LOOKING INTO SOME MAIL FRAUD. WE'RE JUST WONDERING IF YOU RECEIVED ANYTHING OUT OF THE ORDINARY IN THE LAST COUPLE DAYS.
WELL, YES. FUNNY YOU SHOULD ASK.
DARNDEST THING. I FOUND A STRANGE PACKAGE WAITING FOR ME ON MY DOORSTEP WHEN I WOKE UP YESTERDAY.
THOUGHT IT WAS SOME KINDA JOKE. SCARED ME AT FIRST. "I WAS SUPPOSED TO SEND IT TO THE PERSON I HATE THE MOST."

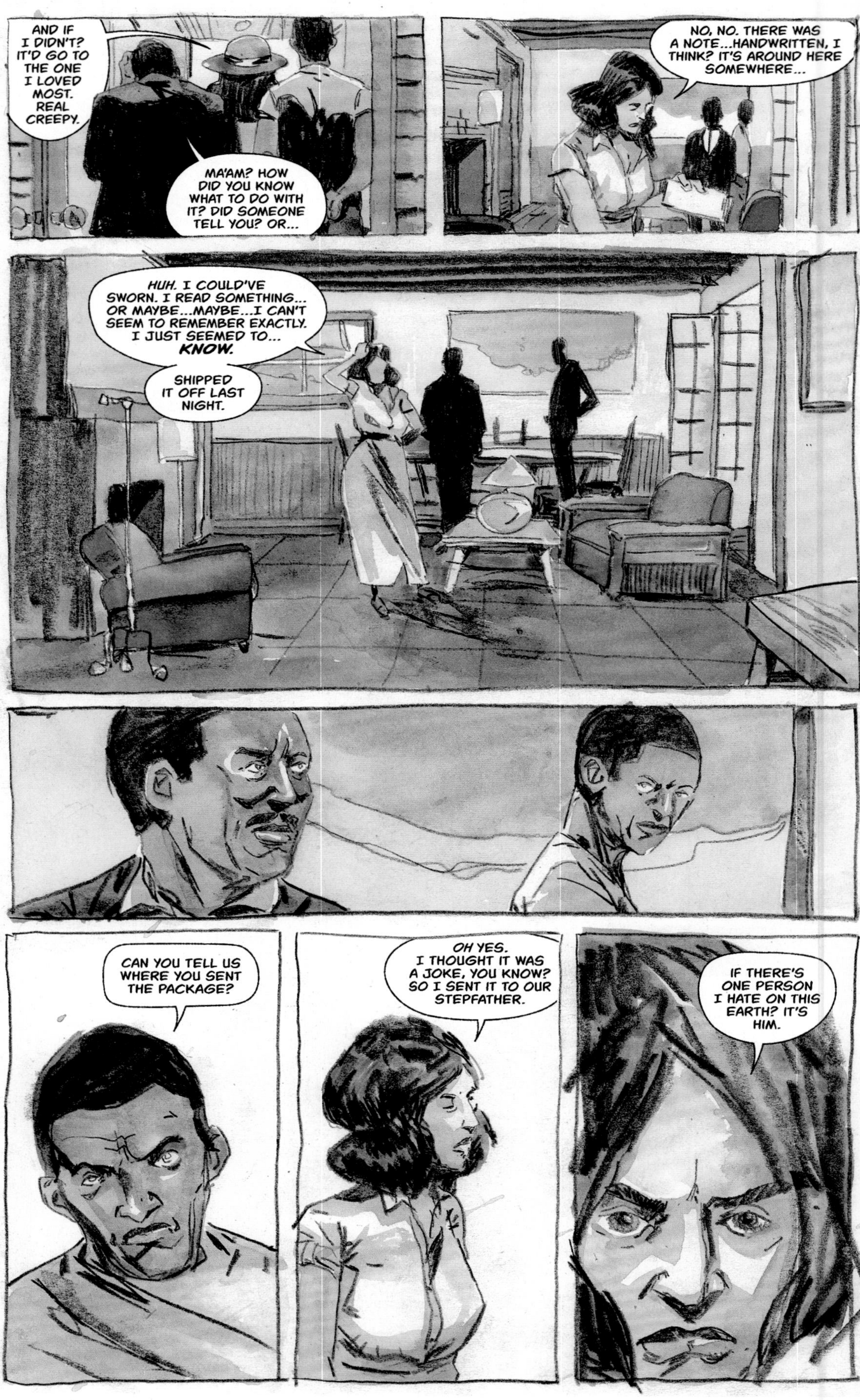
AND IF I DIDN'T? IT'D GO TO THE ONE I LOVED MOST. REAL CREEPY.
MA'AM? HOW DID YOU KNOW WHAT TO DO WITH IT? DID SOMEONE TELL YOU? OR...
NO, NO. THERE WAS A NOTE...HANDWRITTEN, I THINK? IT'S AROUND HERE SOMEWHERE...
HUH. I COULD'VE SWORN. I READ SOMETHING... OR MAYBE...MAYBE...I CAN'T SEEM TO REMEMBER EXACTLY. I JUST SEEMED TO... KNOW.
SHIPPED IT OFF LAST NIGHT.
CAN YOU TELL US WHERE YOU SENT THE PACKAGE?
OH YES. I THOUGHT IT WAS A JOKE, YOU KNOW? SO I SENT IT TO OUR STEPFATHER.
IF THERE'S ONE PERSON I HATE ON THIS EARTH? IT'S HIM.

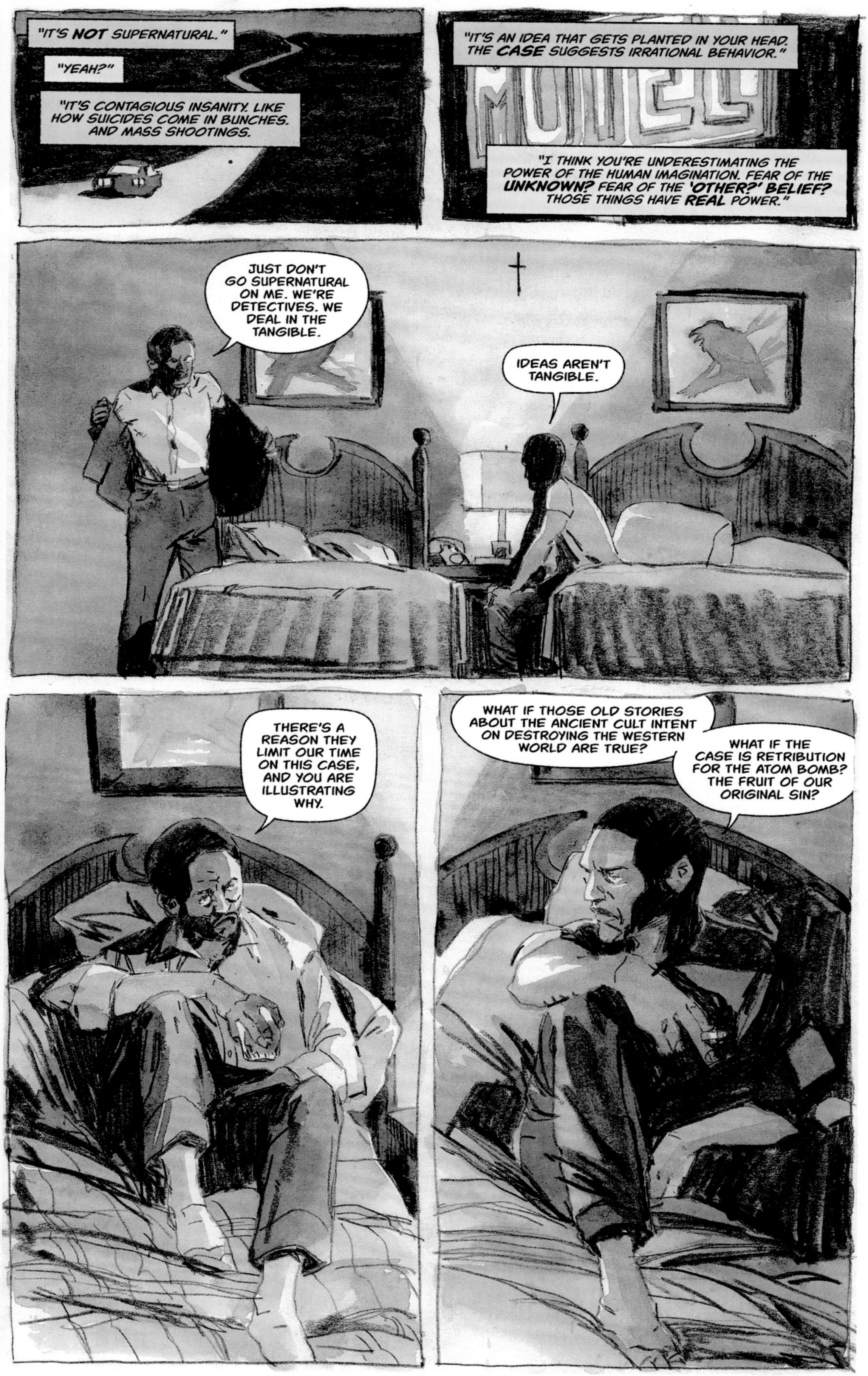
"IT'S NOT SUPERNATURAL."
"YEAH?"
"IT'S CONTAGIOUS INSANITY. LIKE HOW SUICIDES COME IN BUNCHES. AND MASS SHOOTINGS.
"IT'S AN IDEA THAT GETS PLANTED IN YOUR HEAD. THE CASE SUGGESTS IRRATIONAL BEHAVIOR."
"I THINK YOU'RE UNDERESTIMATING THE POWER OF THE HUMAN IMAGINATION. FEAR OF THE UNKNOWN? FEAR OF THE 'OTHER?' BELIEF? THOSE THINGS HAVE REAL POWER."
JUST DON'T GO SUPERNATURAL ON ME. WE'RE DETECTIVES. WE DEAL IN THE TANGIBLE.
IDEAS AREN'T TANGIBLE.
THERE'S A REASON THEY LIMIT OUR TIME ON THIS CASE, AND YOU ARE ILLUSTRATING WHY.
WHAT IF THOSE OLD STORIES ABOUT THE ANCIENT CULT INTENT ON DESTROYING THE WESTERN WORLD ARE TRUE?
WHAT IF THE CASE IS RETRIBUTION FOR THE ATOM BOMB? THE FRUIT OF OUR ORIGINAL SIN?

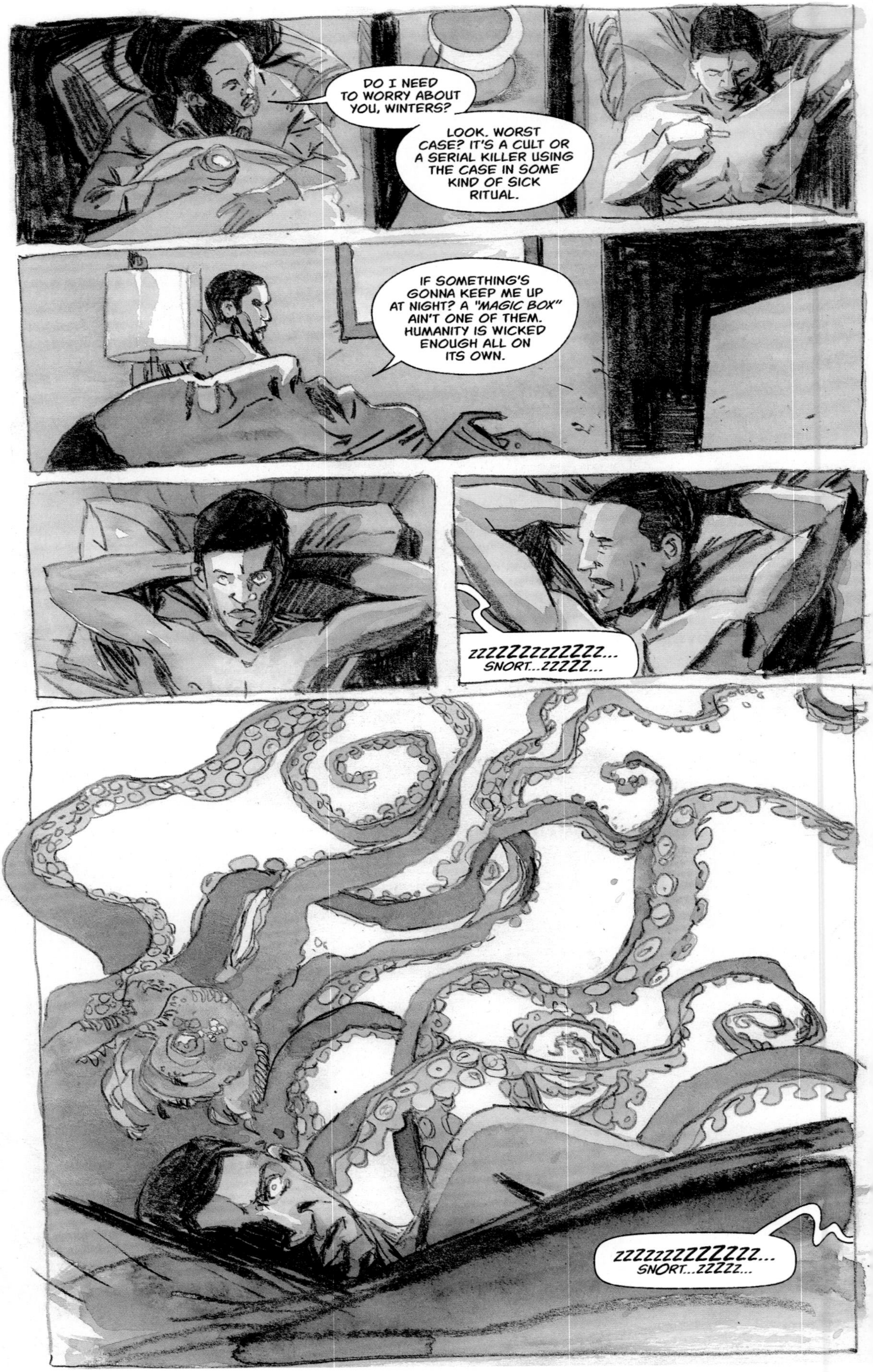
DO I NEED TO WORRY ABOUT YOU, WINTERS?
LOOK. WORST CASE? IT'S A CULT OR A SERIAL KILLER USING THE CASE IN SOME KIND OF SICK RITUAL.
IF SOMETHING'S GONNA KEEP ME UP AT NIGHT? A "MAGIC BOX" AIN'T ONE OF THEM. HUMANITY IS WICKED ENOUGH ALL ON ITS OWN.
zzzZZZzzzzZZZz... SNORT...zzzzz...
zzzzzzzzZZZZzz... SNORT...zzzzz...

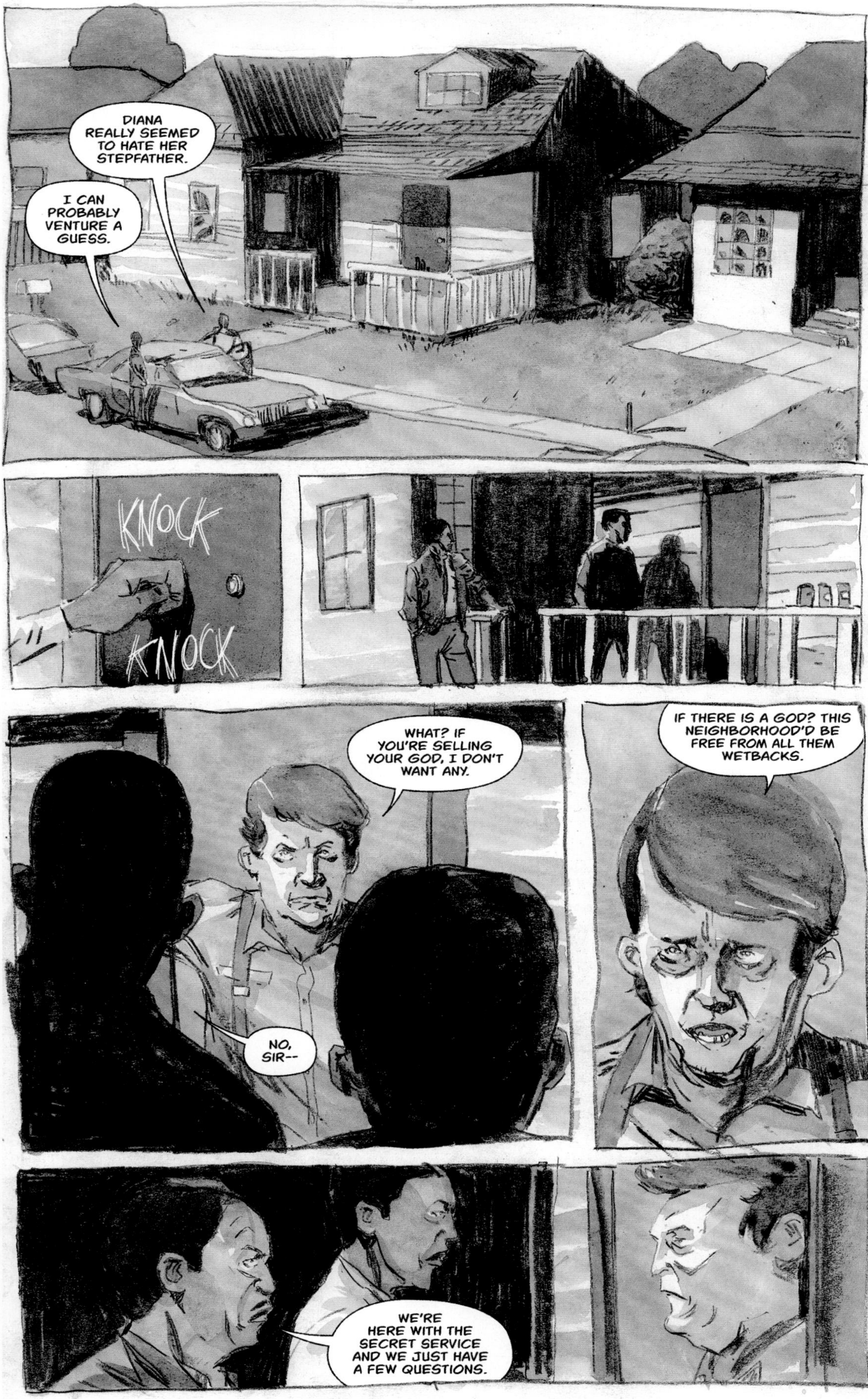
DIANA REALLY SEEMED TO HATE HER STEPFATHER.
I CAN PROBABLY VENTURE A GUESS.
KNOCK
KNOCK
WHAT? IF YOU'RE SELLING YOUR GOD, I DON'T WANT ANY.
NO, SIR--
IF THERE IS A GOD? THIS NEIGHBORHOOD'D BE FREE FROM ALL THEM WETBACKS.
WE'RE HERE WITH THE SECRET SERVICE AND WE JUST HAVE A FEW QUESTIONS.

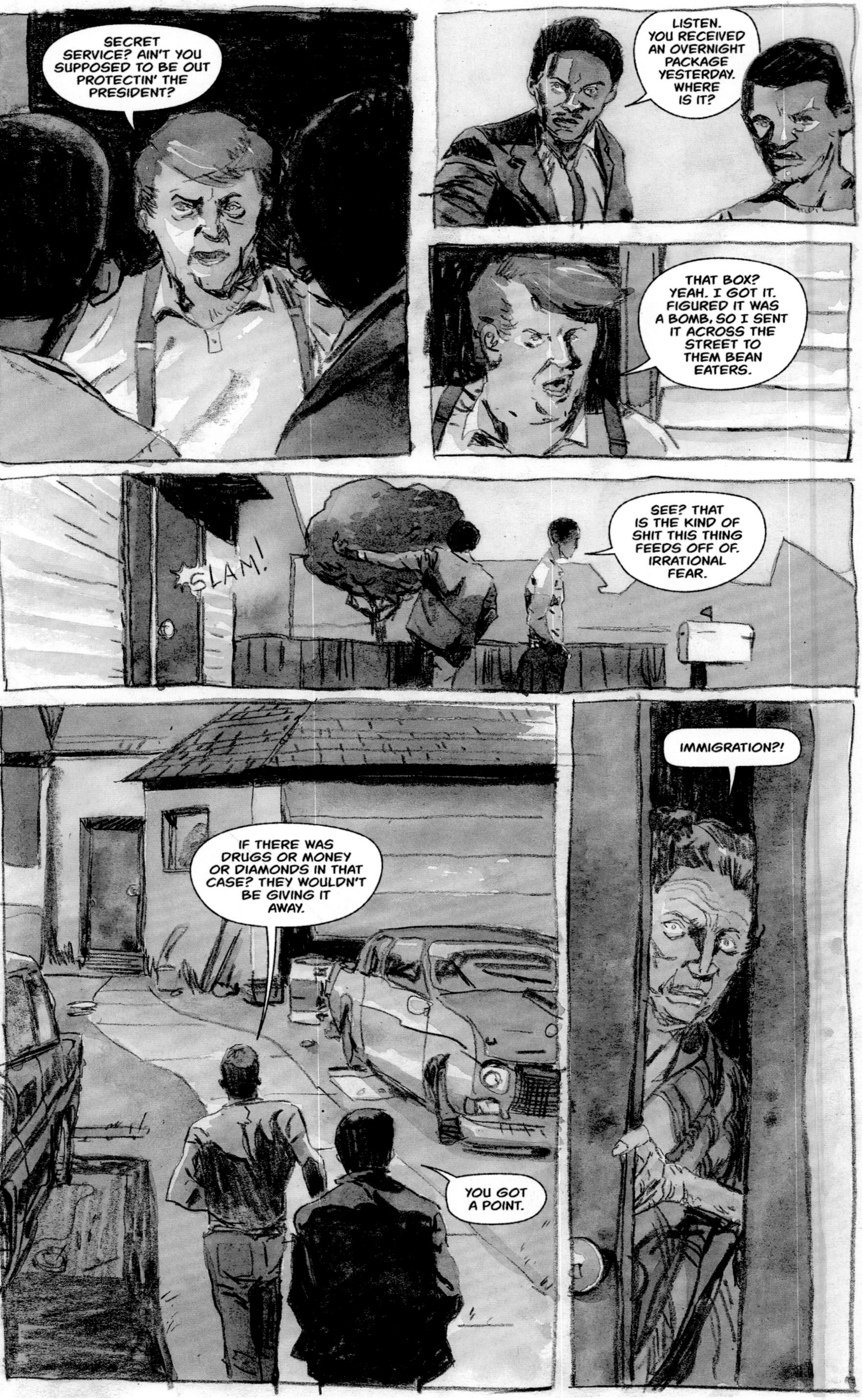
SECRET SERVICE? AIN'T YOU SUPPOSED TO BE OUT PROTECTIN' THE PRESIDENT?
LISTEN. YOU RECEIVED AN OVERNIGHT PACKAGE YESTERDAY. WHERE IS IT?
THAT BOX? YEAH. I GOT IT. FIGURED IT WAS A BOMB, SO I SENT IT ACROSS THE STREET TO THEM BEAN EATERS.
SLAM!
SEE? THAT IS THE KIND OF SHIT THIS THING FEEDS OFF OF. IRRATIONAL FEAR.
IF THERE WAS DRUGS OR MONEY OR DIAMONDS IN THAT CASE? THEY WOULDN'T BE GIVING IT AWAY.
YOU GOT A POINT.
IMMIGRATION?!

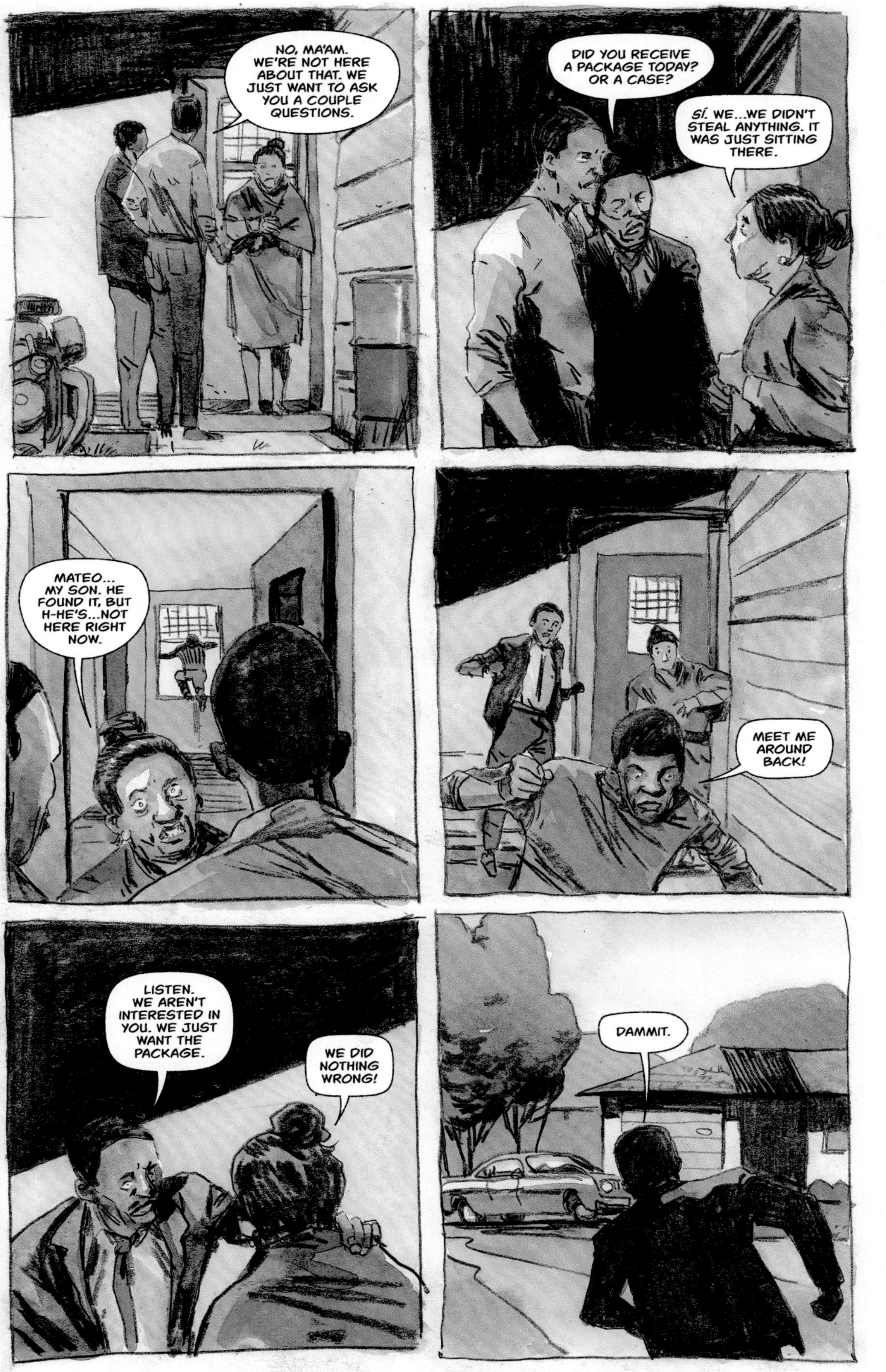
NO, MA'AM. WE'RE NOT HERE ABOUT THAT. WE JUST WANT TO ASK YOU A COUPLE QUESTIONS.
DID YOU RECEIVE A PACKAGE TODAY? OR A CASE?
SÍ. WE...WE DIDN'T STEAL ANYTHING. IT WAS JUST SITTING THERE.
MATEO... MY SON. HE FOUND IT, BUT H-HE'S...NOT HERE RIGHT NOW.
MEET ME AROUND BACK!
LISTEN. WE AREN'T INTERESTED IN YOU. WE JUST WANT THE PACKAGE.
WE DID NOTHING WRONG!
DAMMIT.

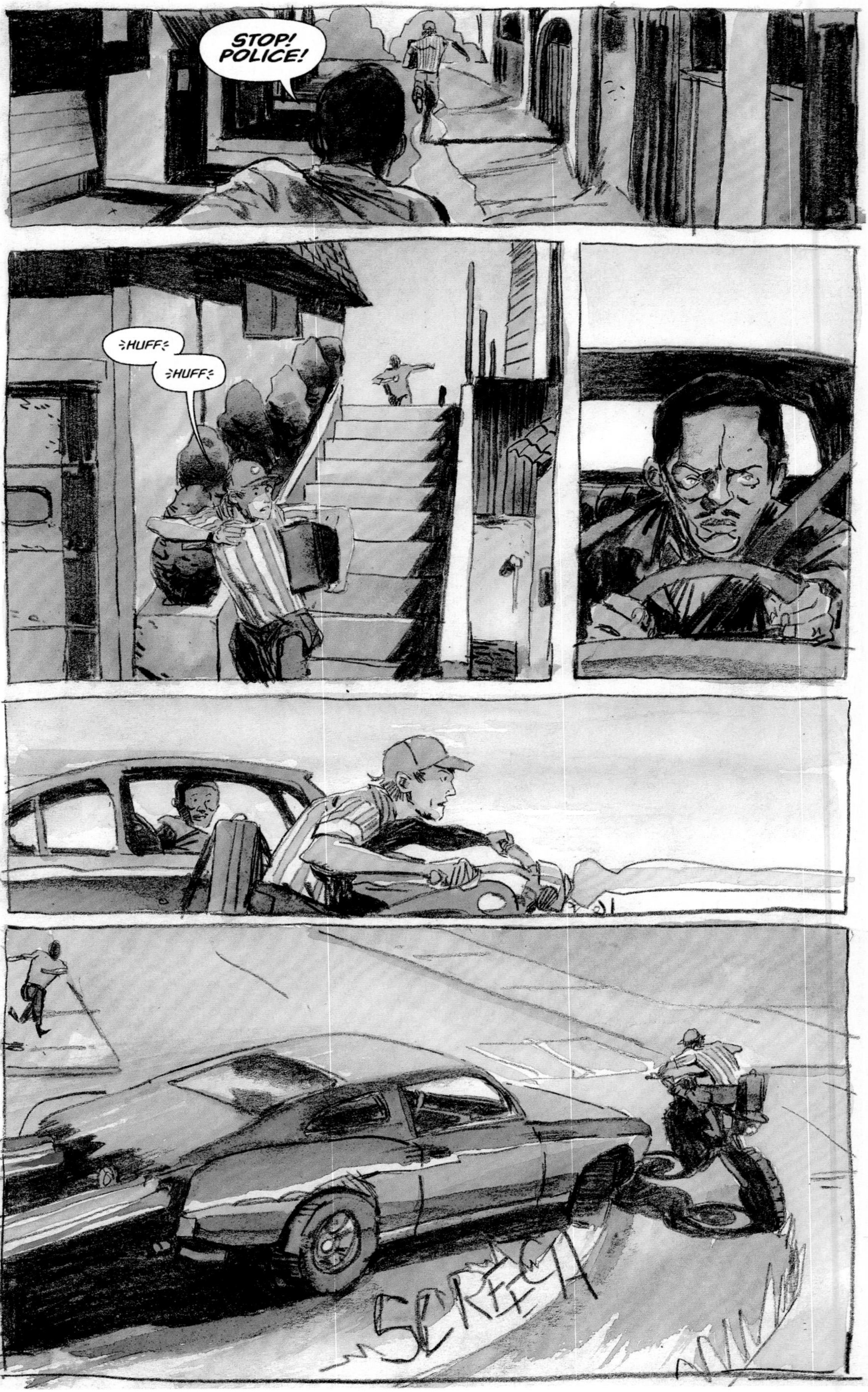
STOP! POLICE!
HUFF
HUFF
SCREECH

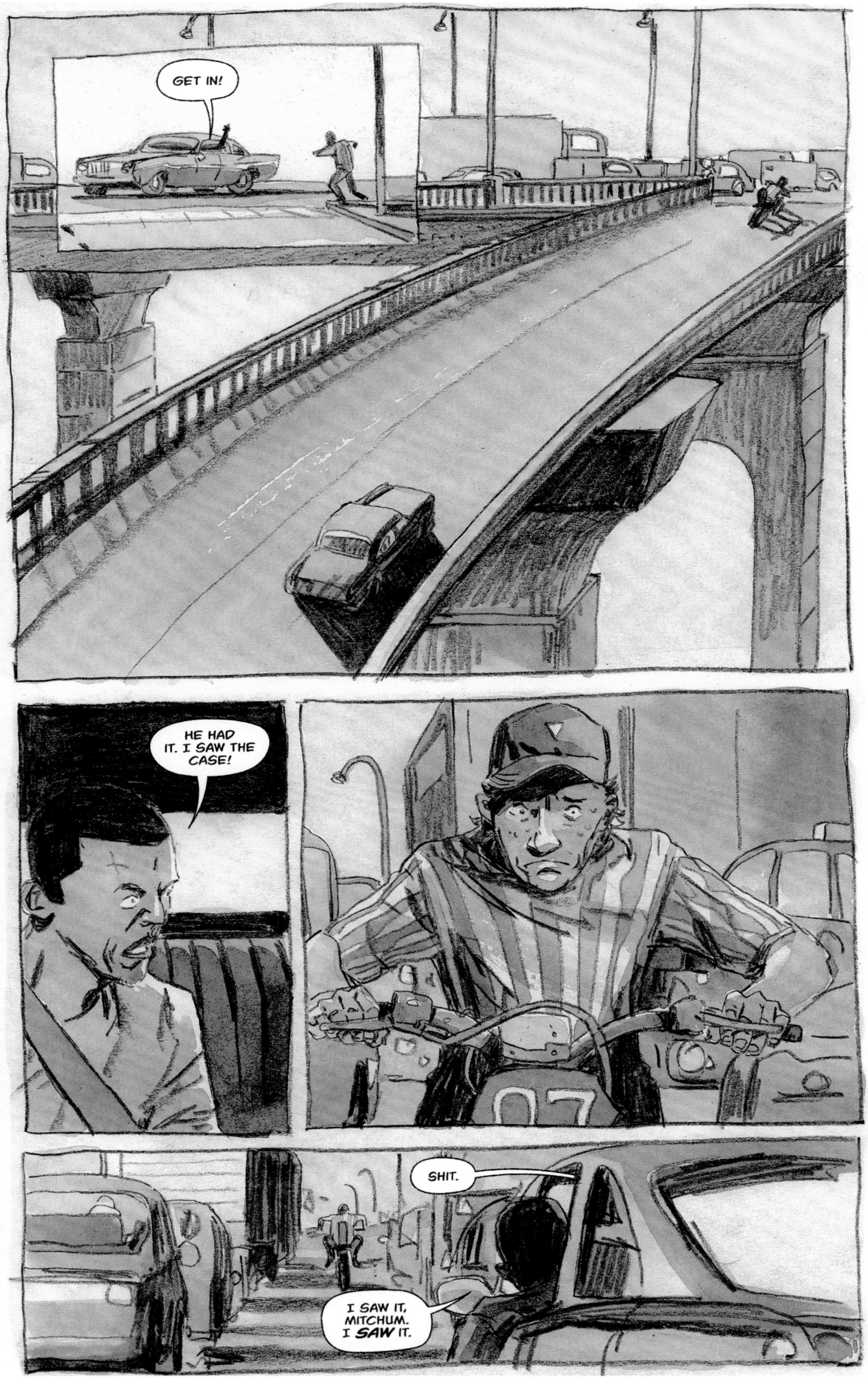
GET IN!
HE HAD IT. I SAW THE CASE!
SHIT.
I SAW IT, MITCHUM. I *SAW* IT.

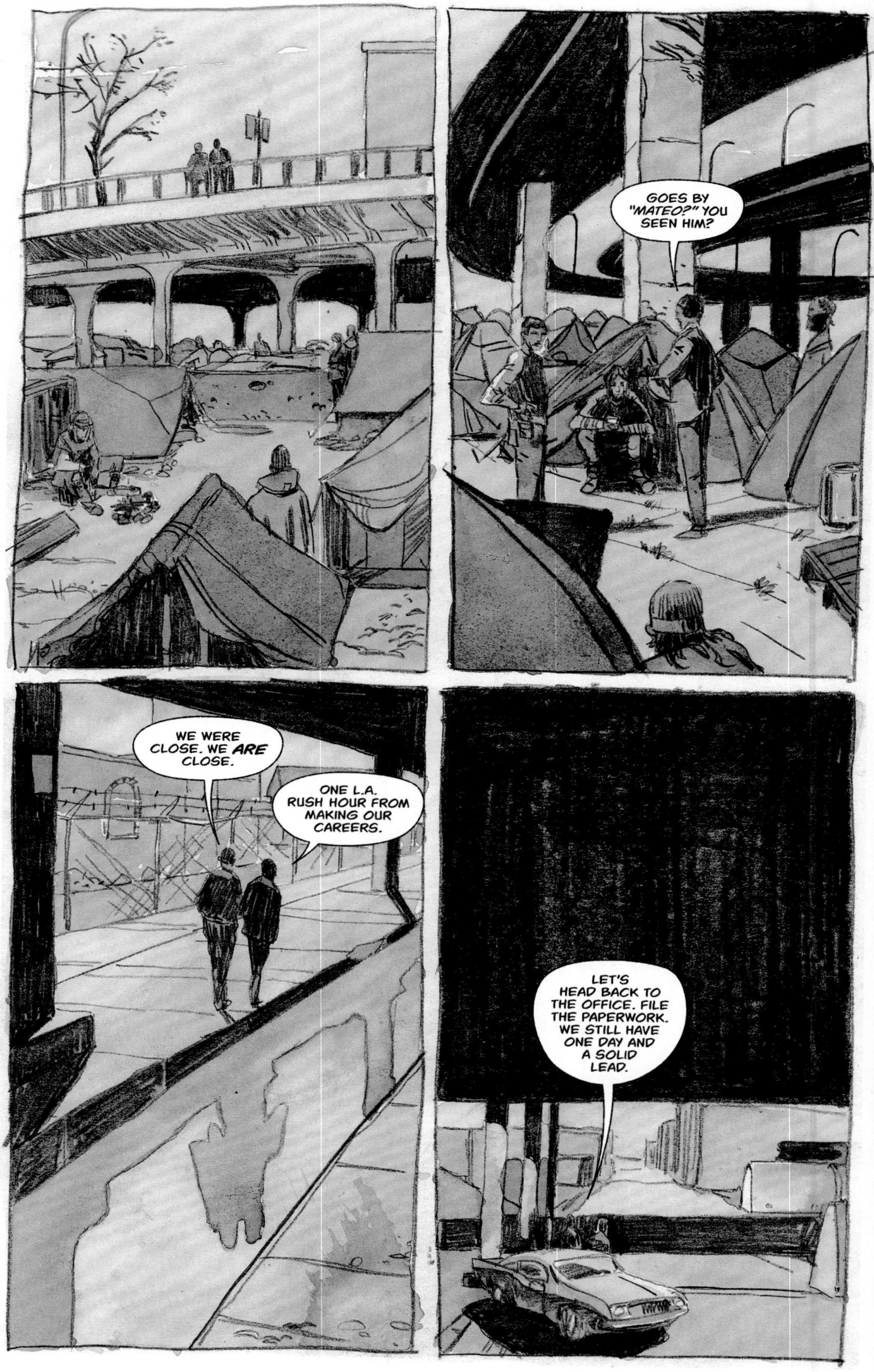
GOES BY "MATEO?" YOU SEEN HIM?
WE WERE CLOSE. WE ARE CLOSE.
ONE L.A. RUSH HOUR FROM MAKING OUR CAREERS.
LET'S HEAD BACK TO THE OFFICE. FILE THE PAPERWORK. WE STILL HAVE ONE DAY AND A SOLID LEAD.

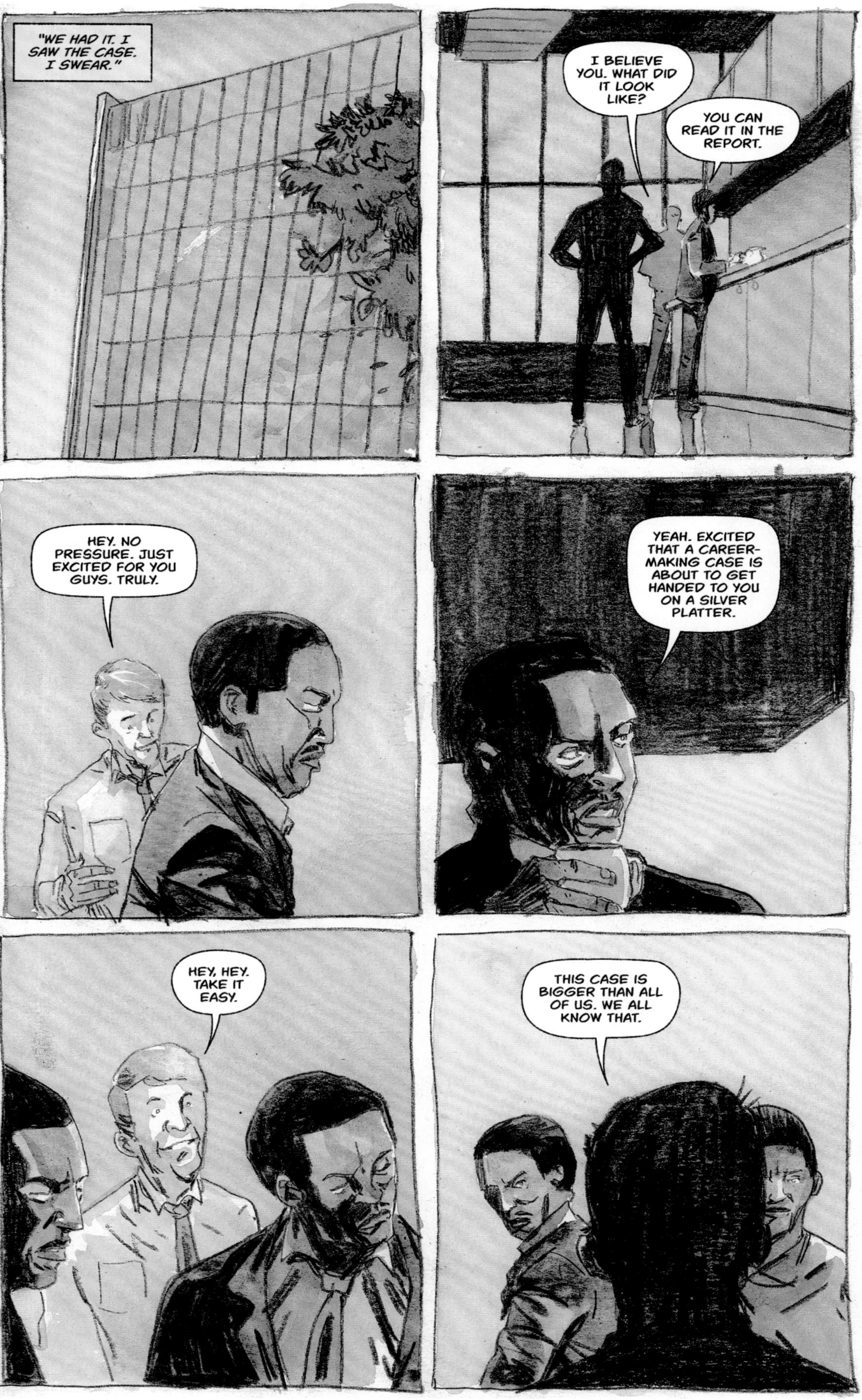
"WE HAD IT. I SAW THE CASE. I SWEAR."
I BELIEVE YOU. WHAT DID IT LOOK LIKE?
YOU CAN READ IT IN THE REPORT.
HEY. NO PRESSURE. JUST EXCITED FOR YOU GUYS. TRULY.
YEAH. EXCITED THAT A CAREER-MAKING CASE IS ABOUT TO GET HANDED TO YOU ON A SILVER PLATTER.
HEY, HEY. TAKE IT EASY.
THIS CASE IS BIGGER THAN ALL OF US. WE ALL KNOW THAT.

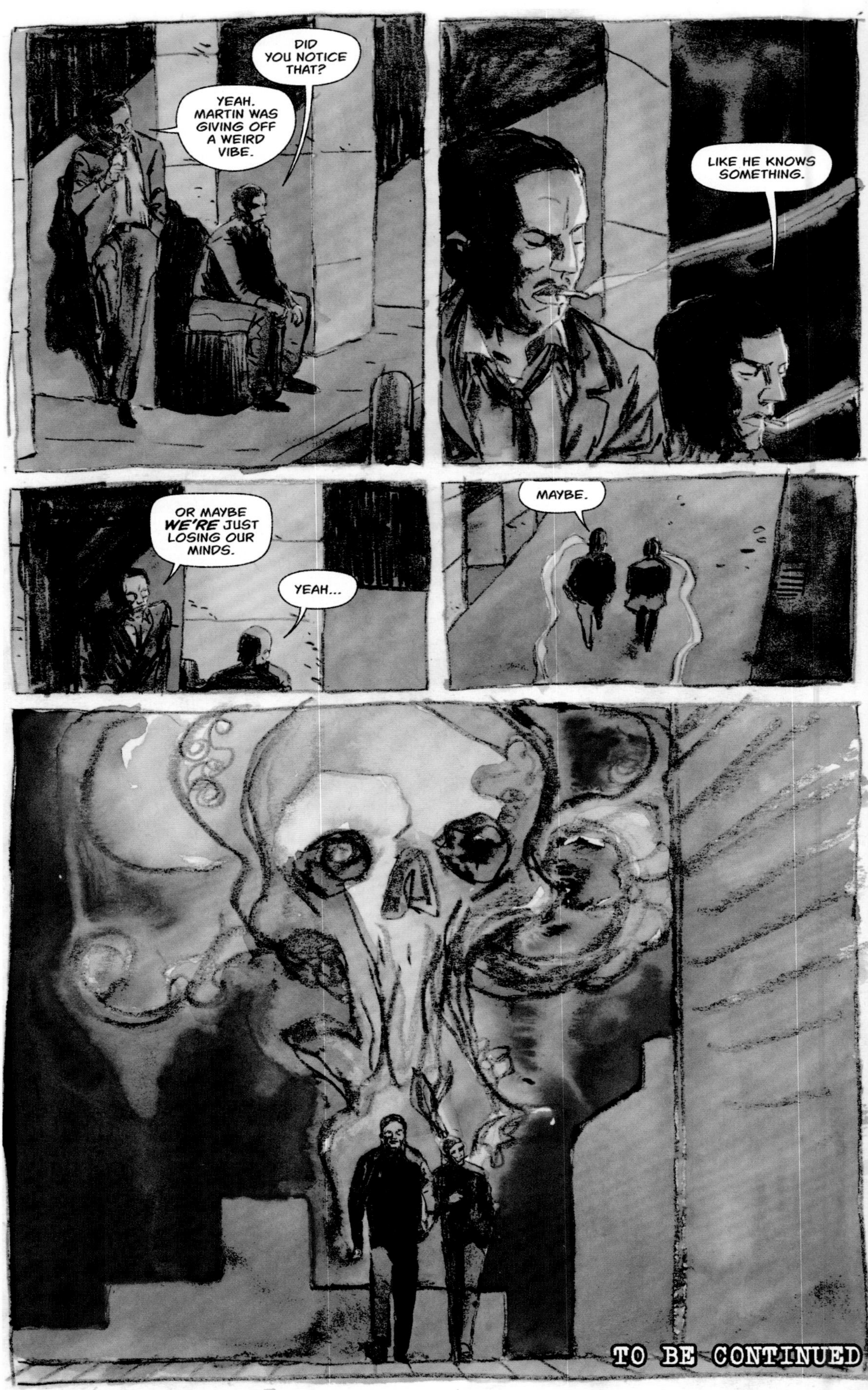
DID YOU NOTICE THAT?
YEAH. MARTIN WAS GIVING OFF A WEIRD VIBE.
LIKE HE KNOWS SOMETHING.
OR MAYBE *WE'RE* JUST LOSING OUR MINDS.
YEAH...
MAYBE.
TO BE CONTINUED

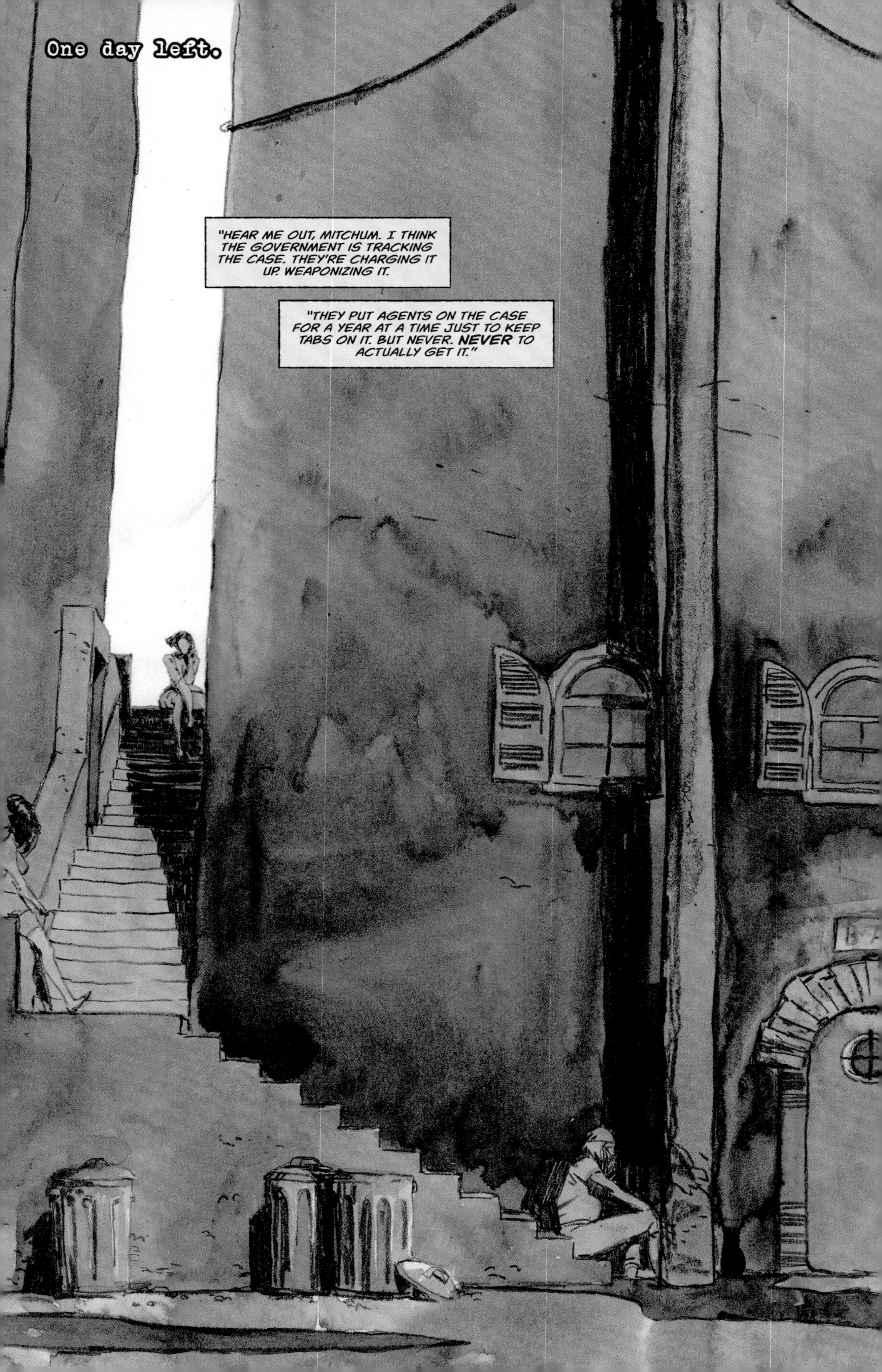
One day left.
"HEAR ME OUT, MITCHUM. I THINK THE GOVERNMENT IS TRACKING THE CASE. THEY'RE CHARGING IT UP. WEAPONIZING IT.
"THEY PUT AGENTS ON THE CASE FOR A YEAR AT A TIME JUST TO KEEP TABS ON IT. BUT NEVER. NEVER TO ACTUALLY GET IT."

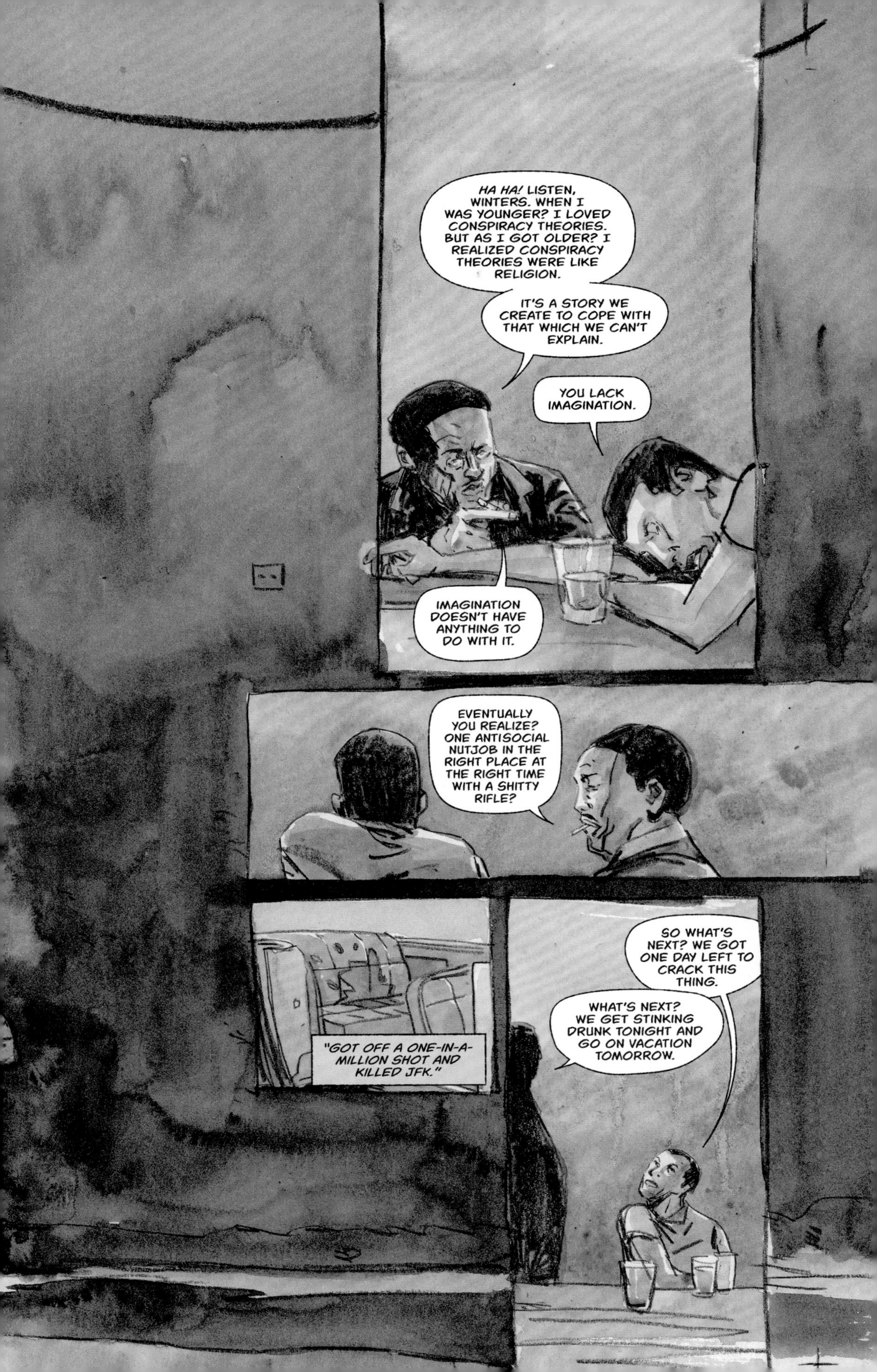

HA HA! LISTEN, WINTERS. WHEN I WAS YOUNGER? I LOVED CONSPIRACY THEORIES. BUT AS I GOT OLDER? I REALIZED CONSPIRACY THEORIES WERE LIKE RELIGION.
IT'S A STORY WE CREATE TO COPE WITH THAT WHICH WE CAN'T EXPLAIN.
YOU LACK IMAGINATION.
IMAGINATION DOESN'T HAVE ANYTHING TO DO WITH IT.
EVENTUALLY YOU REALIZE? ONE ANTISOCIAL NUTJOB IN THE RIGHT PLACE AT THE RIGHT TIME WITH A SHITTY RIFLE?
"GOT OFF A ONE-IN-A-MILLION SHOT AND KILLED JFK."
SO WHAT'S NEXT? WE GOT ONE DAY LEFT TO CRACK THIS THING.
WHAT'S NEXT? WE GET STINKING DRUNK TONIGHT AND GO ON VACATION TOMORROW.

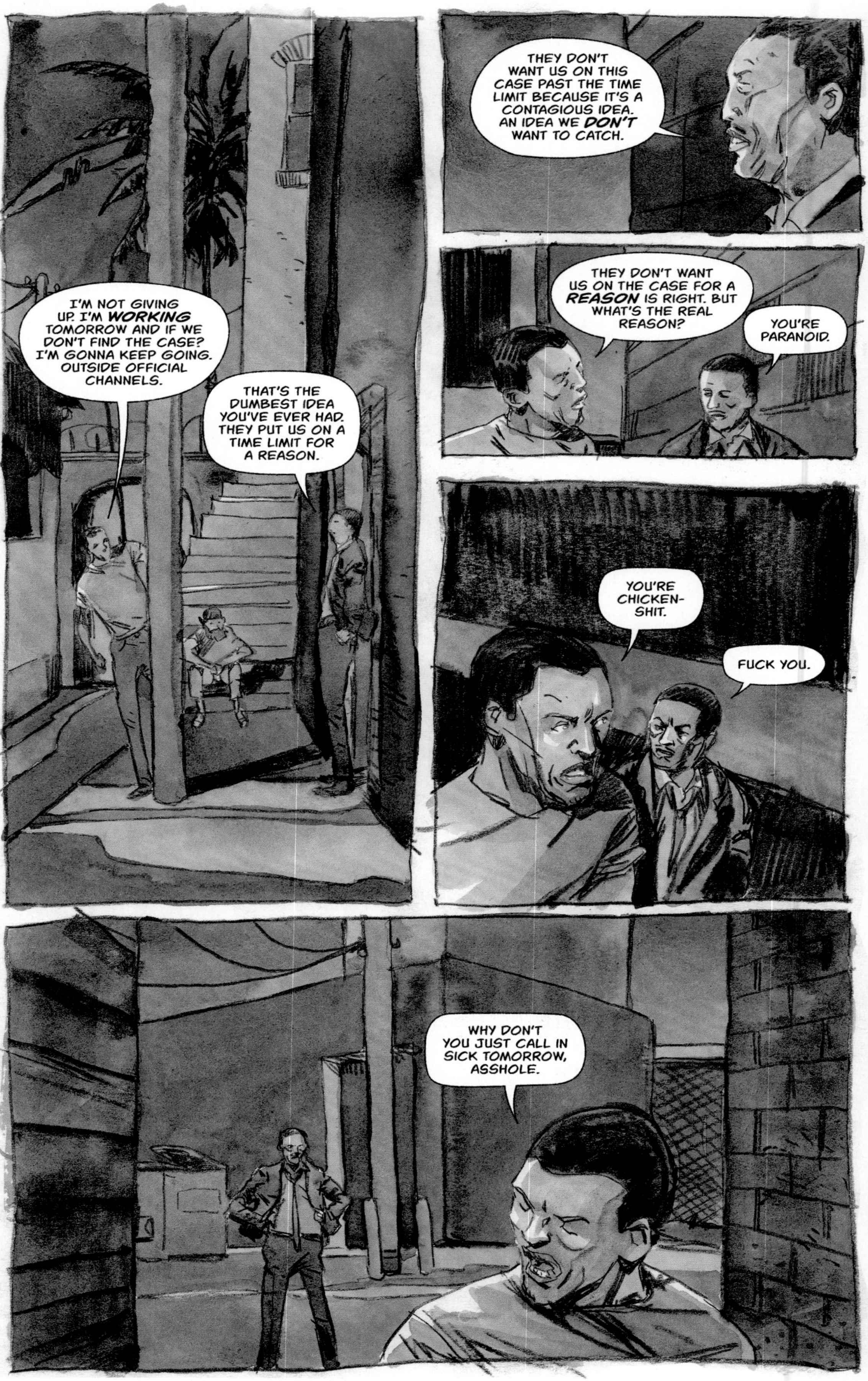
I'M NOT GIVING UP. I'M WORKING TOMORROW AND IF WE DON'T FIND THE CASE? I'M GONNA KEEP GOING. OUTSIDE OFFICIAL CHANNELS.
THAT'S THE DUMBEST IDEA YOU'VE EVER HAD. THEY PUT US ON A TIME LIMIT FOR A REASON.
THEY DON'T WANT US ON THIS CASE PAST THE TIME LIMIT BECAUSE IT'S A CONTAGIOUS IDEA. AN IDEA WE DON'T WANT TO CATCH.
THEY DON'T WANT US ON THE CASE FOR A REASON IS RIGHT. BUT WHAT'S THE REAL REASON?
YOU'RE PARANOID.
YOU'RE CHICKEN-SHIT.
FUCK YOU.
WHY DON'T YOU JUST CALL IN SICK TOMORROW, ASSHOLE.

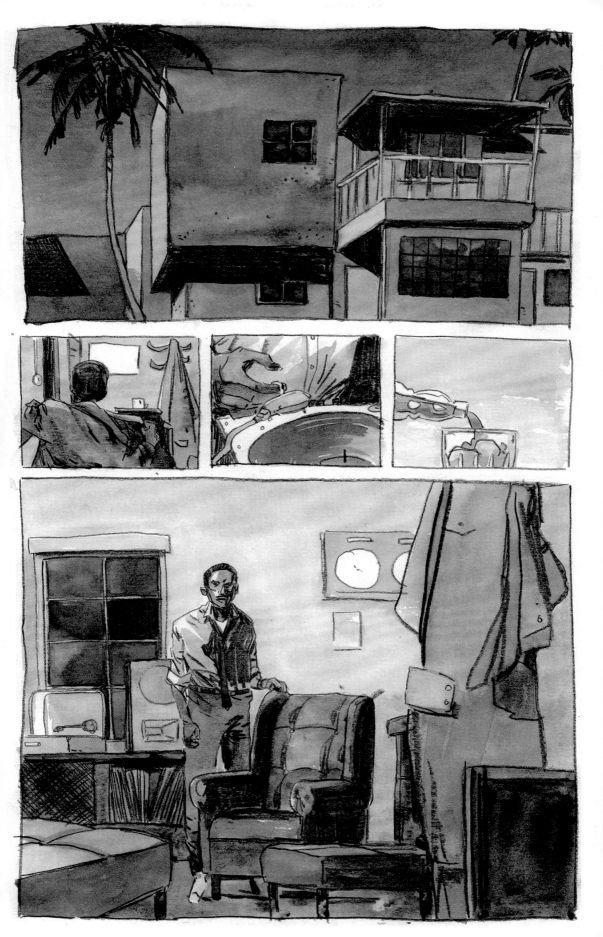

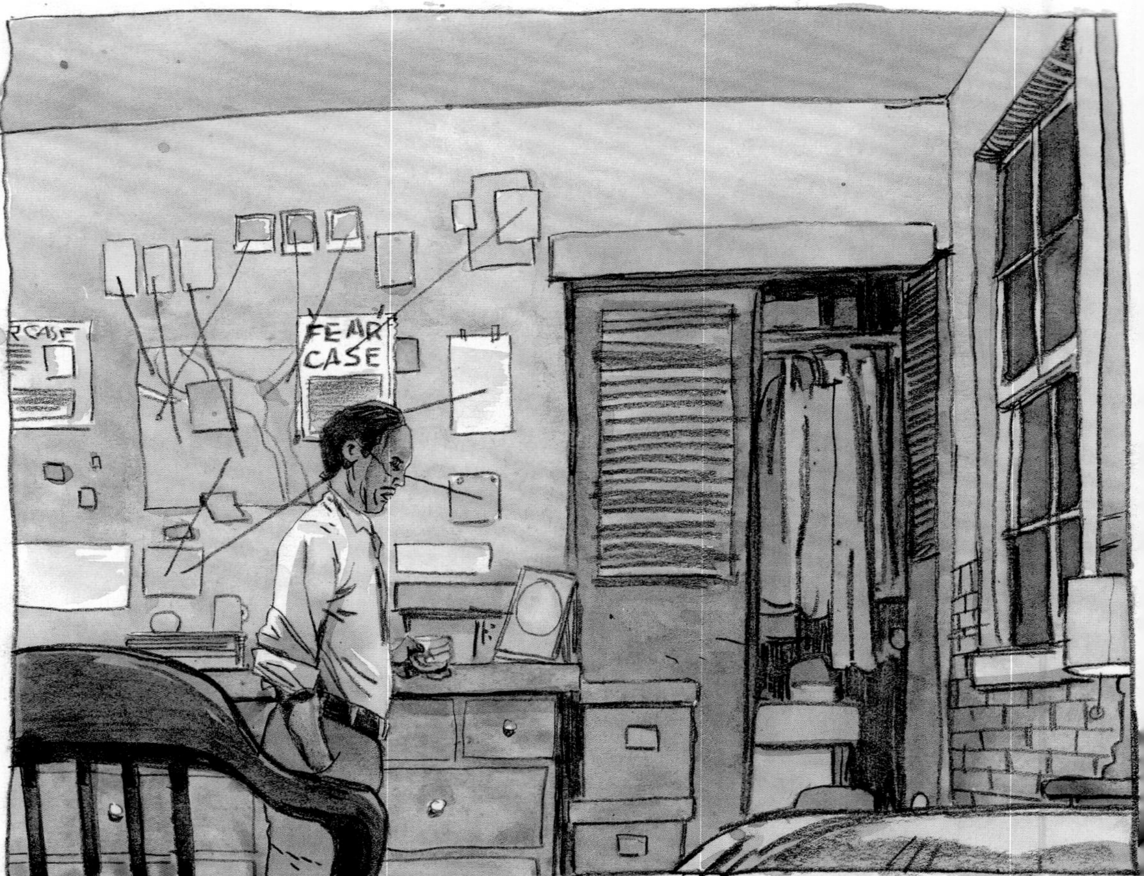
FEAR CASE
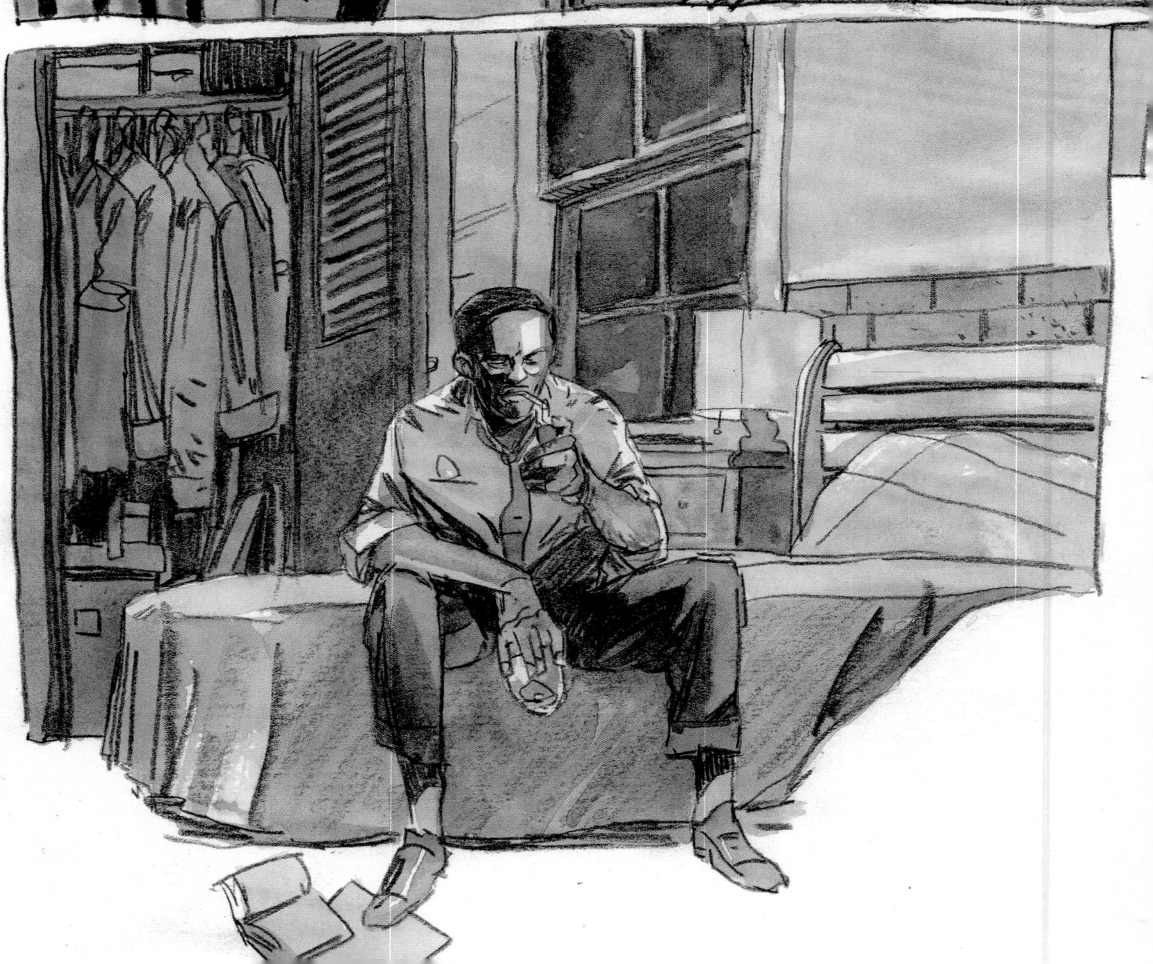

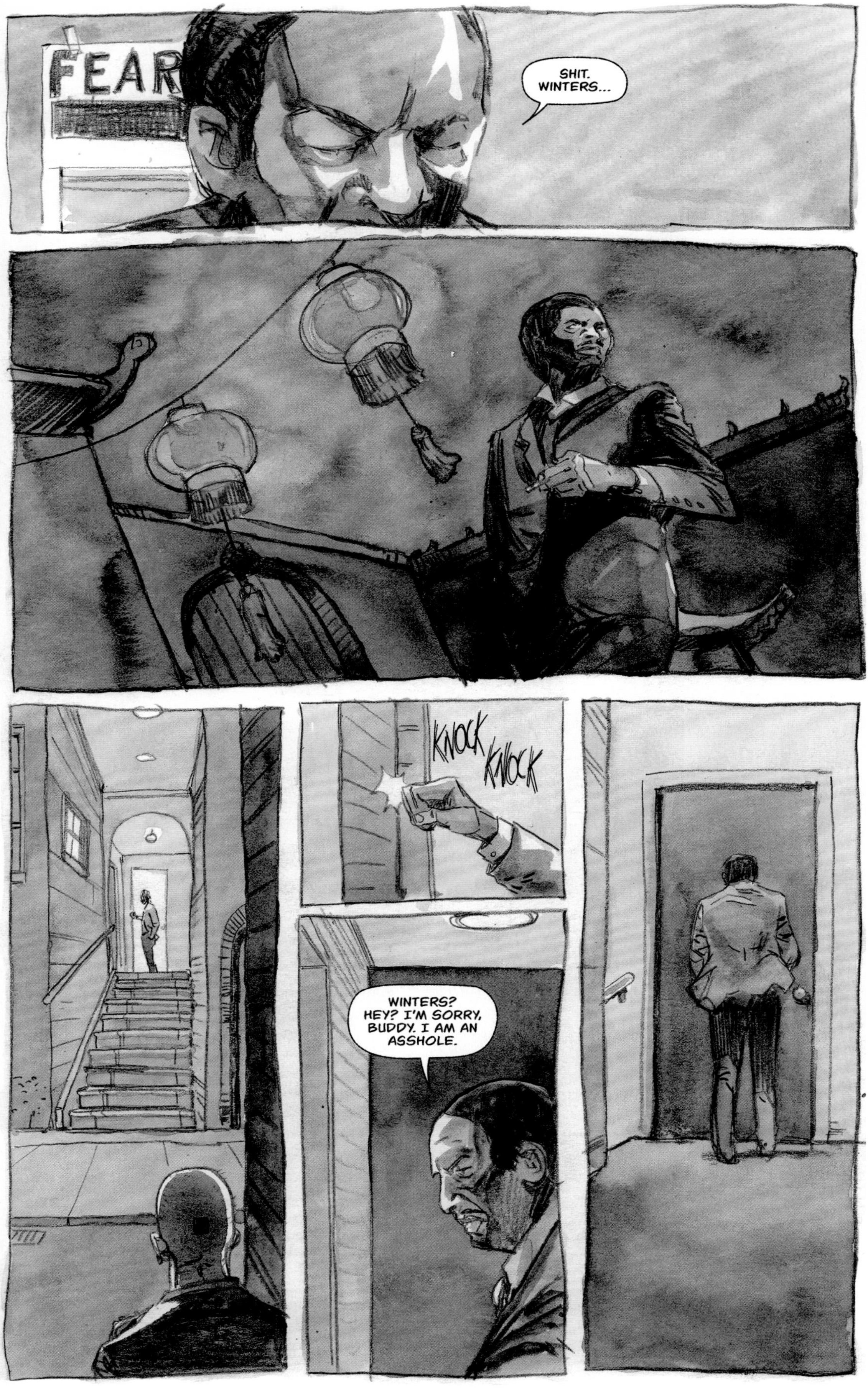
FEAR
SHIT. WINTERS...
KNOCK KNOCK
WINTERS? HEY? I'M SORRY, BUDDY. I AM AN ASSHOLE.

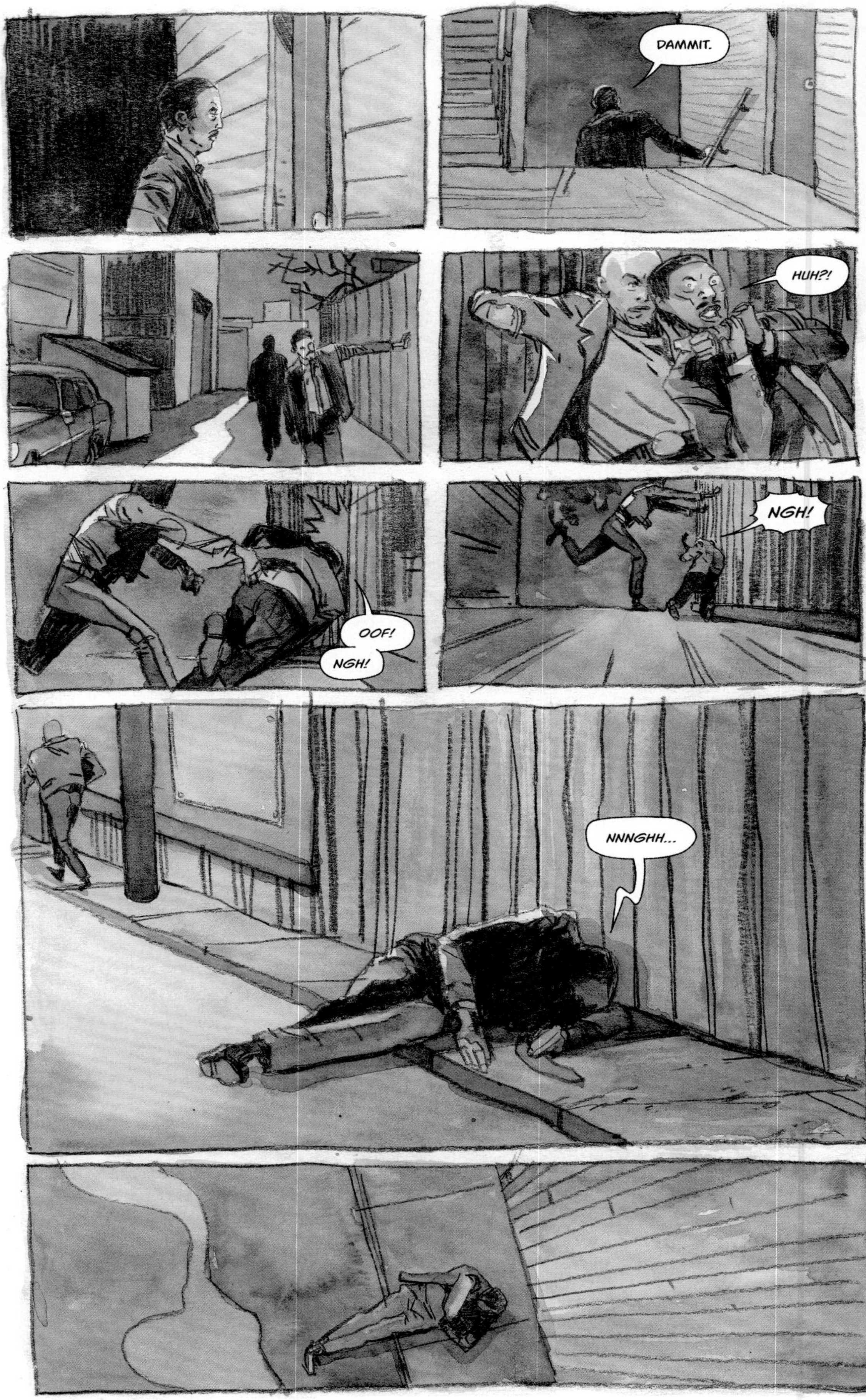
DAMMIT.
HUH?!
OOF!
NGH!
NGH!
NNNGHH...

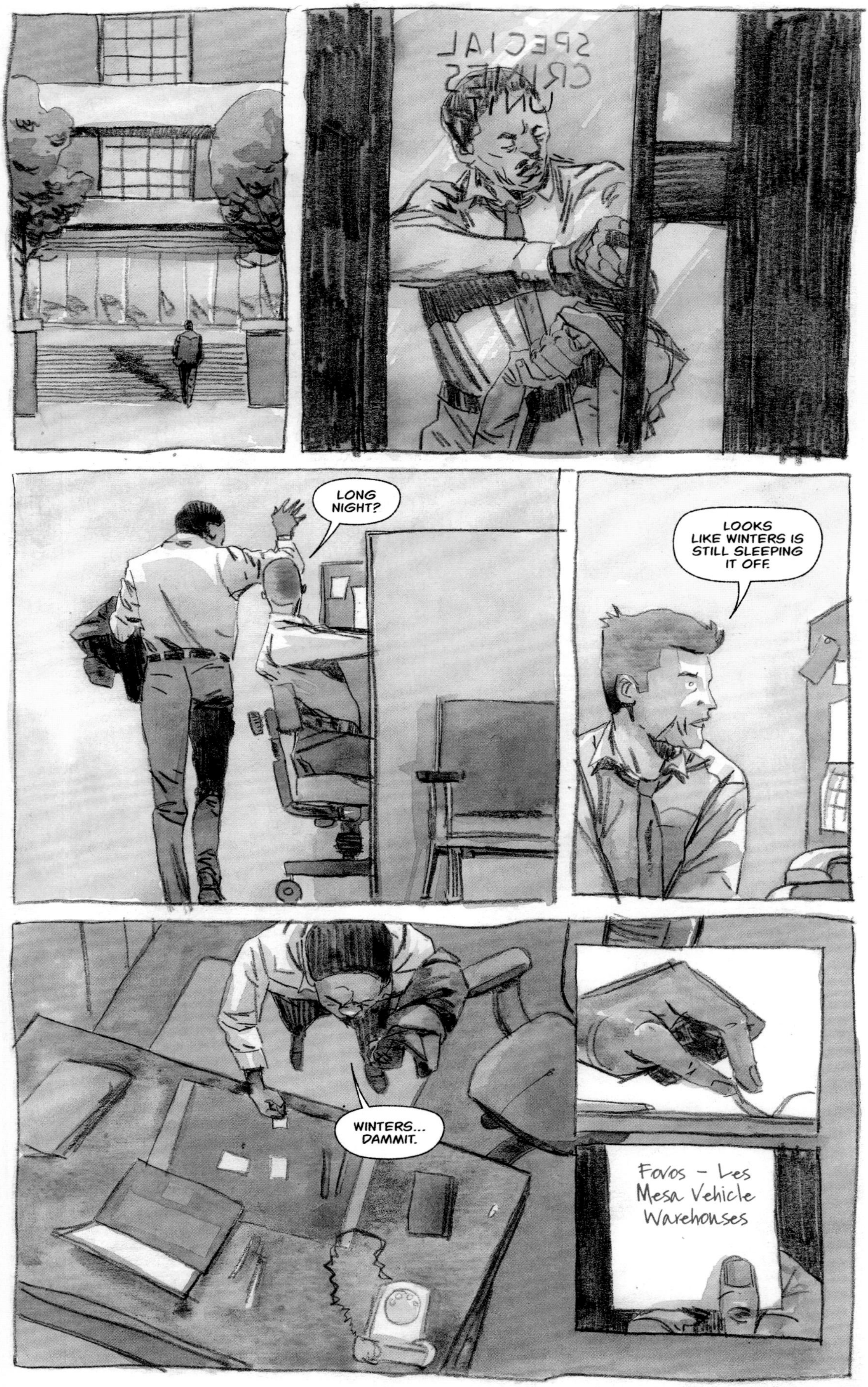
SPECIAL CRIMES UNIT
LONG NIGHT?
LOOKS LIKE WINTERS IS STILL SLEEPING IT OFF.
WINTERS... DAMMIT.
Fovos - Les Mesa Vehicle Warehouses

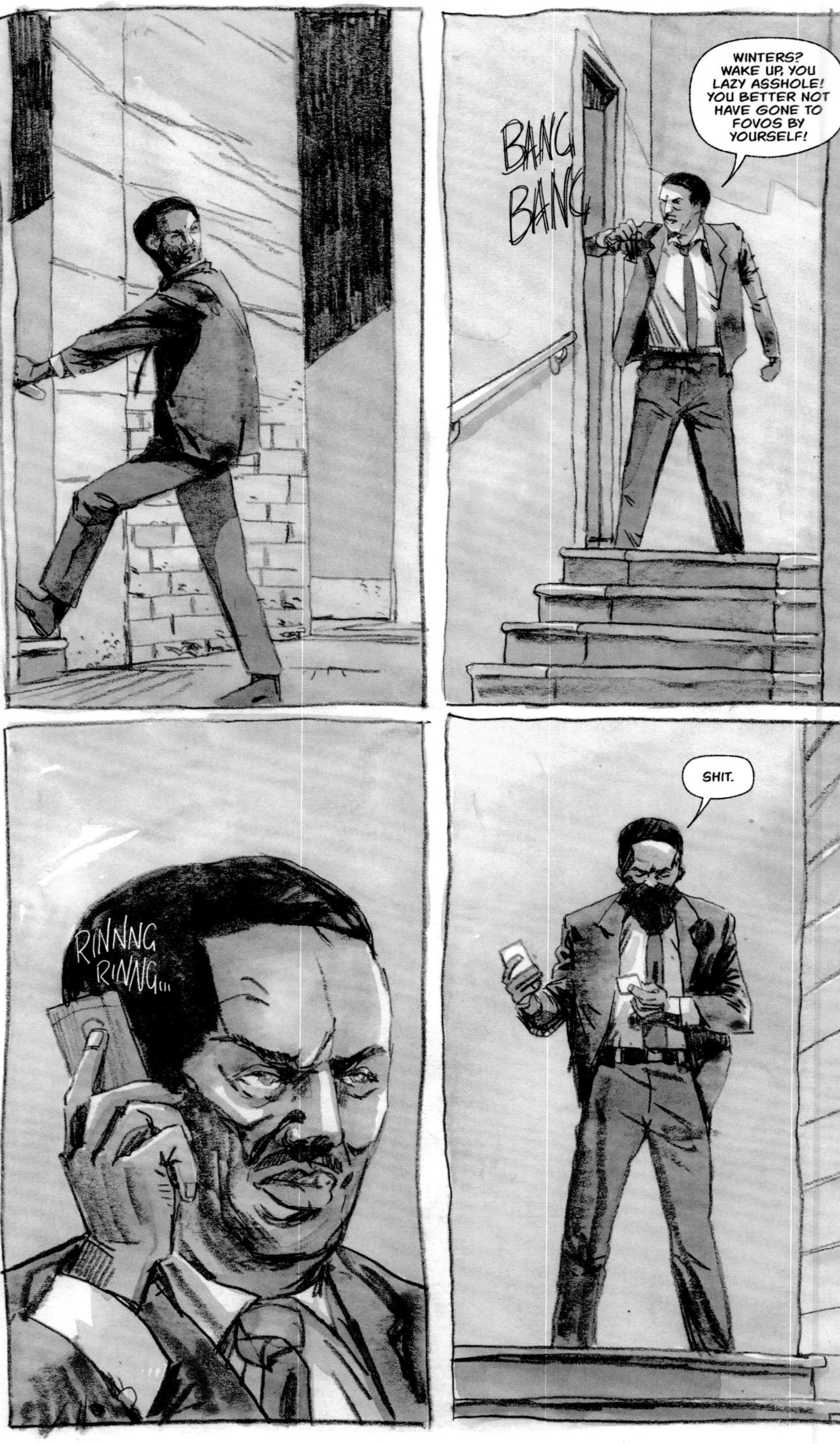
BANG
BANG
WINTERS? WAKE UP, YOU LAZY ASSHOLE! YOU BETTER NOT HAVE GONE TO FOVOS BY YOURSELF!
RINNNG RINNG...
SHIT.

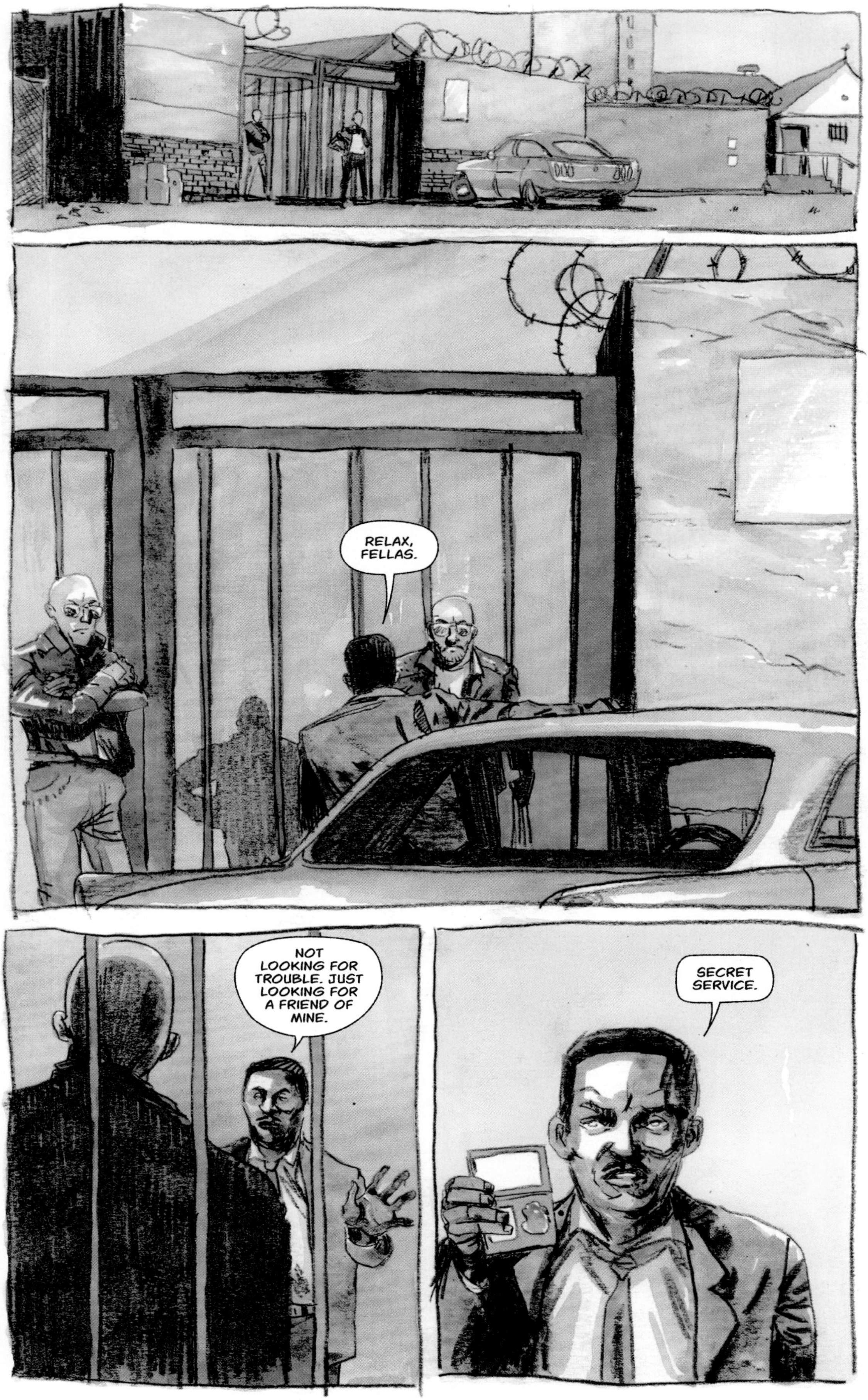
RELAX, FELLAS.
NOT LOOKING FOR TROUBLE. JUST LOOKING FOR A FRIEND OF MINE.
SECRET SERVICE.

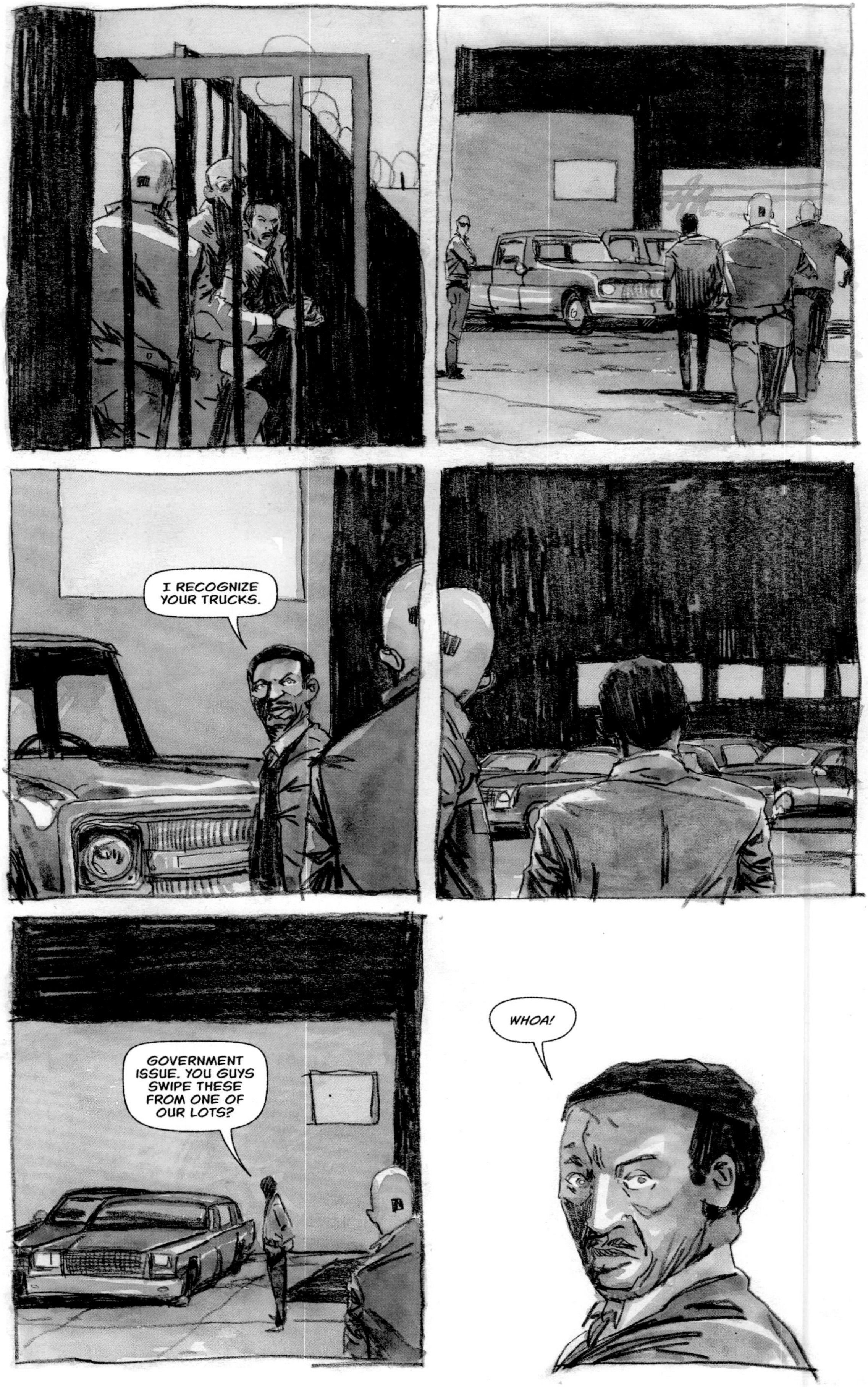
I RECOGNIZE YOUR TRUCKS.
GOVERNMENT ISSUE. YOU GUYS SWIPE THESE FROM ONE OF OUR LOTS?
WHOA!

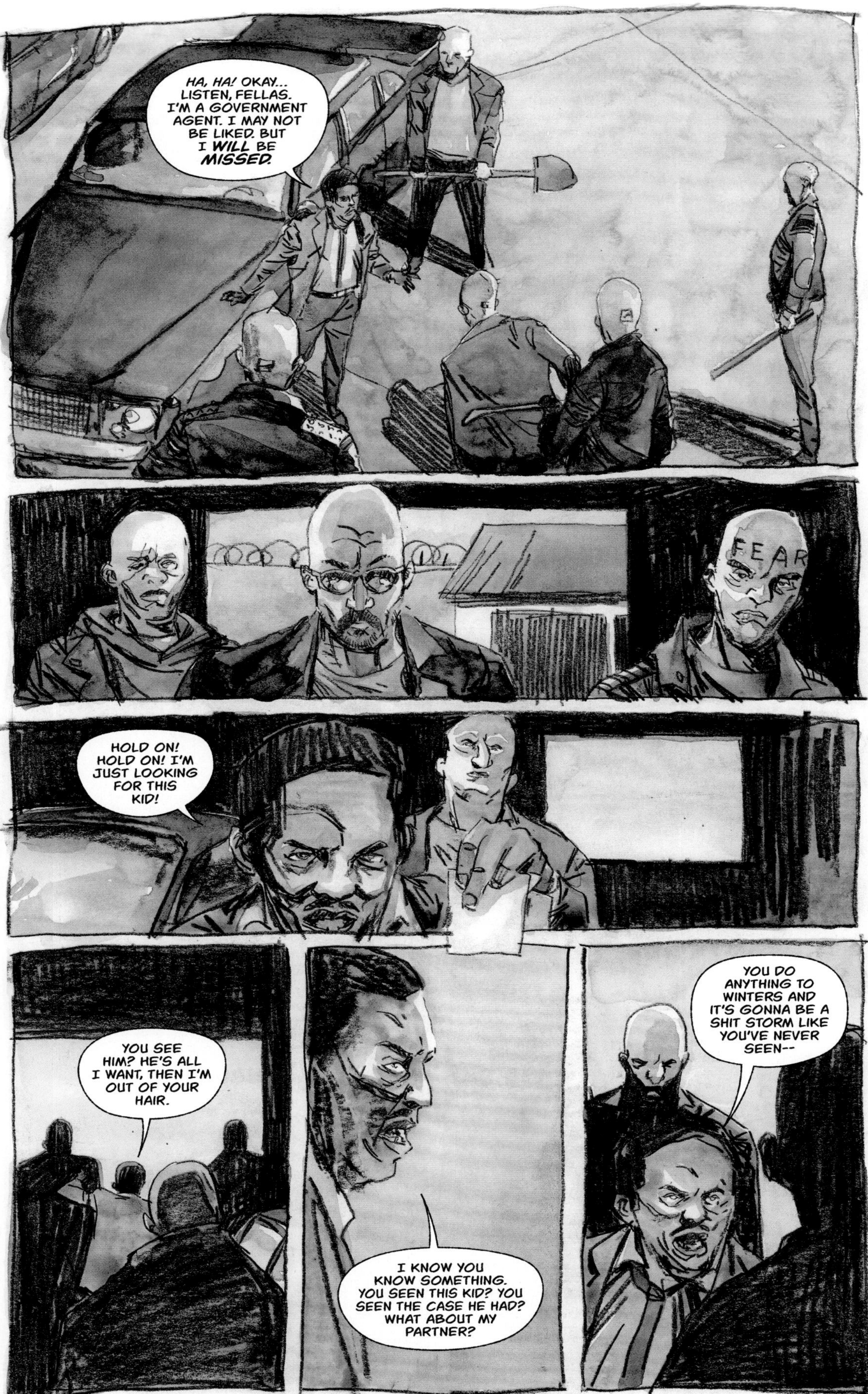
HA, HA! OKAY... LISTEN, FELLAS. I'M A GOVERNMENT AGENT. I MAY NOT BE LIKED. BUT I WILL BE MISSED.
FEAR
HOLD ON! HOLD ON! I'M JUST LOOKING FOR THIS KID!
YOU SEE HIM? HE'S ALL I WANT, THEN I'M OUT OF YOUR HAIR.
I KNOW YOU KNOW SOMETHING. YOU SEEN THIS KID? YOU SEEN THE CASE HE HAD? WHAT ABOUT MY PARTNER?
YOU DO ANYTHING TO WINTERS AND IT'S GONNA BE A SHIT STORM LIKE YOU'VE NEVER SEEN--

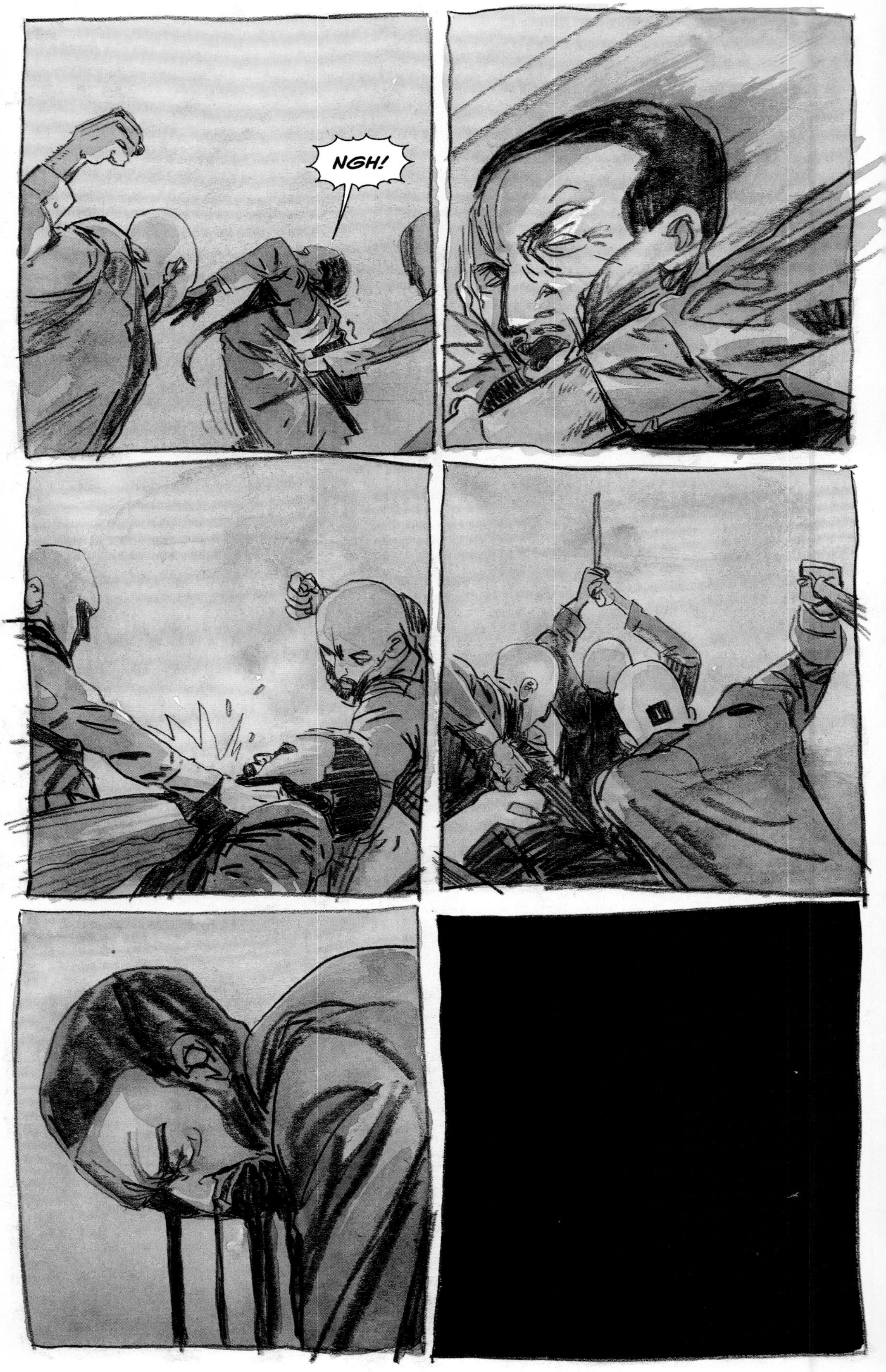
NGH!

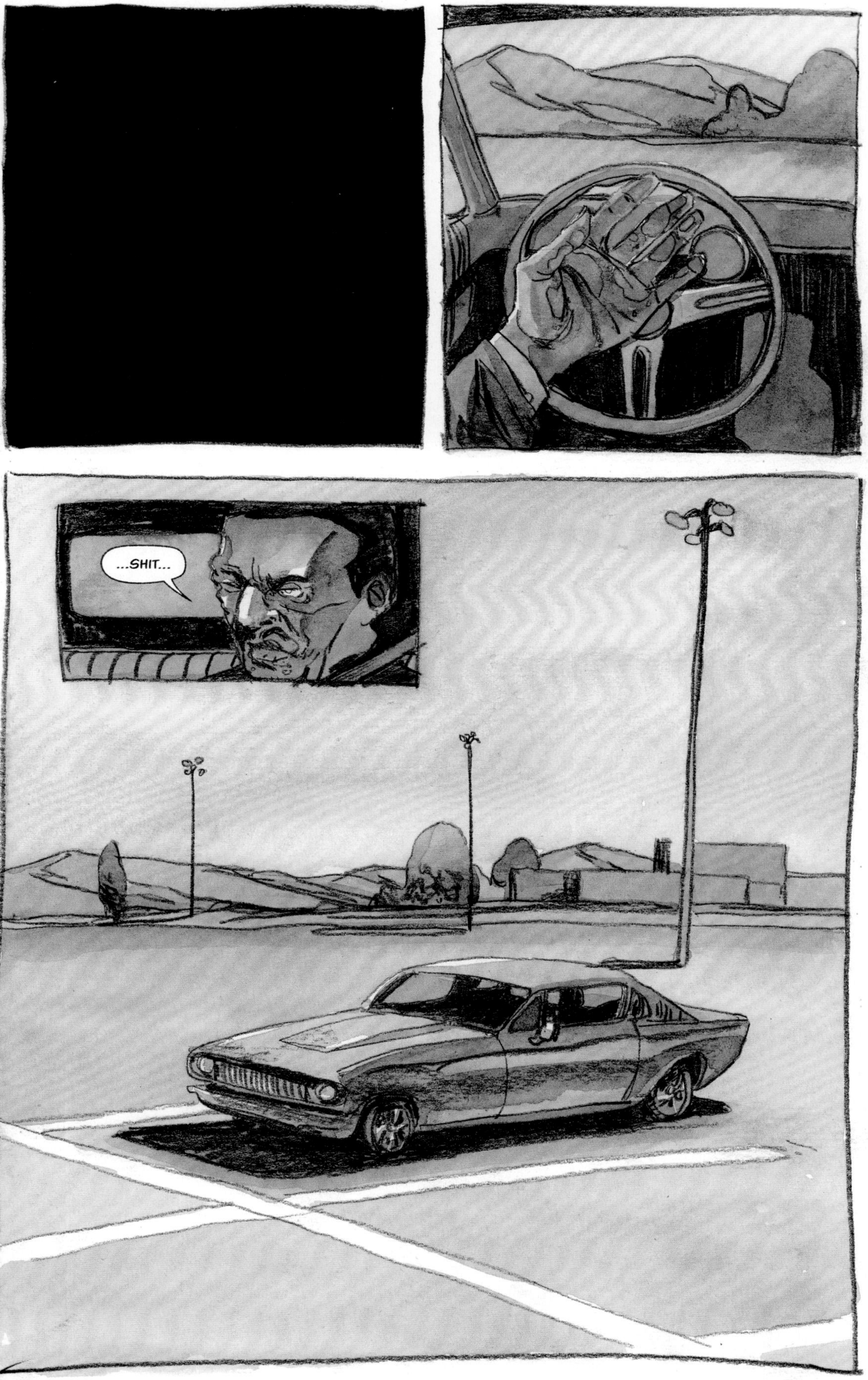
...SHIT...

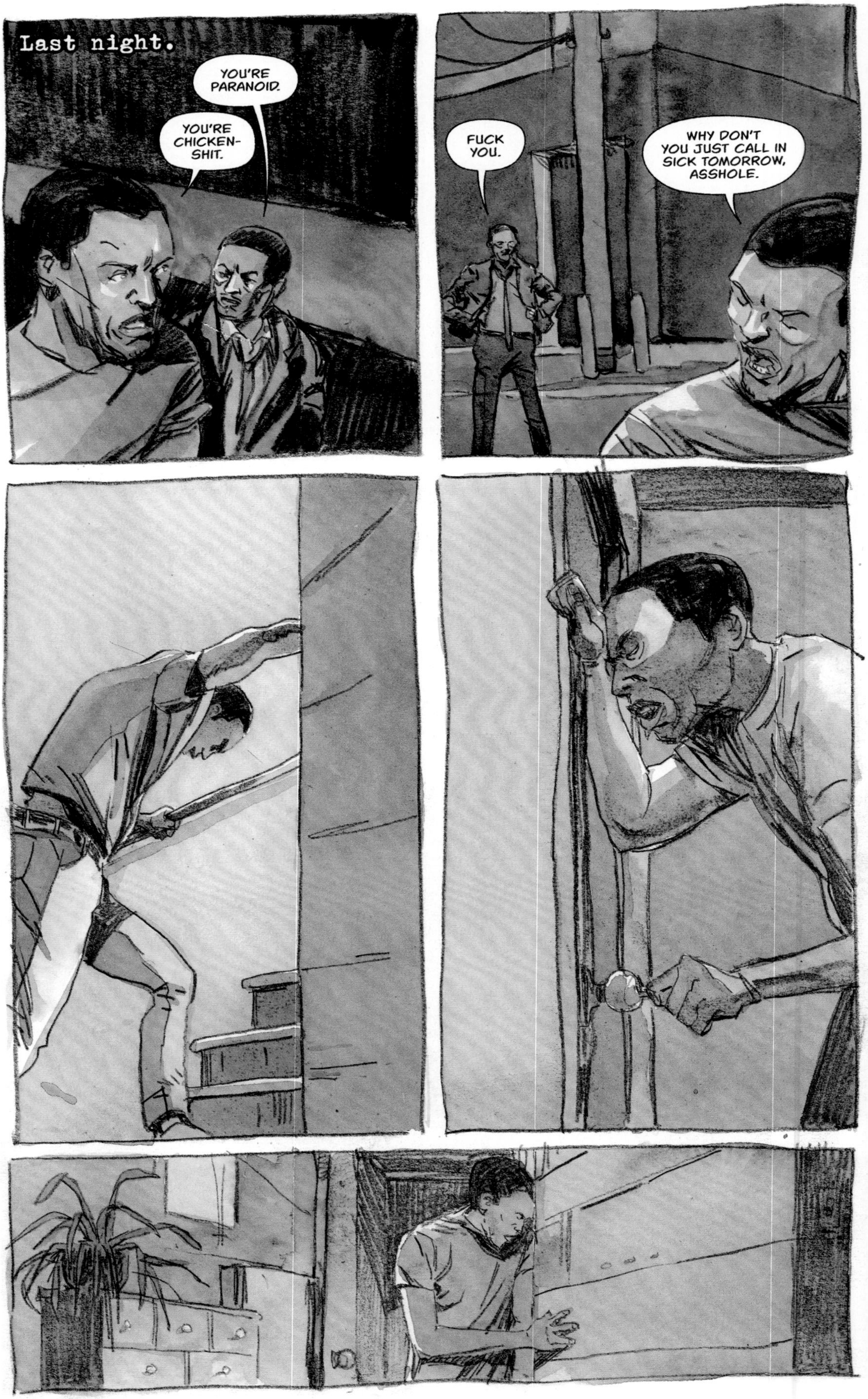
Last night.
YOU'RE PARANOID.
YOU'RE CHICKEN-SHIT.
FUCK YOU.
WHY DON'T YOU JUST CALL IN SICK TOMORROW, ASSHOLE.

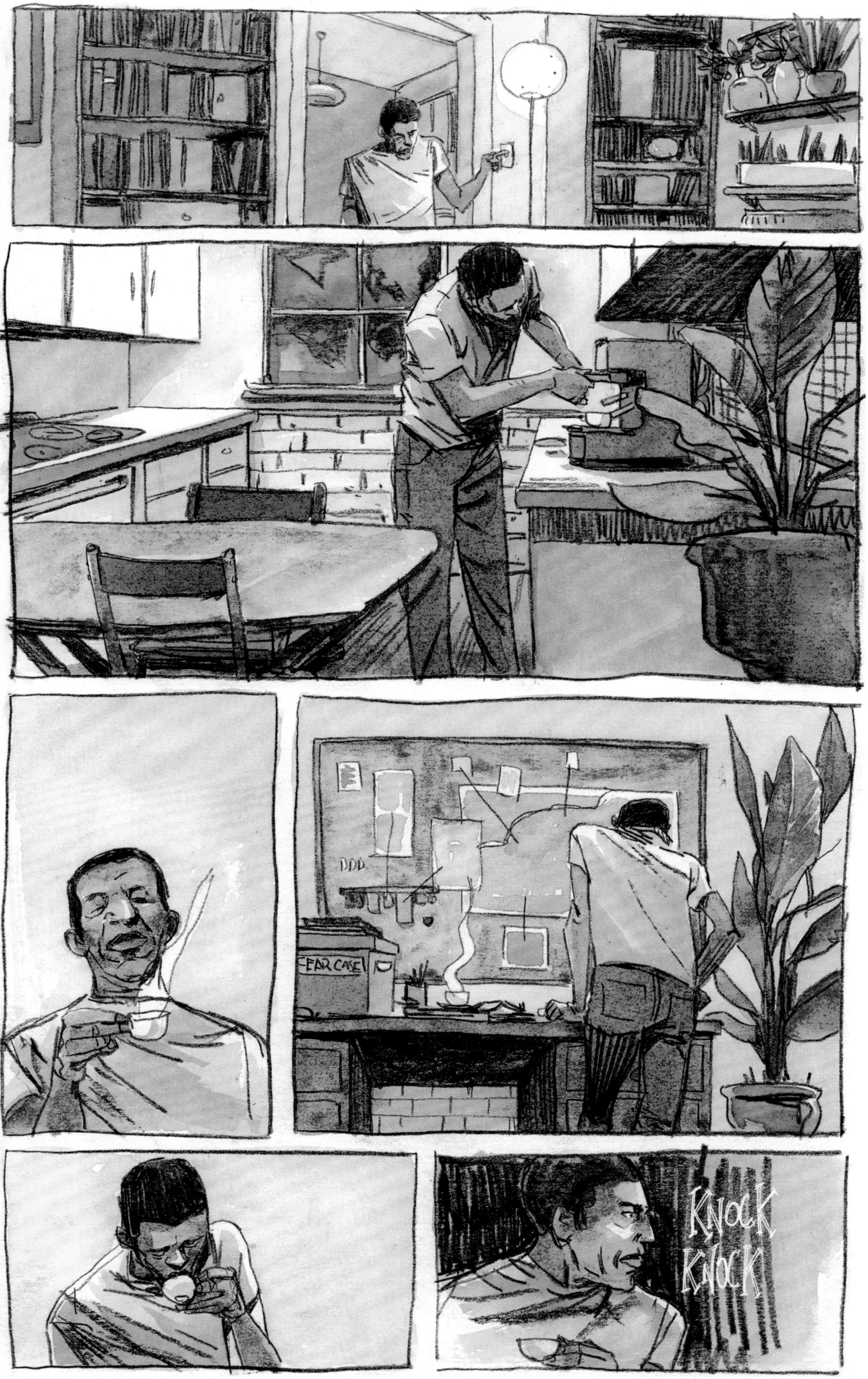
FEAR CASE
KNOCK
KNOCK

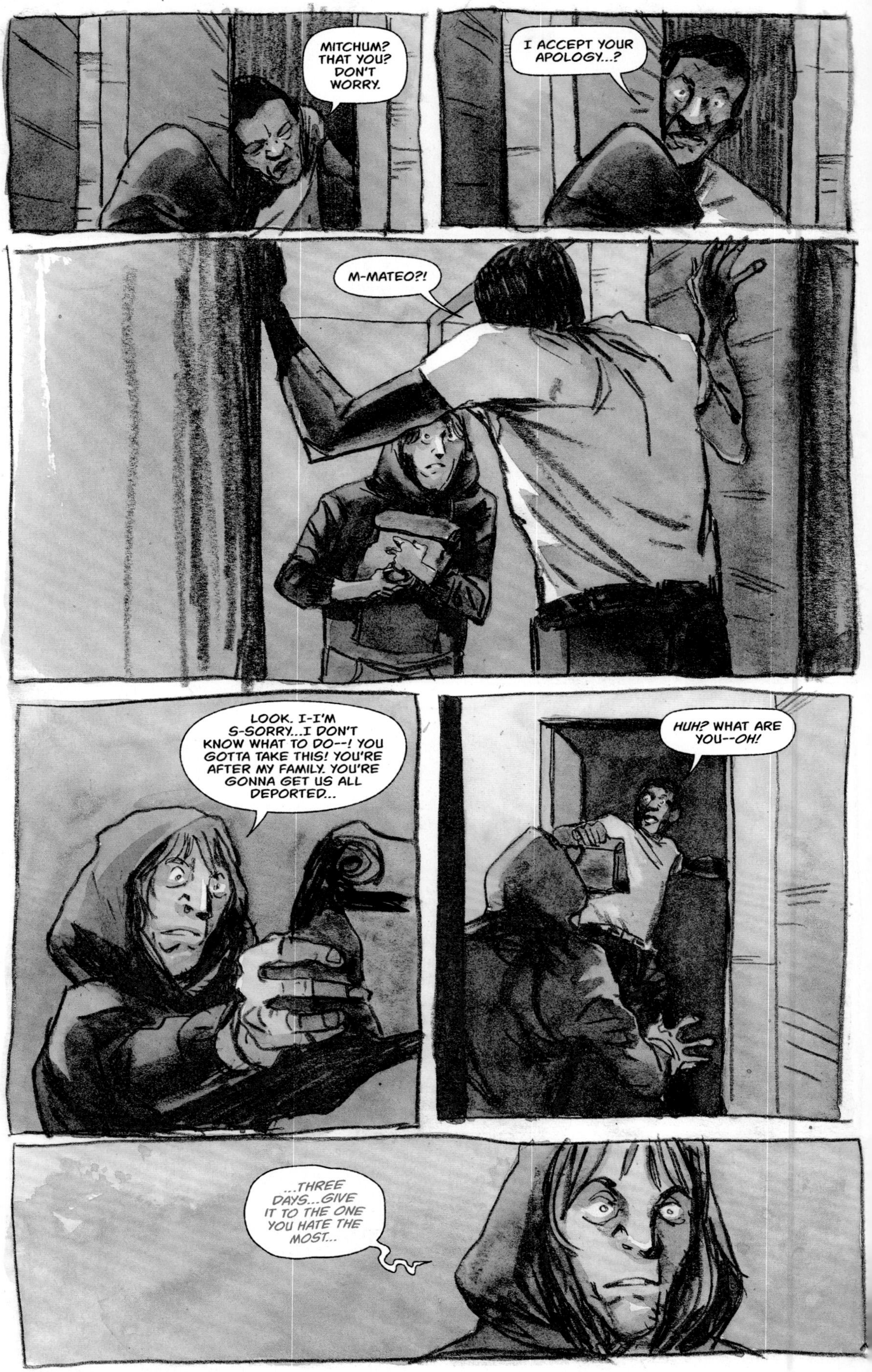
MITCHUM? THAT YOU? DON'T WORRY.
I ACCEPT YOUR APOLOGY...?
M-MATEO?!
LOOK. I-I'M S-SORRY...I DON'T KNOW WHAT TO DO--! YOU GOTTA TAKE THIS! YOU'RE AFTER MY FAMILY. YOU'RE GONNA GET US ALL DEPORTED...
HUH? WHAT ARE YOU--OH!
...THREE DAYS...GIVE IT TO THE ONE YOU HATE THE MOST...

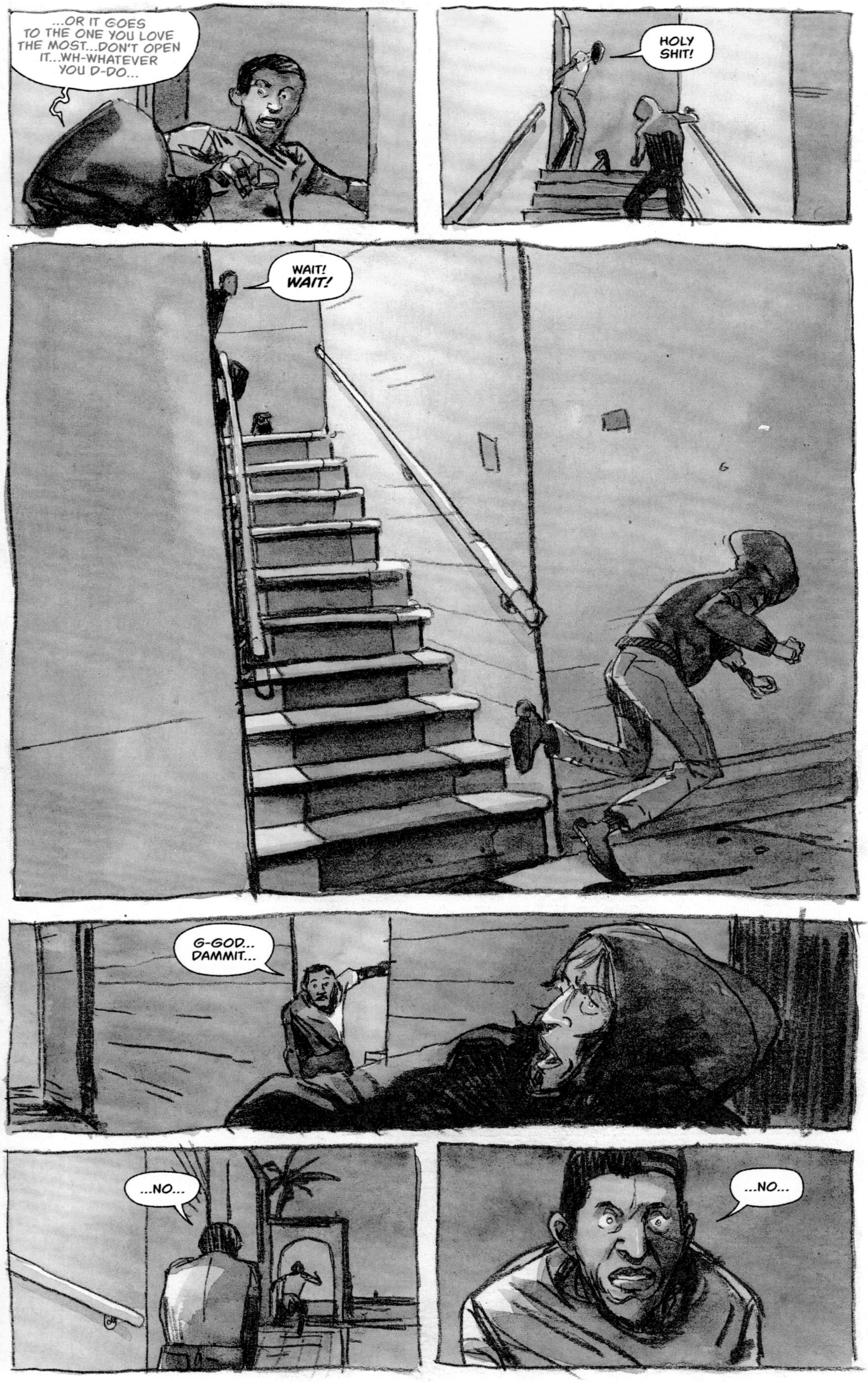
...OR IT GOES TO THE ONE YOU LOVE THE MOST...DON'T OPEN IT...WH-WHATEVER YOU D-DO...
HOLY SHIT!
WAIT! WAIT!
G-GOD... DAMMIT...
...NO...
...NO...

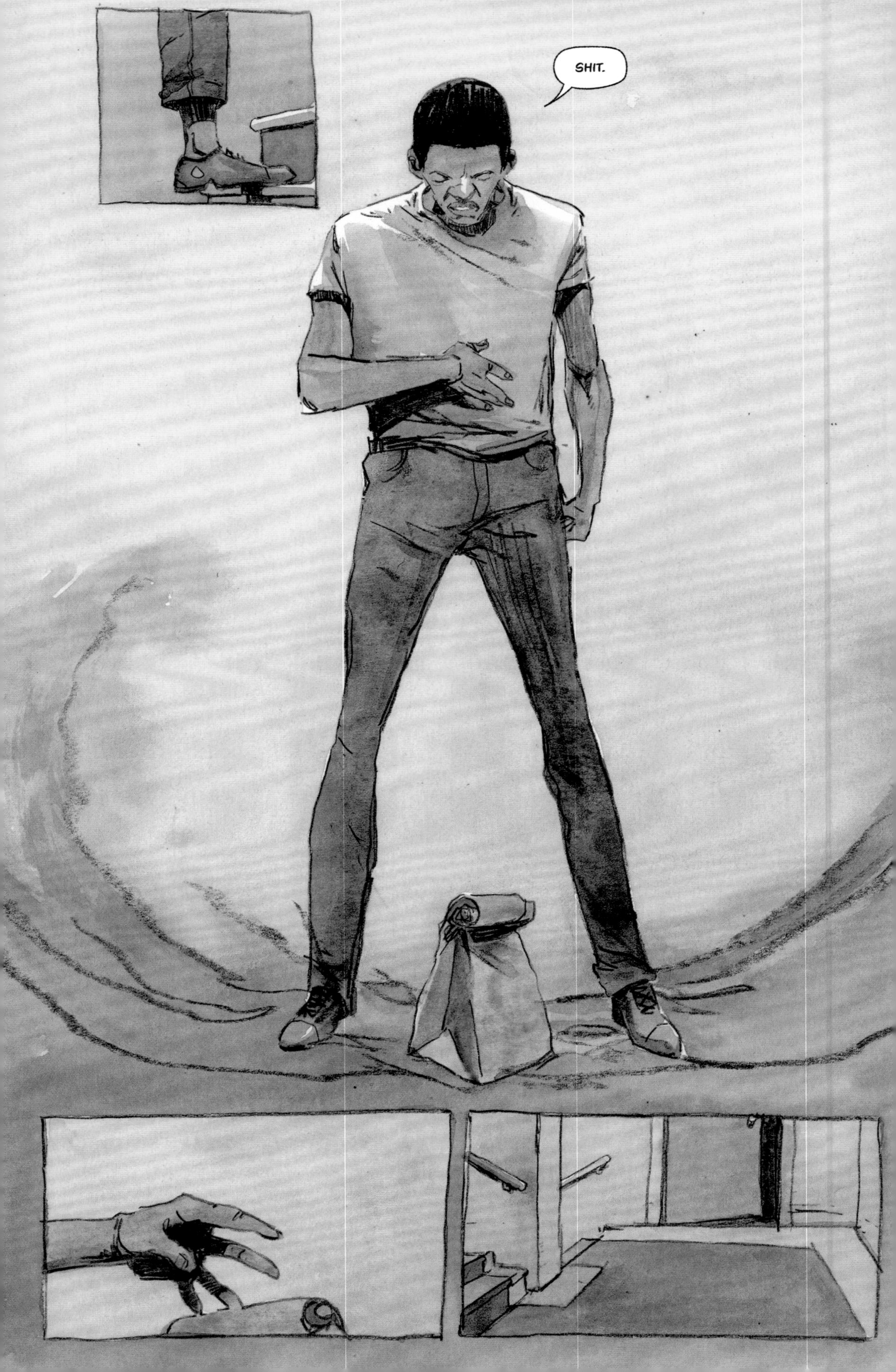
SHIT.

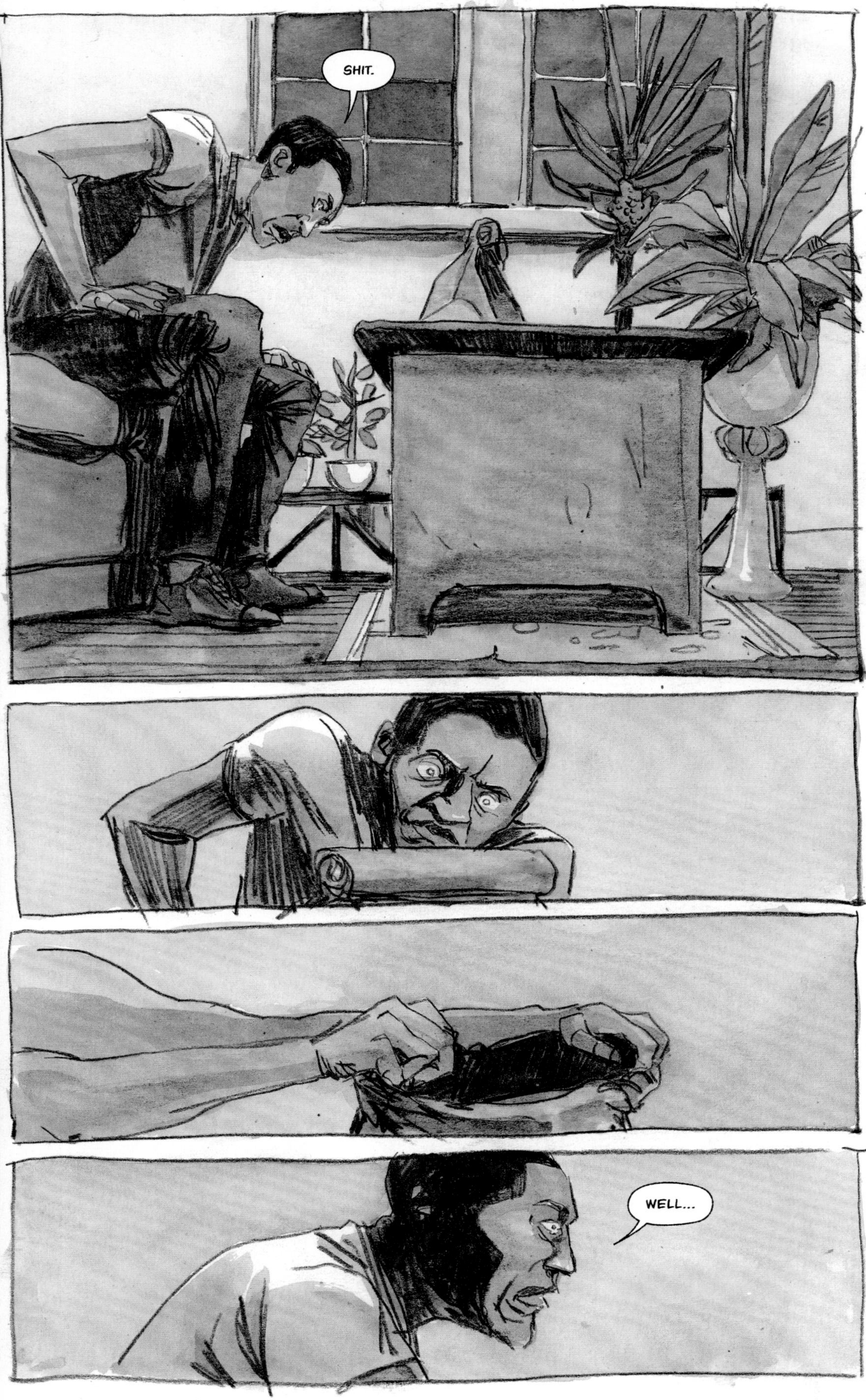
SHIT.
WELL...

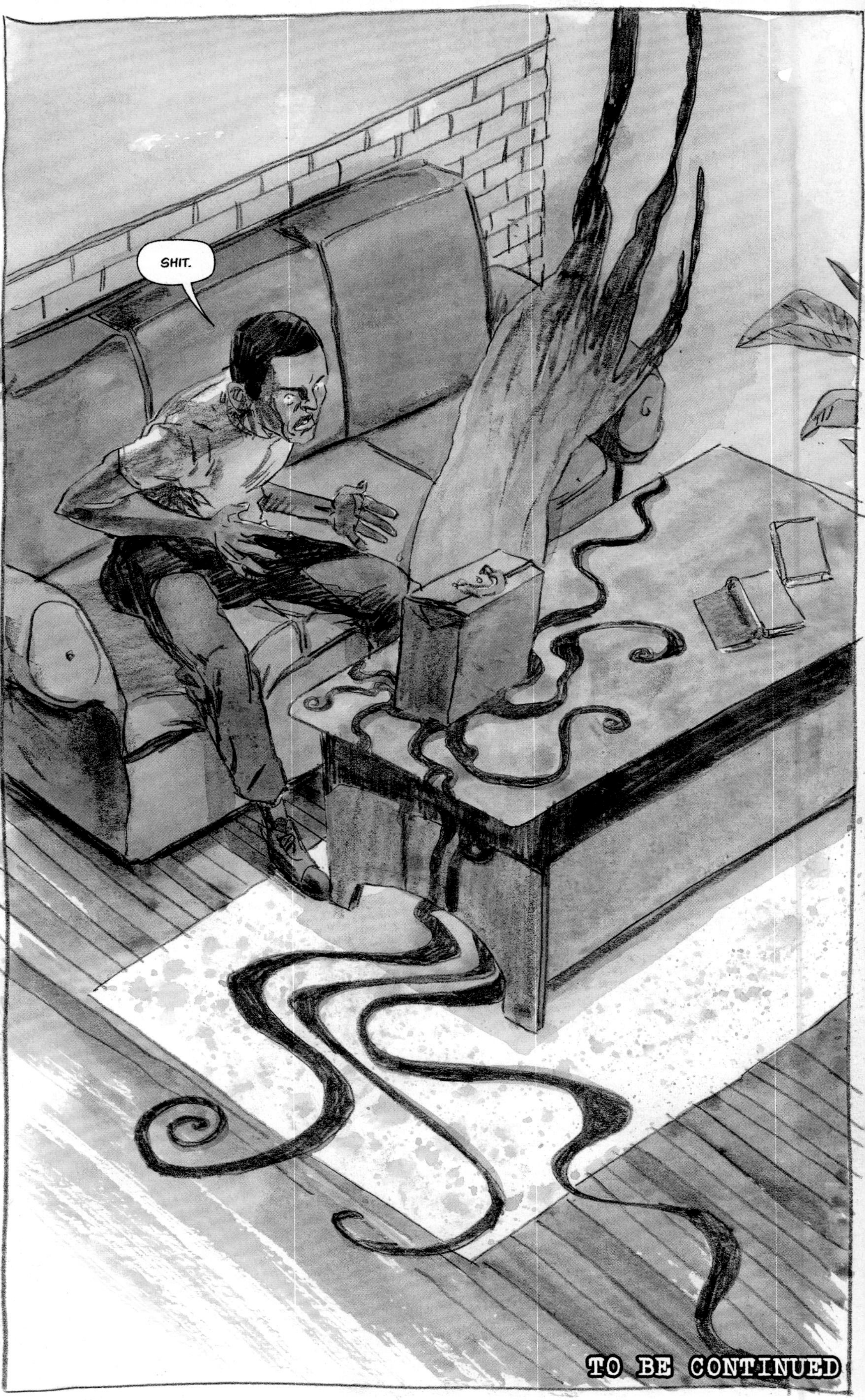
SHIT.
TO BE CONTINUED

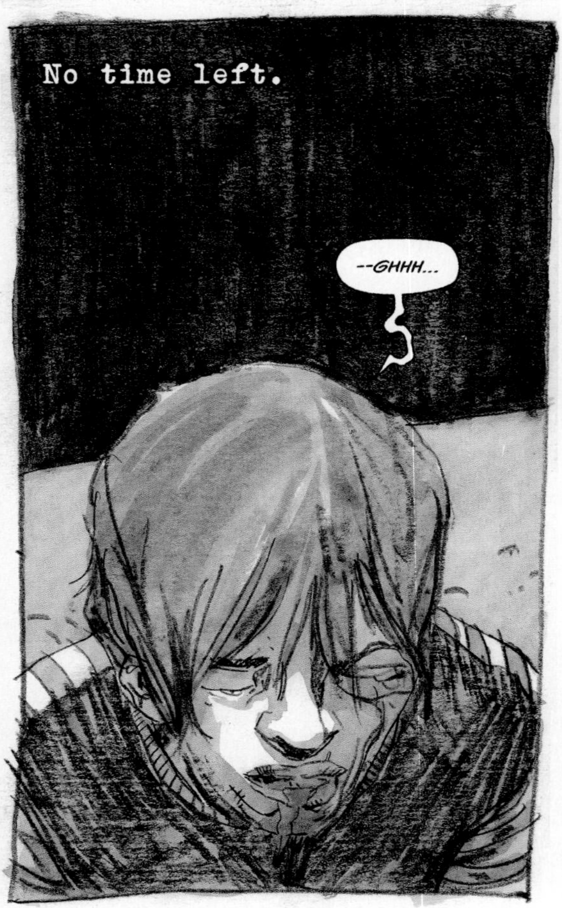
No time left.
--GHHH...
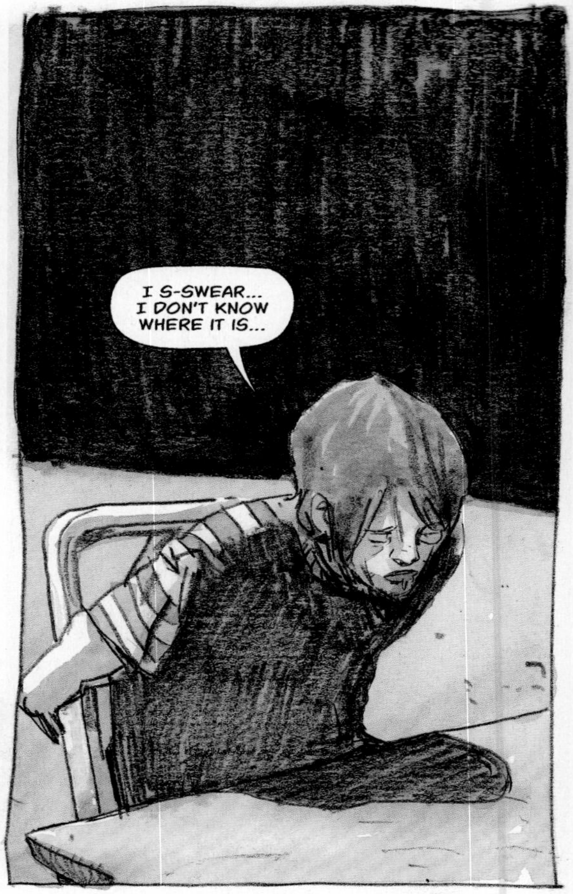
I S-SWEAR... I DON'T KNOW WHERE IT IS...

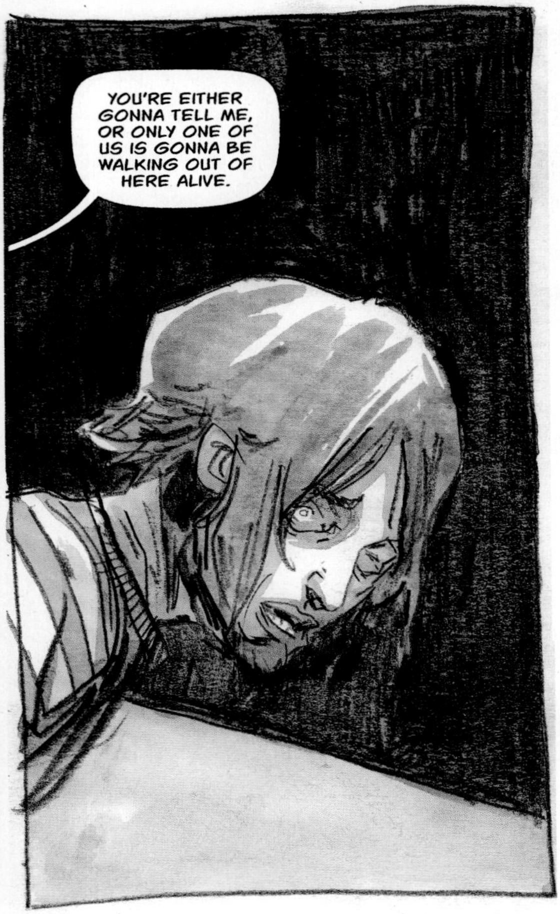
YOU'RE EITHER GONNA TELL ME, OR ONLY ONE OF US IS GONNA BE WALKING OUT OF HERE ALIVE.

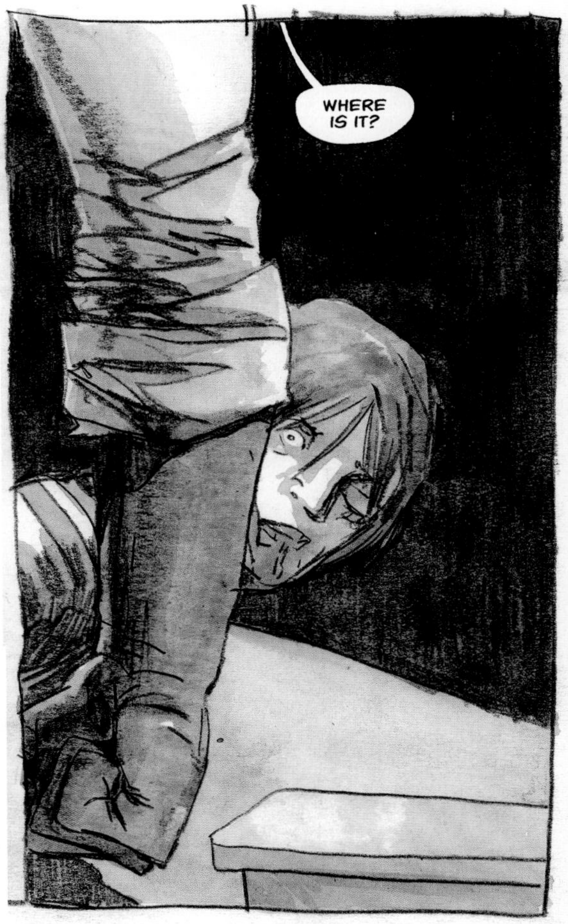
WHERE IS IT?

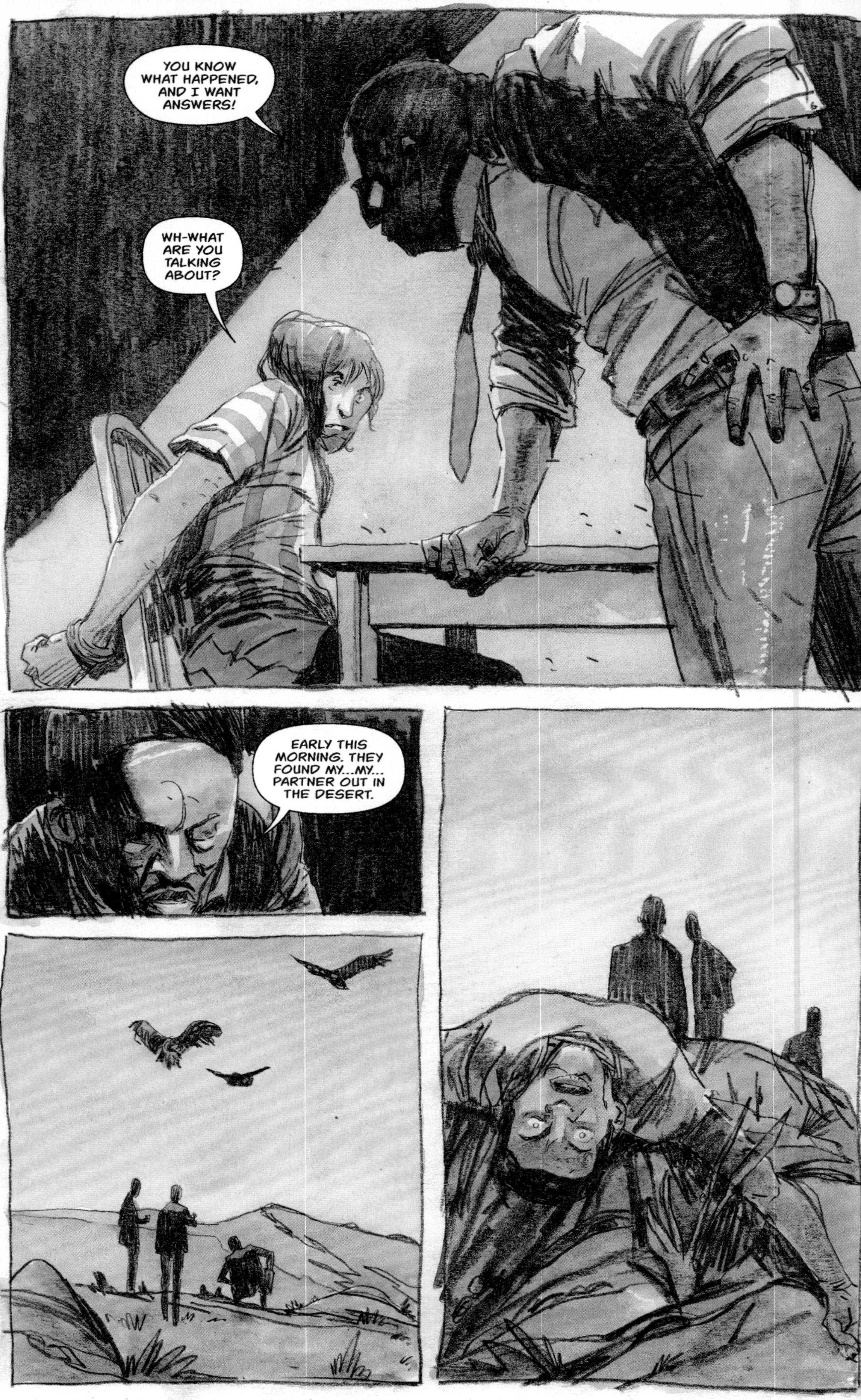
YOU KNOW WHAT HAPPENED, AND I WANT ANSWERS!
WH-WHAT ARE YOU TALKING ABOUT?
EARLY THIS MORNING. THEY FOUND MY...MY... PARTNER OUT IN THE DESERT.

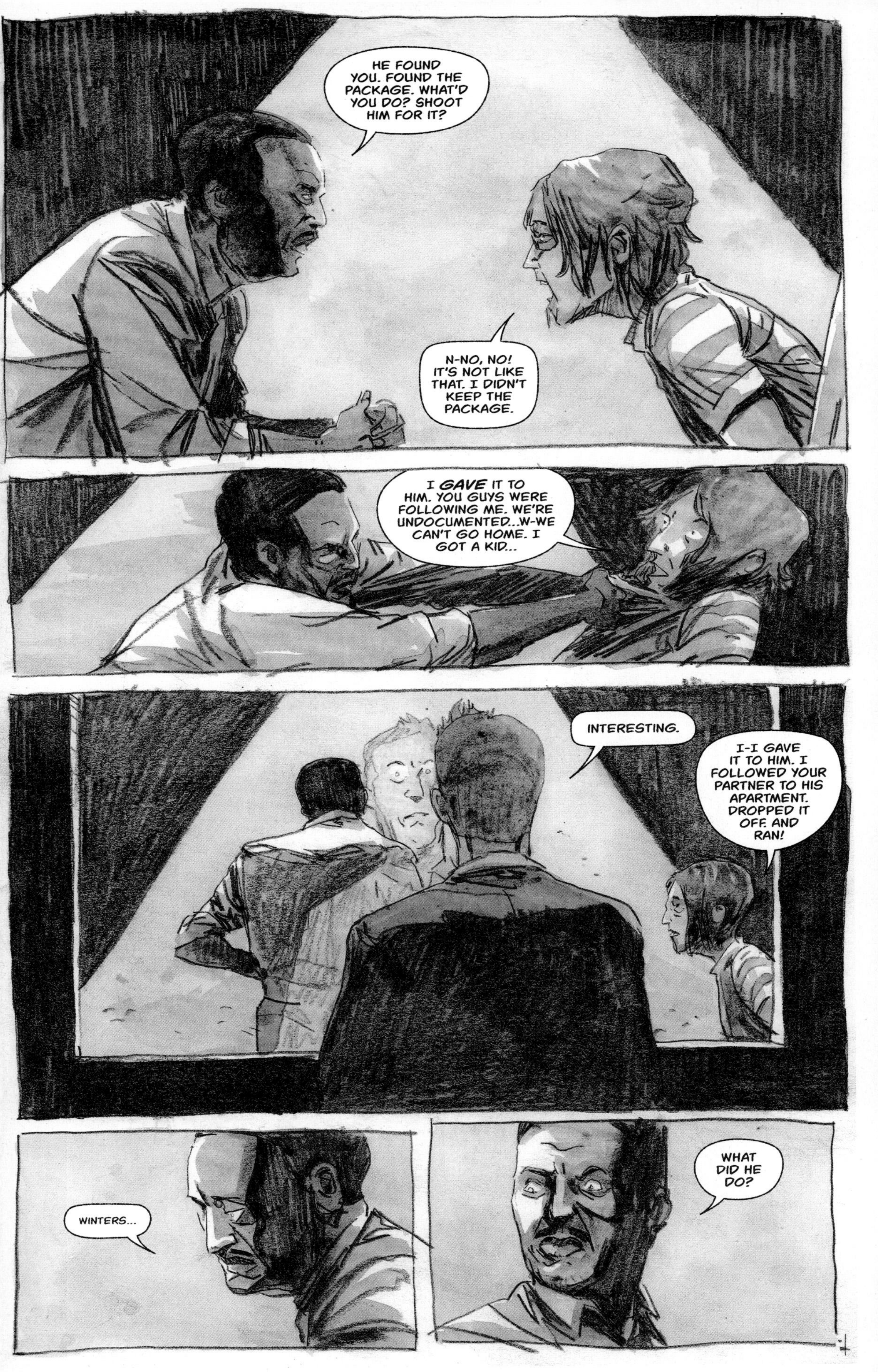
HE FOUND YOU. FOUND THE PACKAGE. WHAT'D YOU DO? SHOOT HIM FOR IT?
N-NO, NO! IT'S NOT LIKE THAT. I DIDN'T KEEP THE PACKAGE.
I GAVE IT TO HIM. YOU GUYS WERE FOLLOWING ME. WE'RE UNDOCUMENTED...W-WE CAN'T GO HOME. I GOT A KID...
INTERESTING.
I-I GAVE IT TO HIM. I FOLLOWED YOUR PARTNER TO HIS APARTMENT. DROPPED IT OFF. AND RAN!
WINTERS...
WHAT DID HE DO?

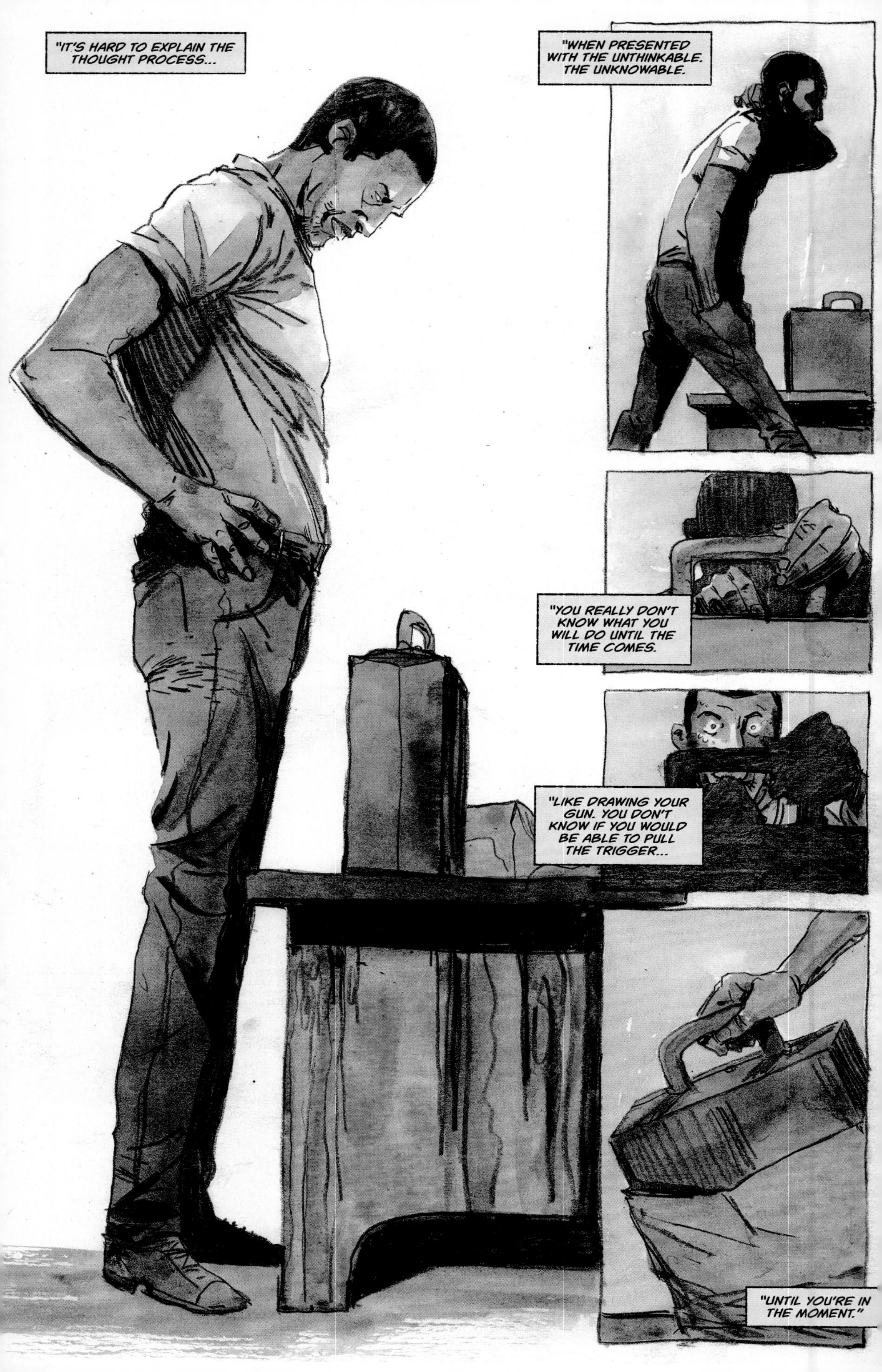
"IT'S HARD TO EXPLAIN THE THOUGHT PROCESS...
"WHEN PRESENTED WITH THE UNTHINKABLE. THE UNKNOWABLE.
"YOU REALLY DON'T KNOW WHAT YOU WILL DO UNTIL THE TIME COMES.
"LIKE DRAWING YOUR GUN. YOU DON'T KNOW IF YOU WOULD BE ABLE TO PULL THE TRIGGER...
"UNTIL YOU'RE IN THE MOMENT."

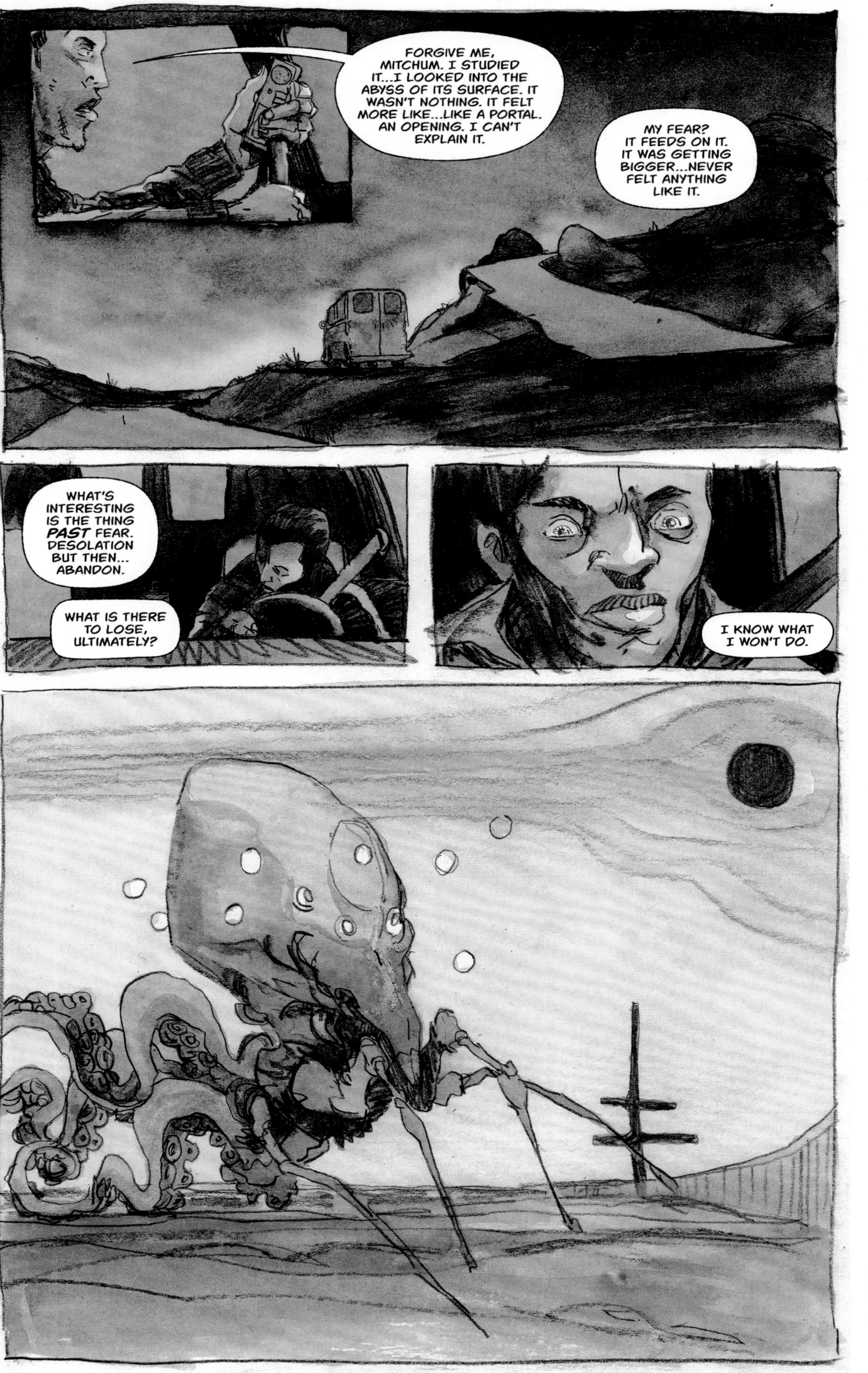

FORGIVE ME, MITCHUM. I STUDIED IT...I LOOKED INTO THE ABYSS OF ITS SURFACE. IT WASN'T NOTHING. IT FELT MORE LIKE...LIKE A PORTAL. AN OPENING. I CAN'T EXPLAIN IT.
MY FEAR? IT FEEDS ON IT. IT WAS GETTING BIGGER...NEVER FELT ANYTHING LIKE IT.
WHAT'S INTERESTING IS THE THING PAST FEAR. DESOLATION BUT THEN... ABANDON.
WHAT IS THERE TO LOSE, ULTIMATELY?
I KNOW WHAT I WON'T DO.

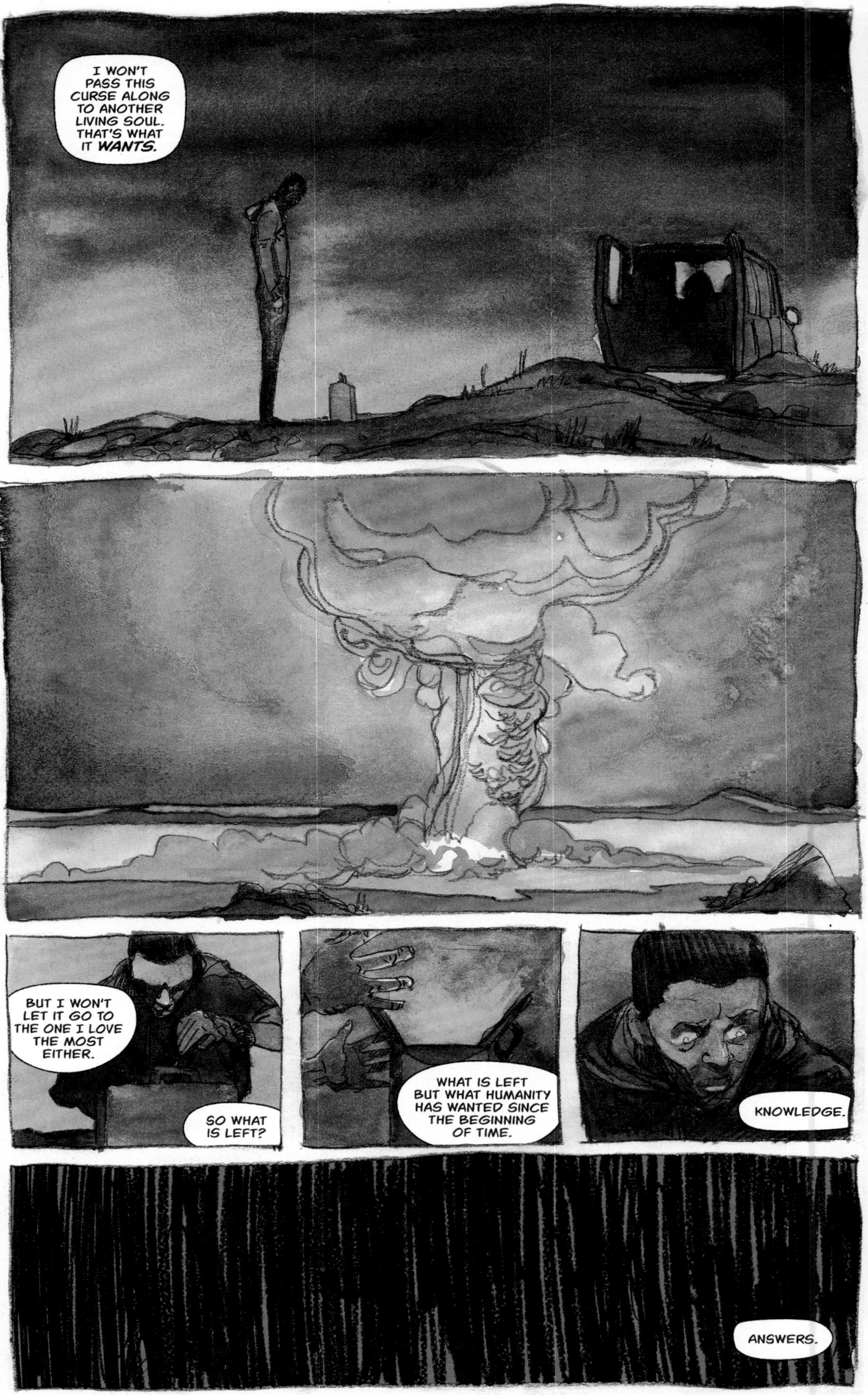
I WON'T PASS THIS CURSE ALONG TO ANOTHER LIVING SOUL. THAT'S WHAT IT WANTS.
BUT I WON'T LET IT GO TO THE ONE I LOVE THE MOST EITHER.
SO WHAT IS LEFT?
WHAT IS LEFT BUT WHAT HUMANITY HAS WANTED SINCE THE BEGINNING OF TIME.
KNOWLEDGE.
ANSWERS.

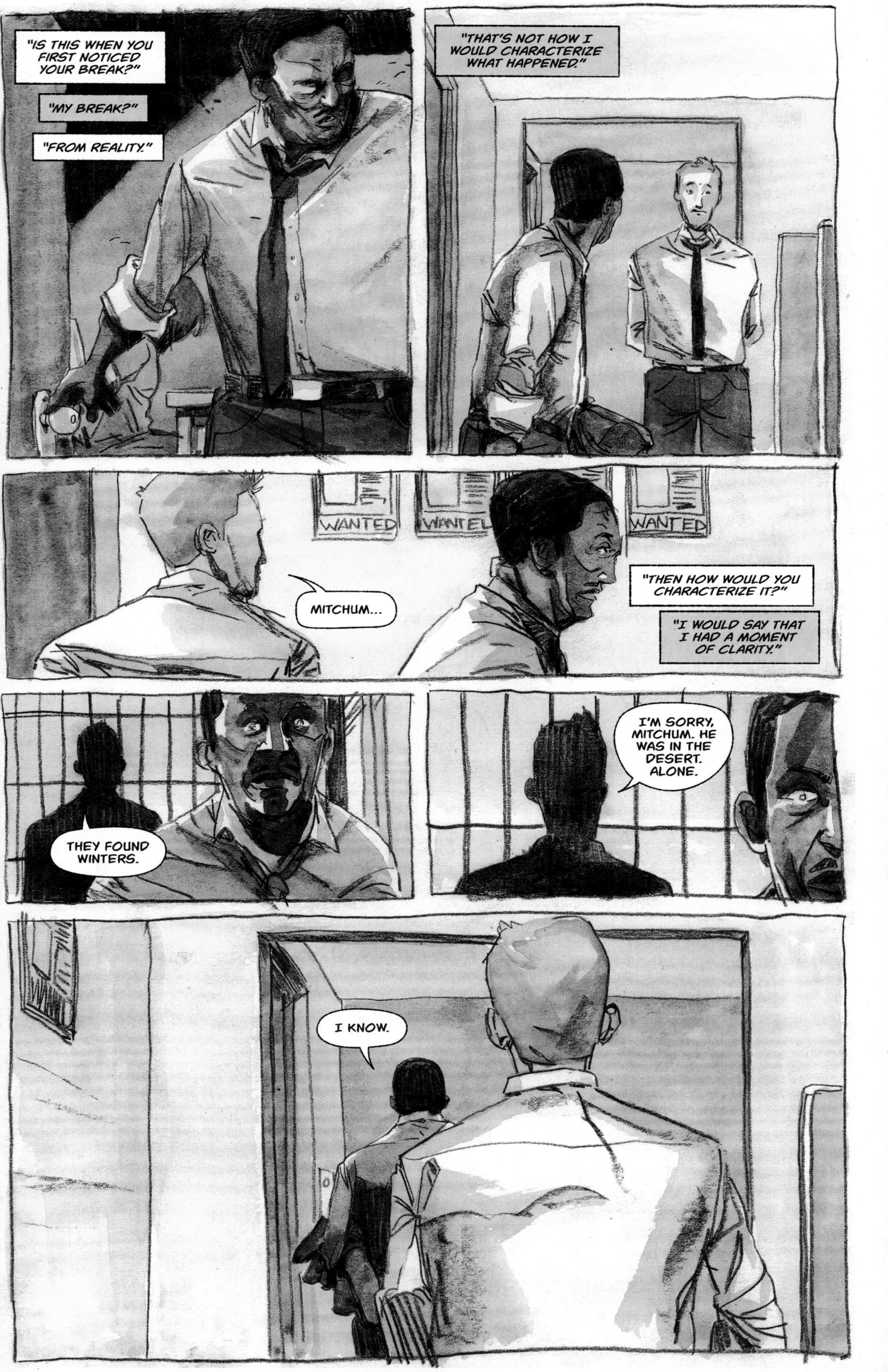
"IS THIS WHEN YOU FIRST NOTICED YOUR BREAK?"
"MY BREAK?"
"FROM REALITY."
"THAT'S NOT HOW I WOULD CHARACTERIZE WHAT HAPPENED."
WANTED
WANTED
WANTED
MITCHUM...
"THEN HOW WOULD YOU CHARACTERIZE IT?"
"I WOULD SAY THAT I HAD A MOMENT OF CLARITY."
THEY FOUND WINTERS.
I'M SORRY, MITCHUM. HE WAS IN THE DESERT. ALONE.
I KNOW.

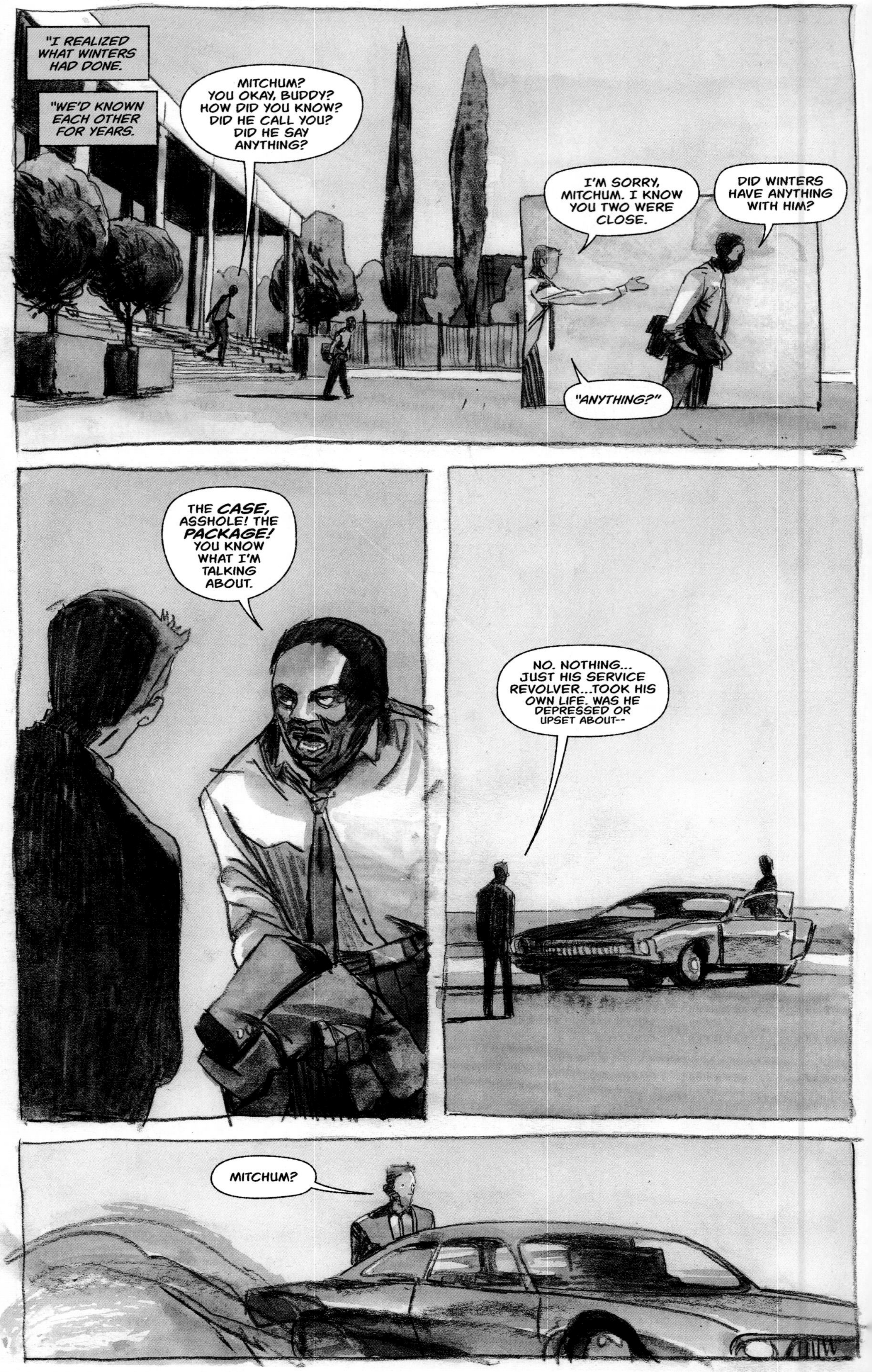
"I REALIZED WHAT WINTERS HAD DONE.
"WE'D KNOWN EACH OTHER FOR YEARS.
MITCHUM? YOU OKAY, BUDDY? HOW DID YOU KNOW? DID HE CALL YOU? DID HE SAY ANYTHING?
I'M SORRY, MITCHUM. I KNOW YOU TWO WERE CLOSE.
DID WINTERS HAVE ANYTHING WITH HIM?
"ANYTHING?"
THE CASE, ASSHOLE! THE PACKAGE! YOU KNOW WHAT I'M TALKING ABOUT.
NO. NOTHING... JUST HIS SERVICE REVOLVER...TOOK HIS OWN LIFE. WAS HE DEPRESSED OR UPSET ABOUT--
MITCHUM?

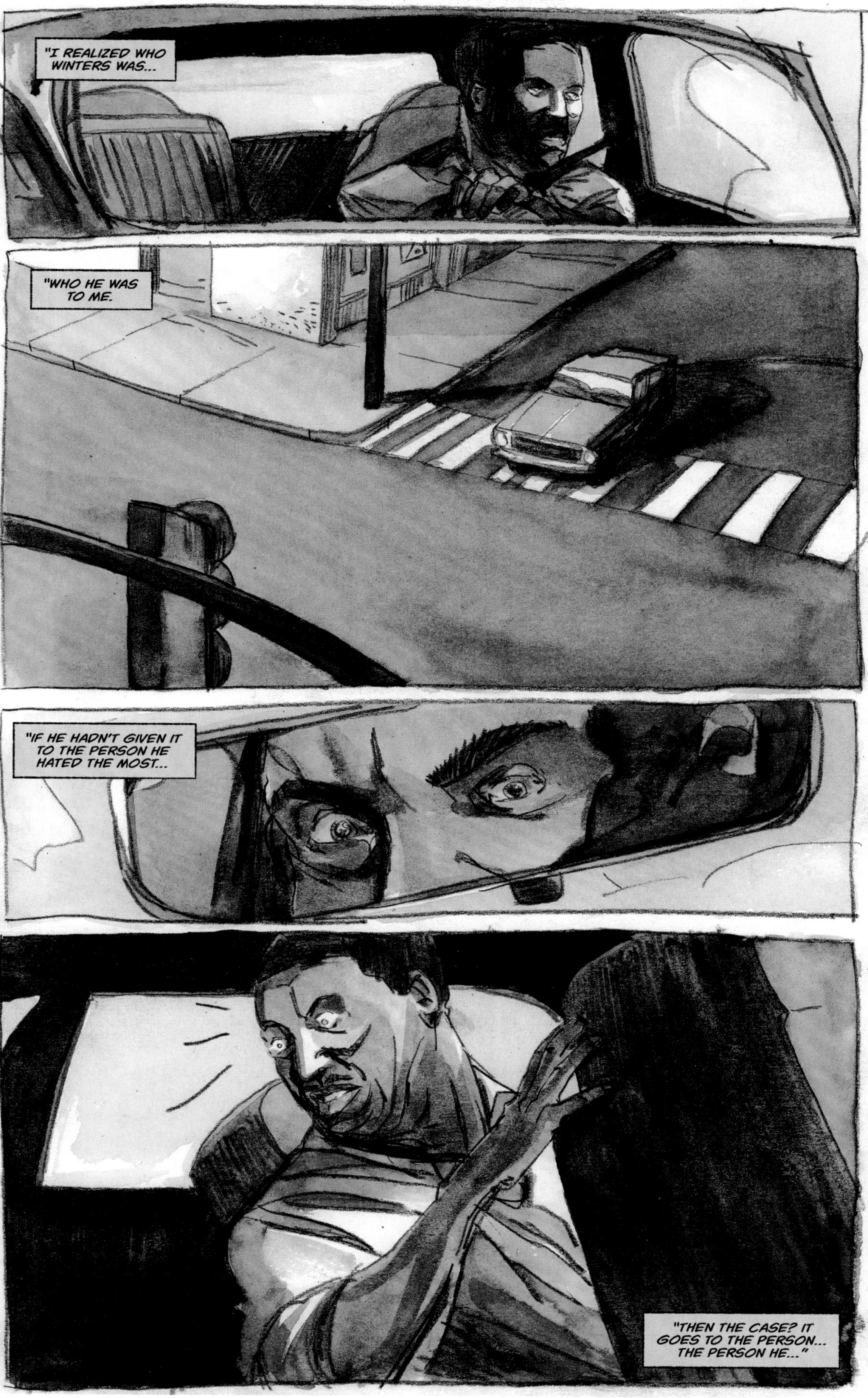
"I REALIZED WHO WINTERS WAS...
"WHO HE WAS TO ME.
"IF HE HADN'T GIVEN IT TO THE PERSON HE HATED THE MOST...
"THEN THE CASE? IT GOES TO THE PERSON... THE PERSON HE..."

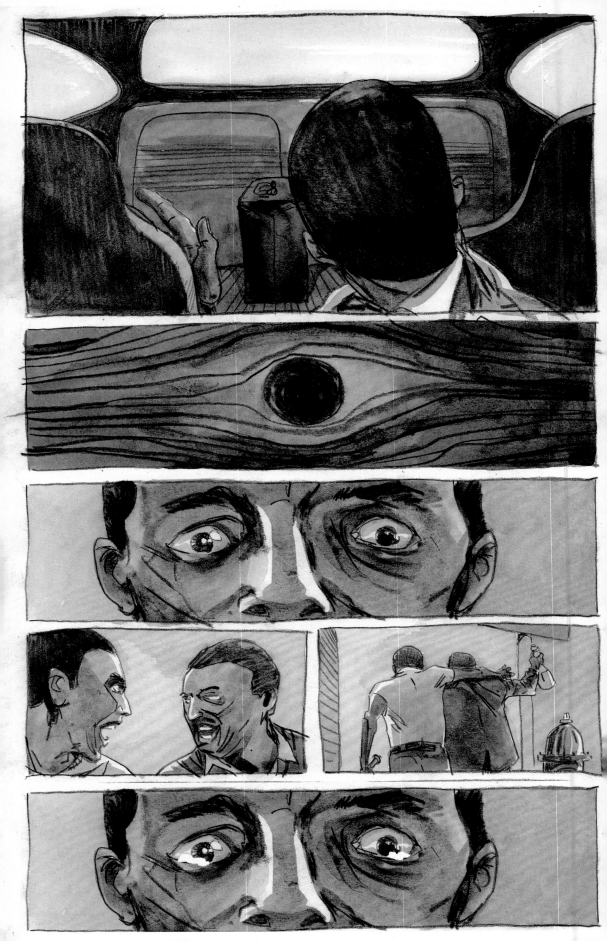

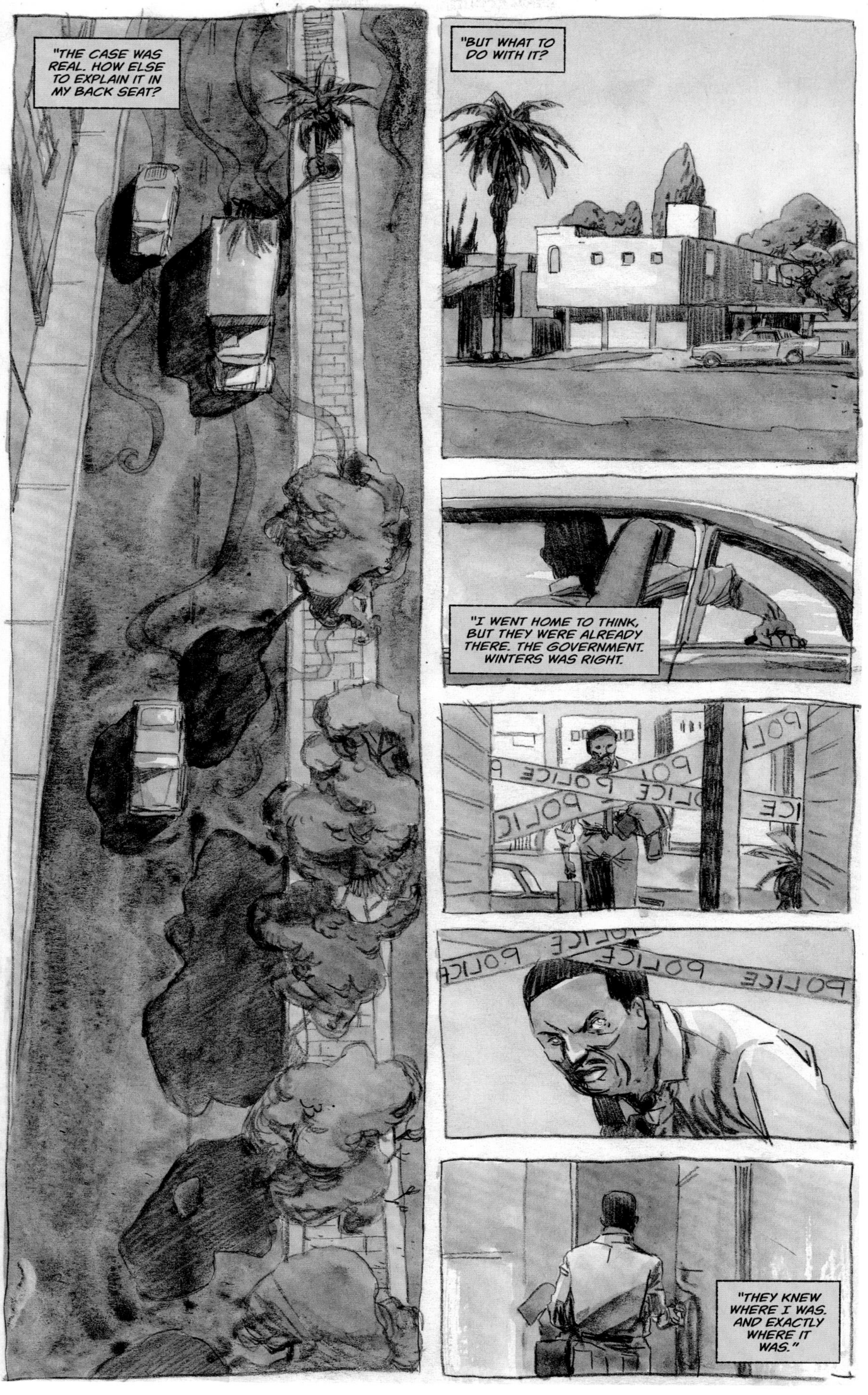
"THE CASE WAS REAL. HOW ELSE TO EXPLAIN IT IN MY BACK SEAT?
"BUT WHAT TO DO WITH IT?
"I WENT HOME TO THINK, BUT THEY WERE ALREADY THERE. THE GOVERNMENT. WINTERS WAS RIGHT.
POLICE
POLICE
"THEY KNEW WHERE I WAS. AND EXACTLY WHERE IT WAS."

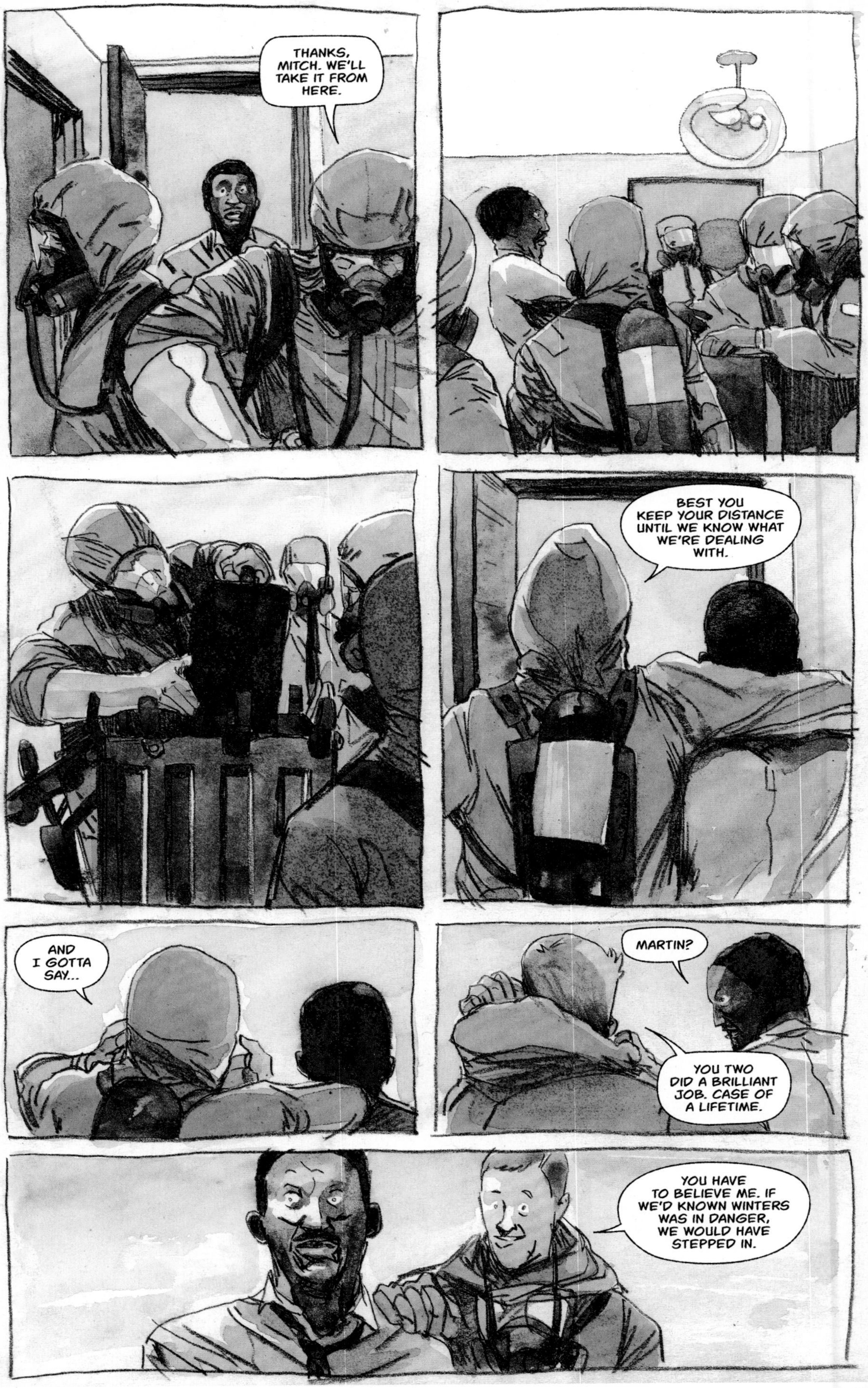
THANKS, MITCH. WE'LL TAKE IT FROM HERE.
BEST YOU KEEP YOUR DISTANCE UNTIL WE KNOW WHAT WE'RE DEALING WITH.
AND I GOTTA SAY...
MARTIN?
YOU TWO DID A BRILLIANT JOB. CASE OF A LIFETIME.
YOU HAVE TO BELIEVE ME. IF WE'D KNOWN WINTERS WAS IN DANGER, WE WOULD HAVE STEPPED IN.

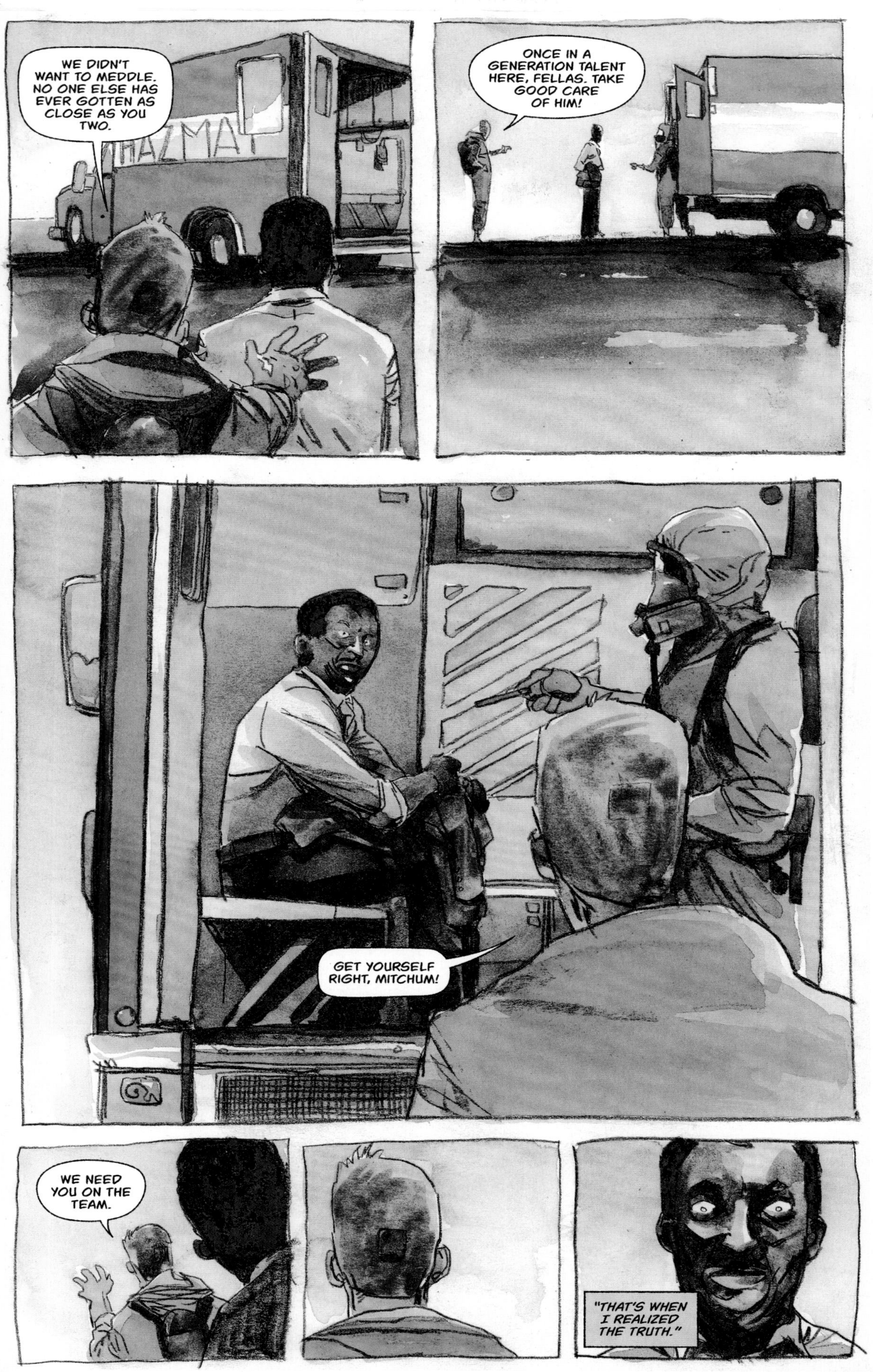
WE DIDN'T WANT TO MEDDLE. NO ONE ELSE HAS EVER GOTTEN AS CLOSE AS YOU TWO.
HAZMAT
ONCE IN A GENERATION TALENT HERE, FELLAS. TAKE GOOD CARE OF HIM!
GET YOURSELF RIGHT, MITCHUM!
WE NEED YOU ON THE TEAM.
"THAT'S WHEN I REALIZED THE TRUTH."

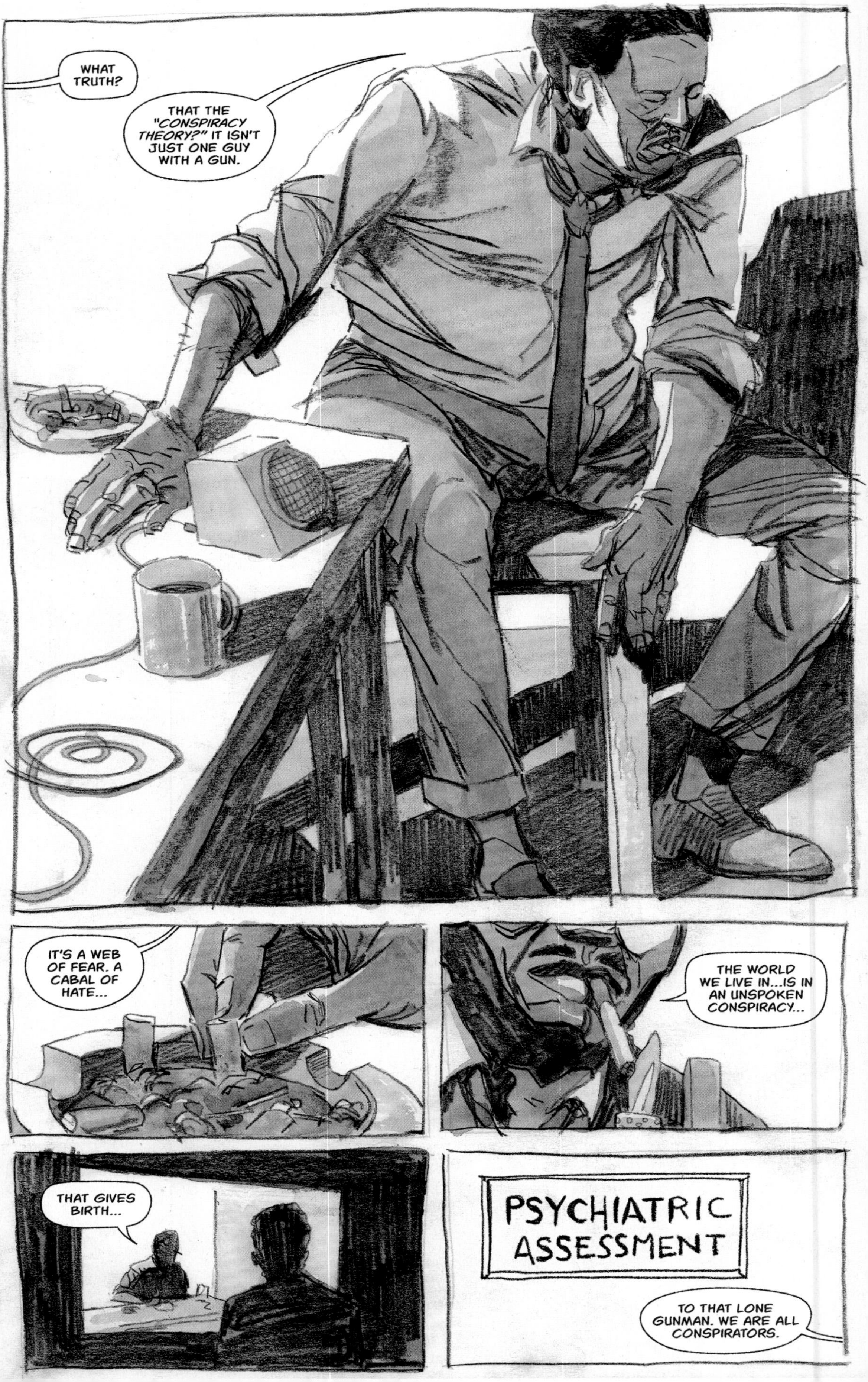
WHAT TRUTH?
THAT THE "CONSPIRACY THEORY?" IT ISN'T JUST ONE GUY WITH A GUN.
IT'S A WEB OF FEAR. A CABAL OF HATE...
THE WORLD WE LIVE IN...IS IN AN UNSPOKEN CONSPIRACY...
THAT GIVES BIRTH...
PSYCHIATRIC ASSESSMENT
TO THAT LONE GUNMAN. WE ARE ALL CONSPIRATORS.

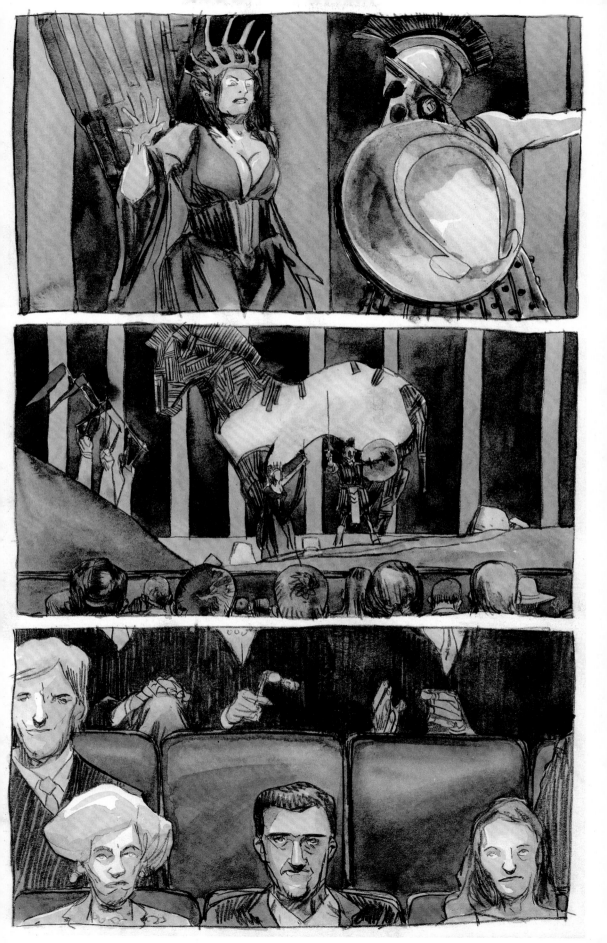

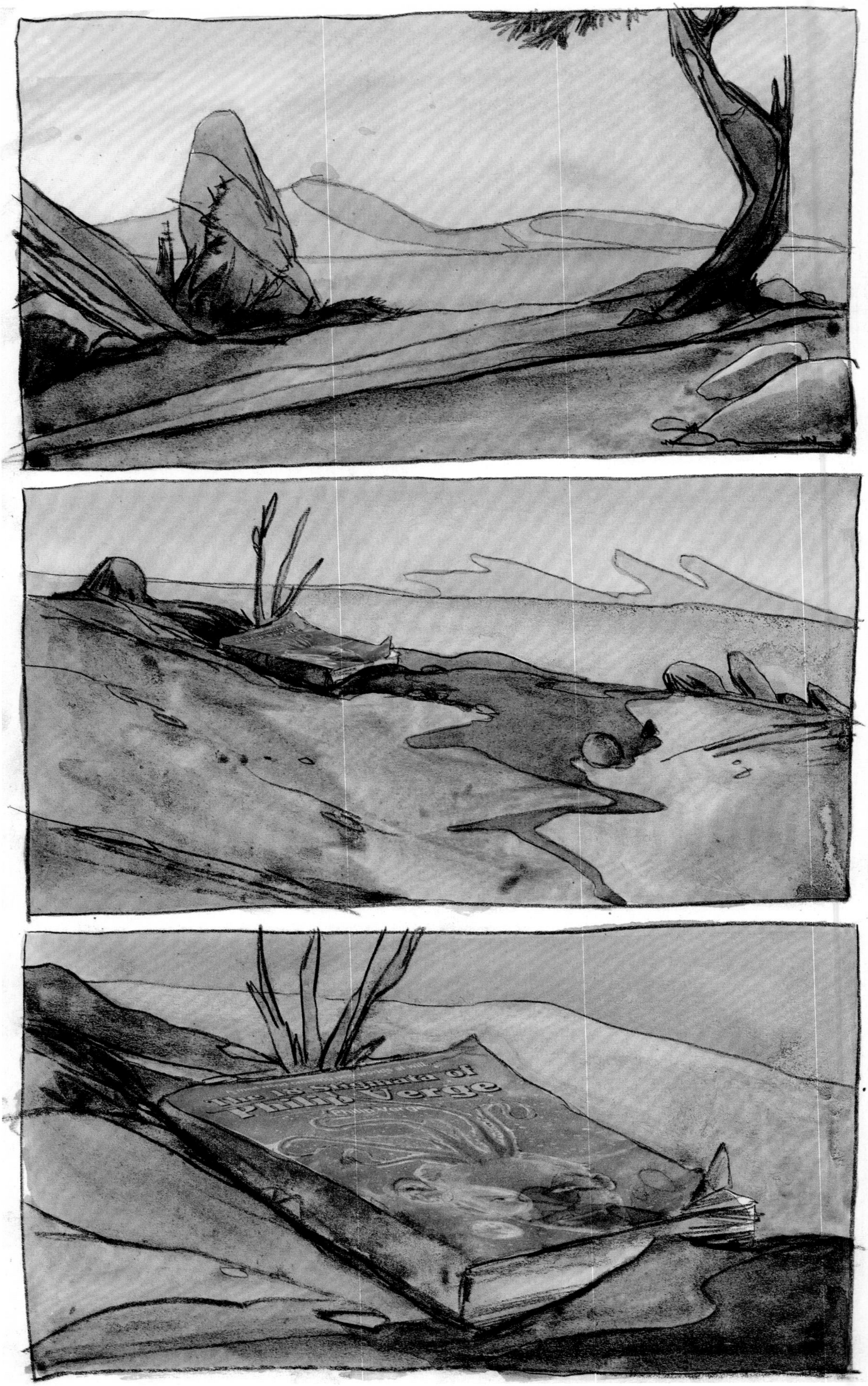
The 13 Stigmata of
Philip Verge

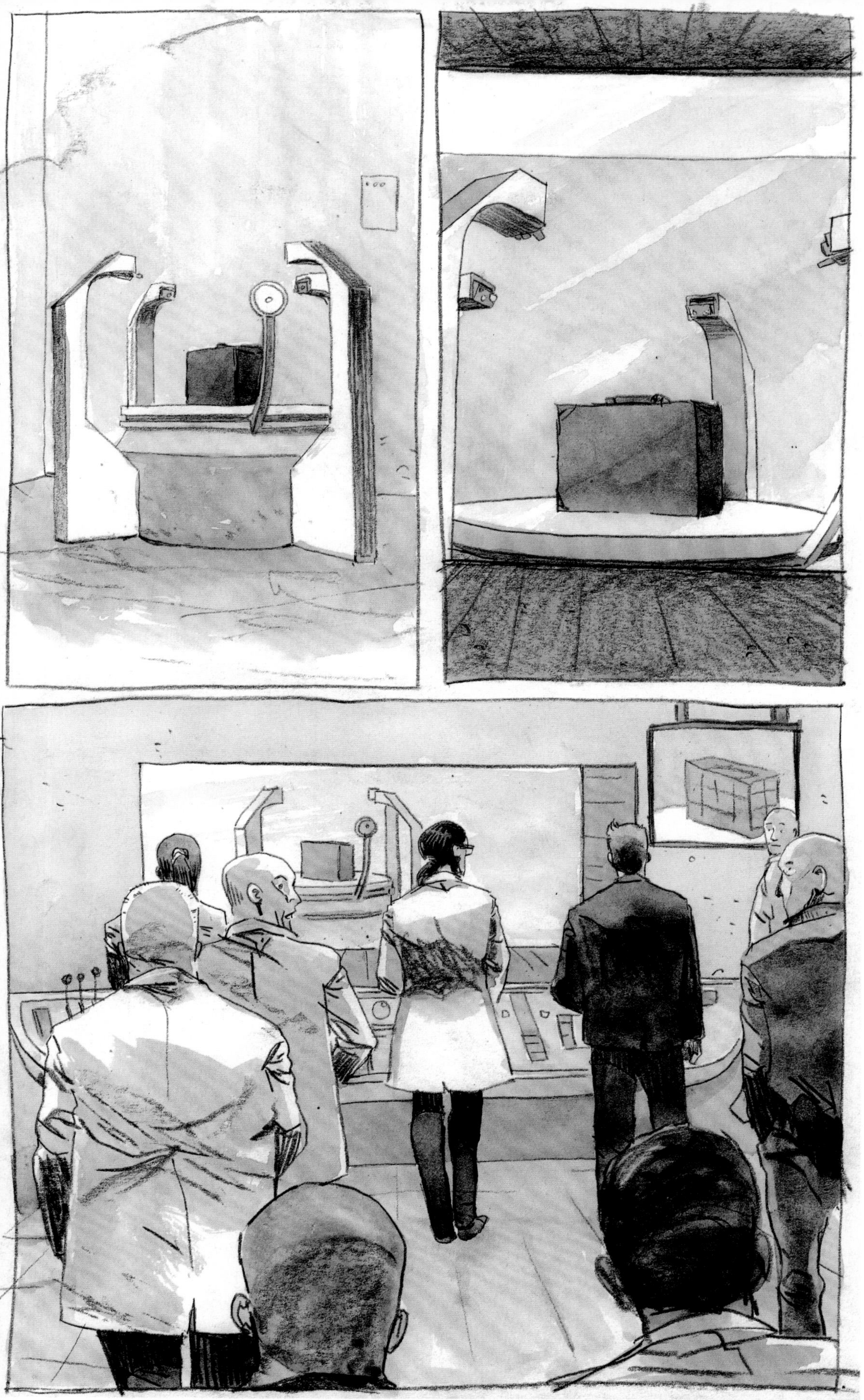

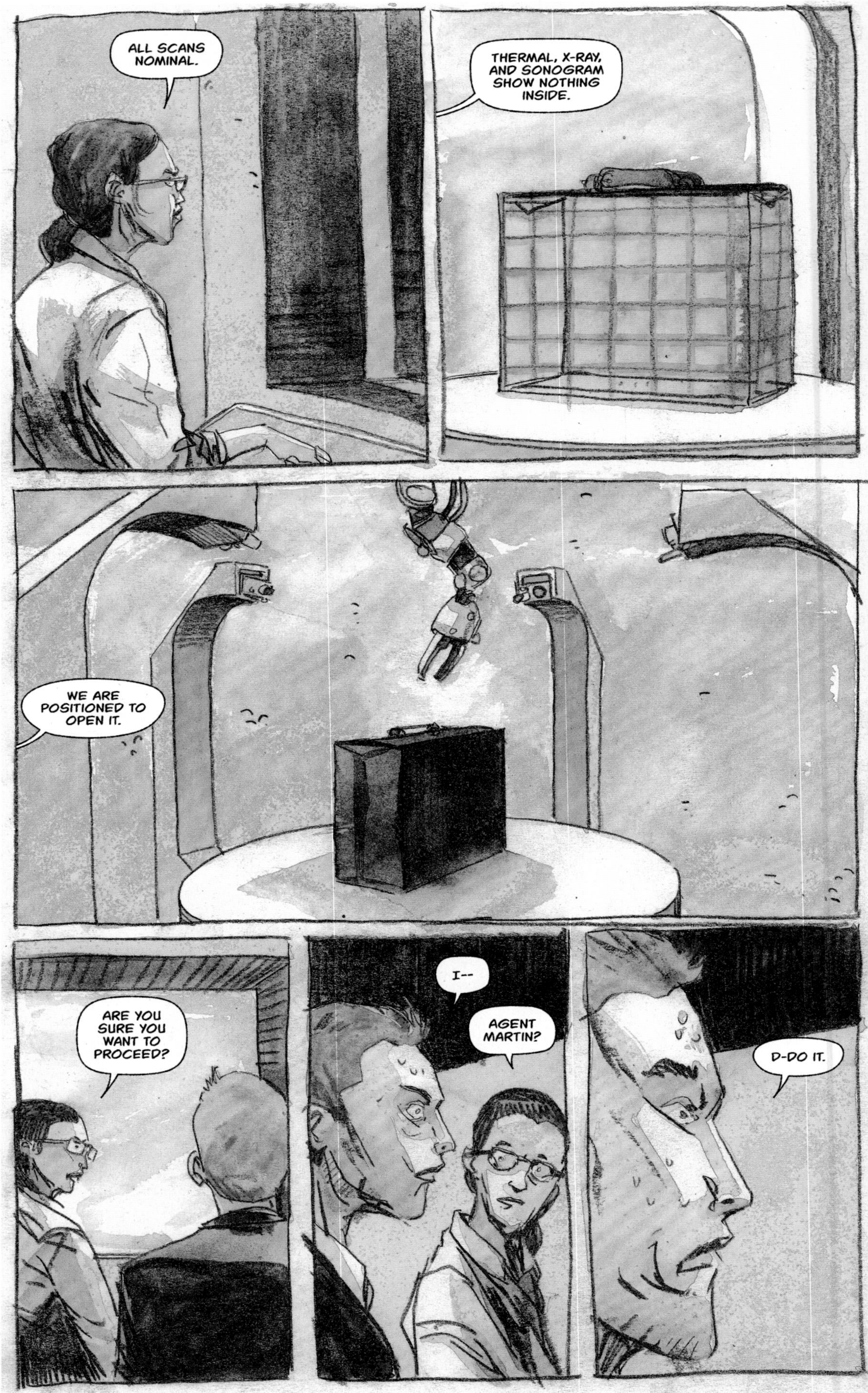
ALL SCANS NOMINAL.
THERMAL, X-RAY, AND SONOGRAM SHOW NOTHING INSIDE.
WE ARE POSITIONED TO OPEN IT.
ARE YOU SURE YOU WANT TO PROCEED?
I--
AGENT MARTIN?
D-DO IT.

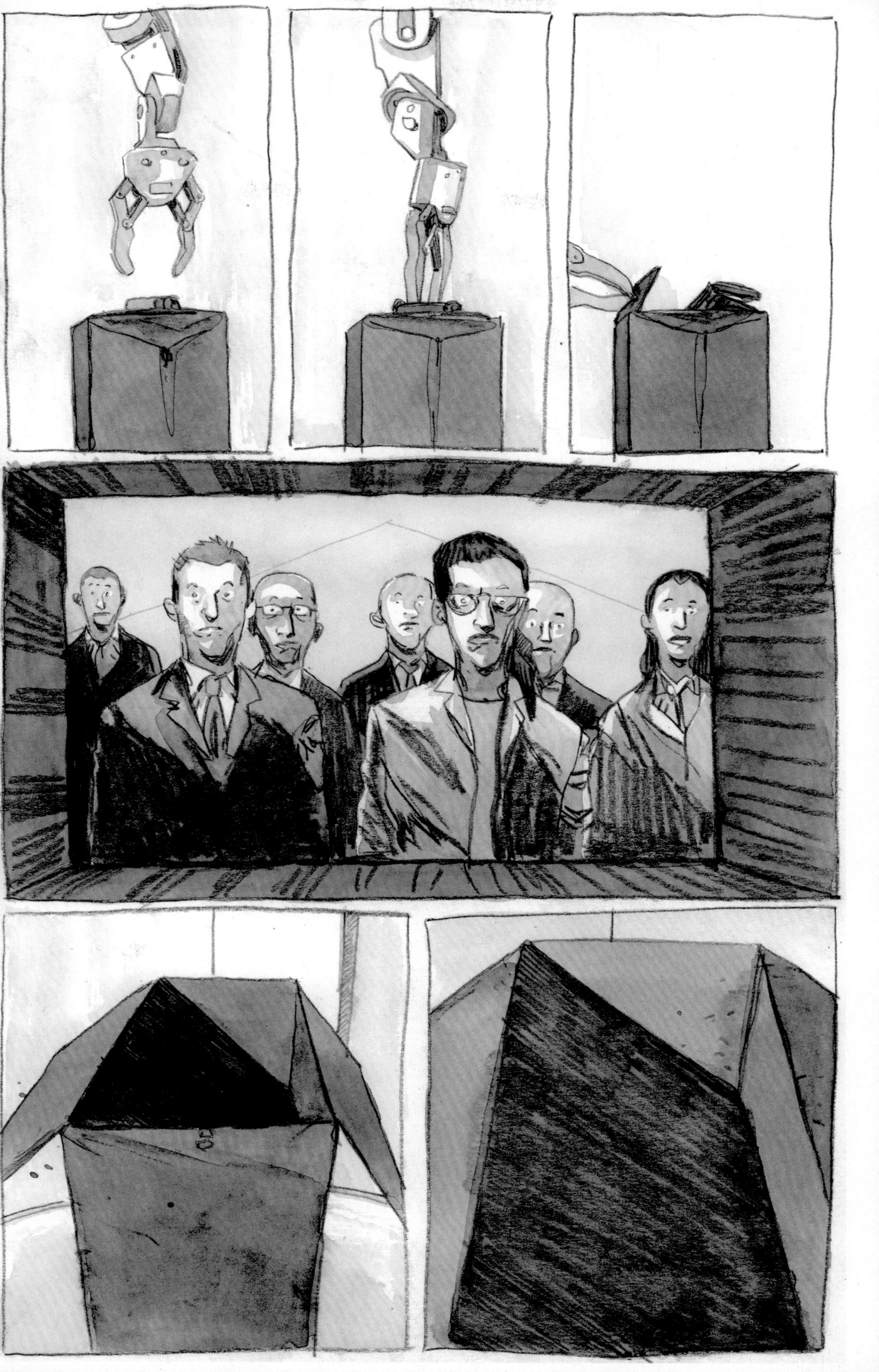

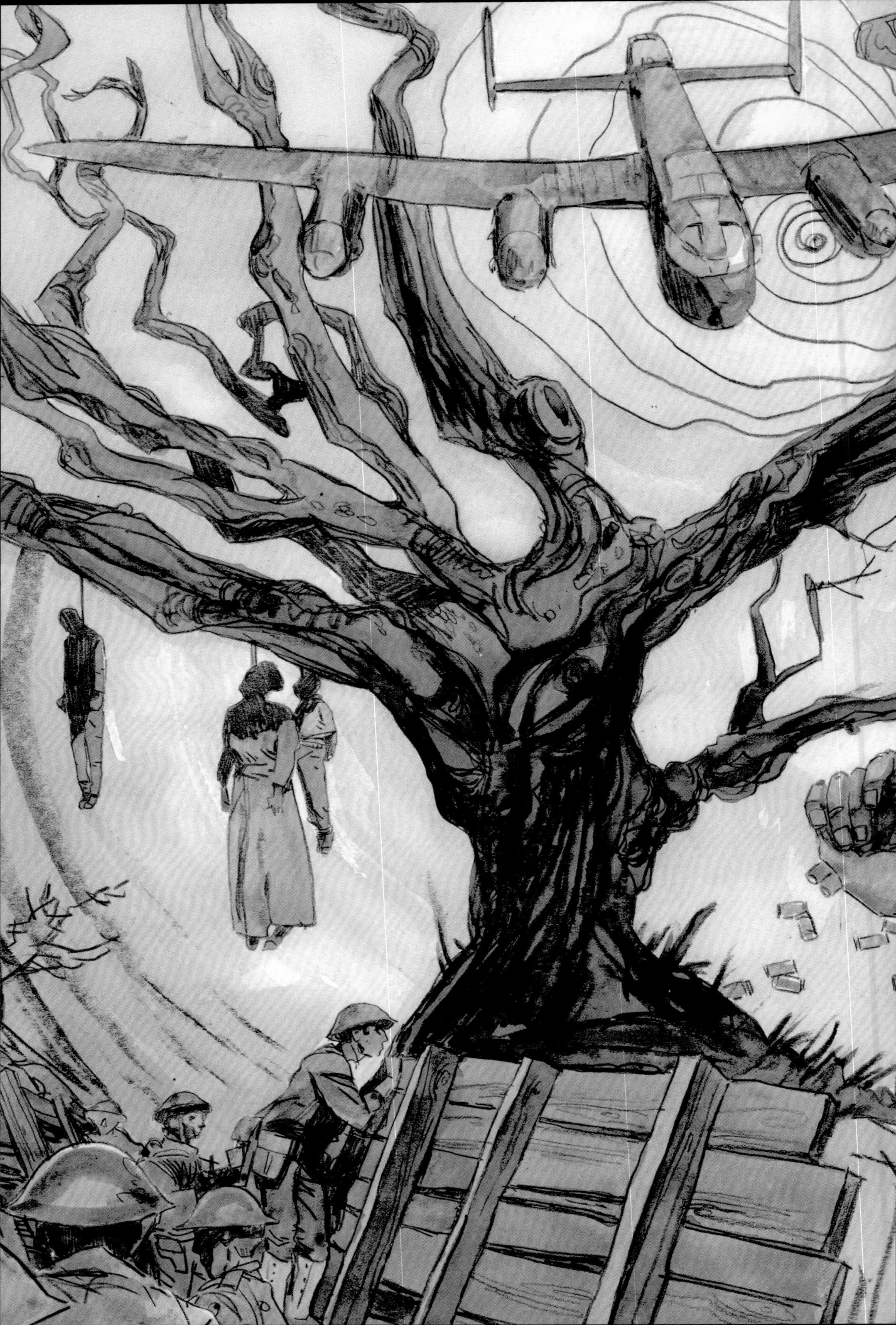

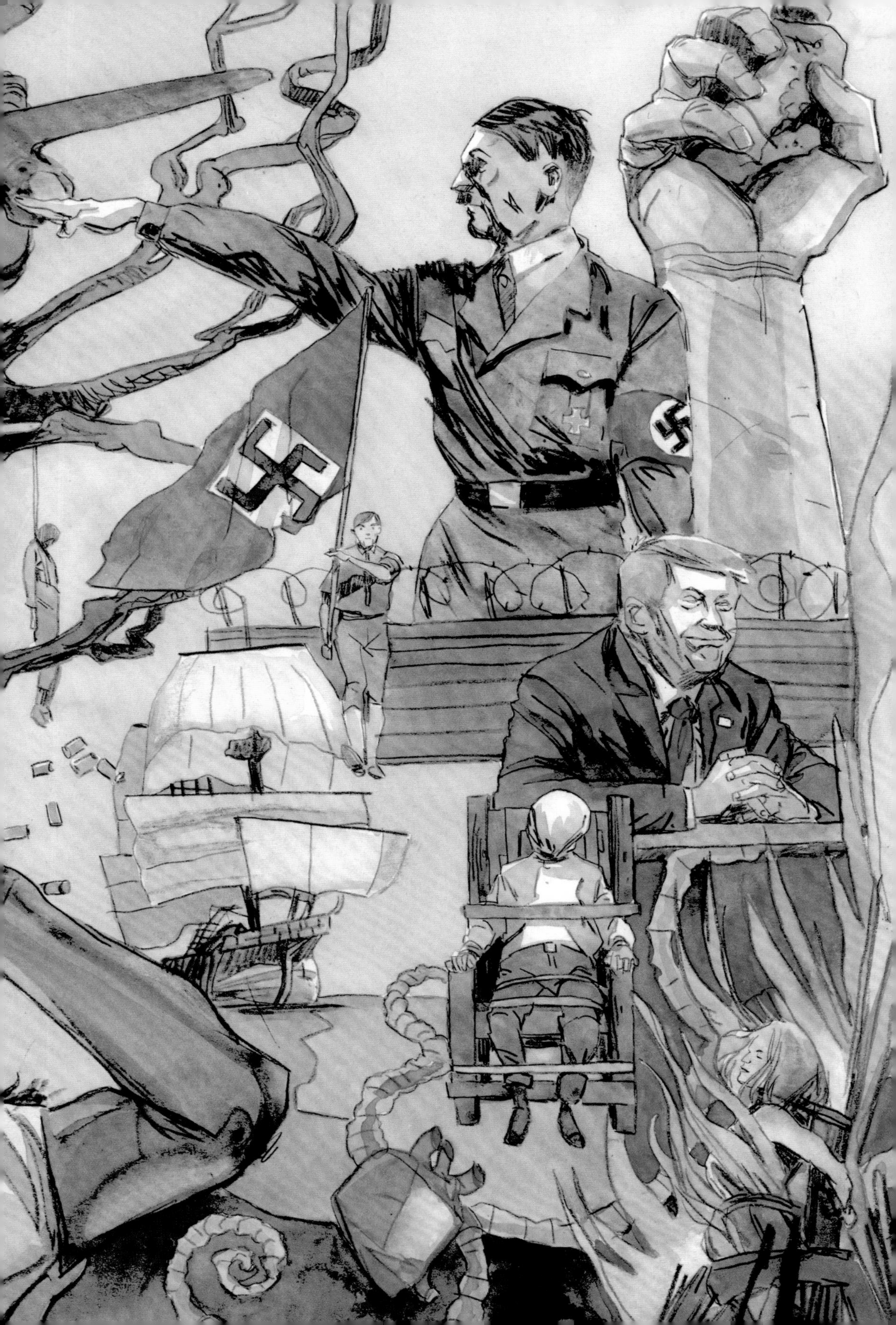

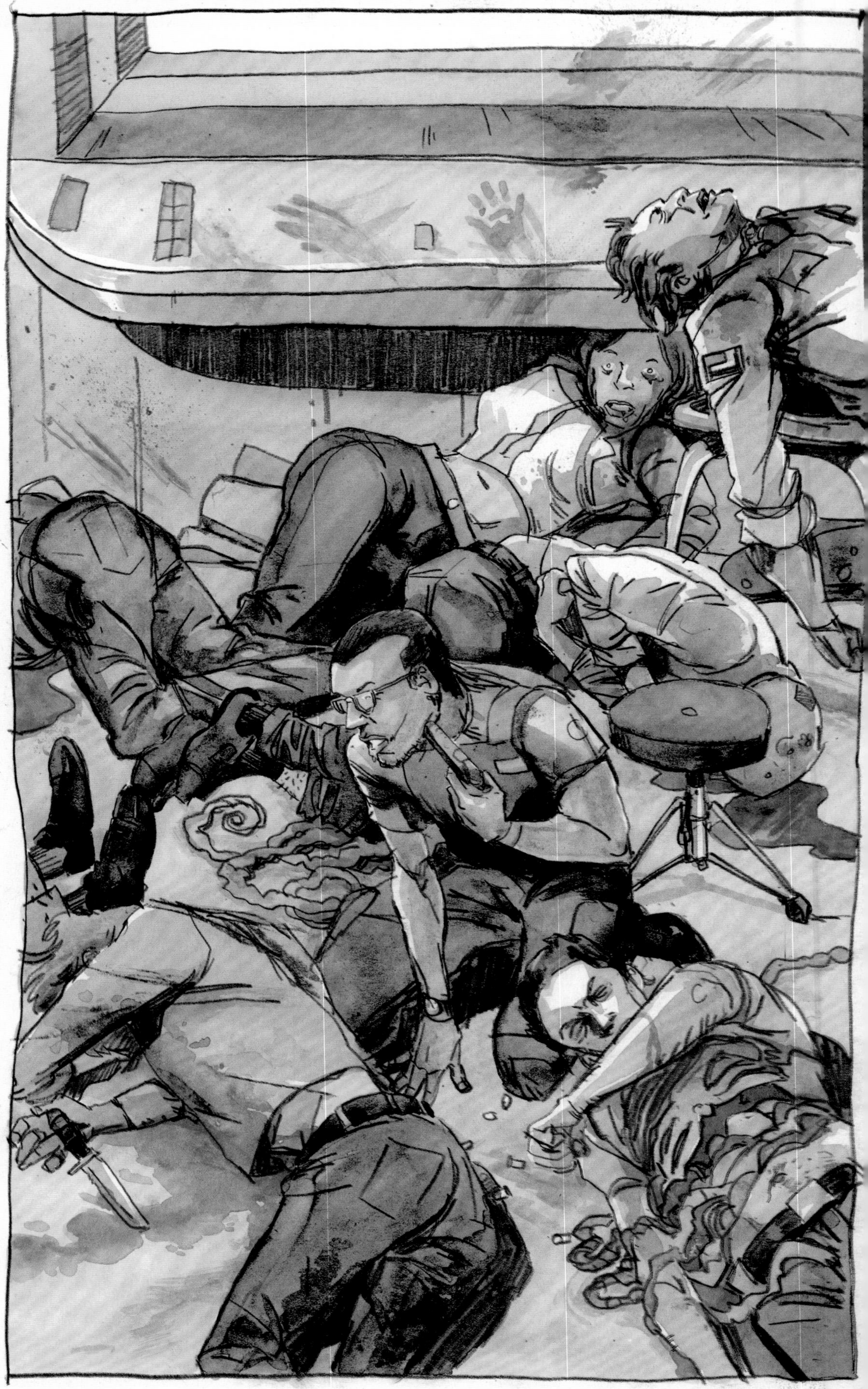

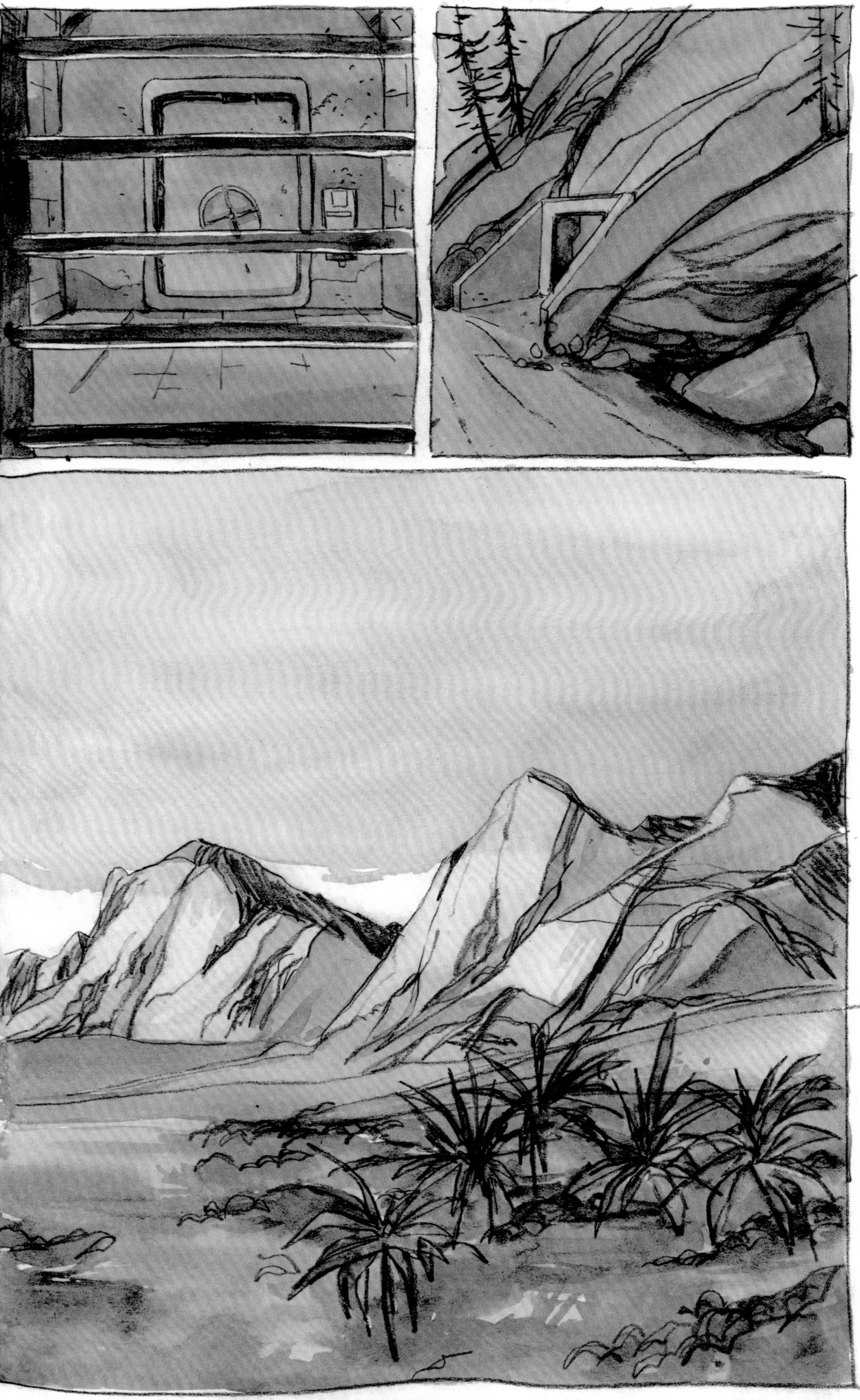

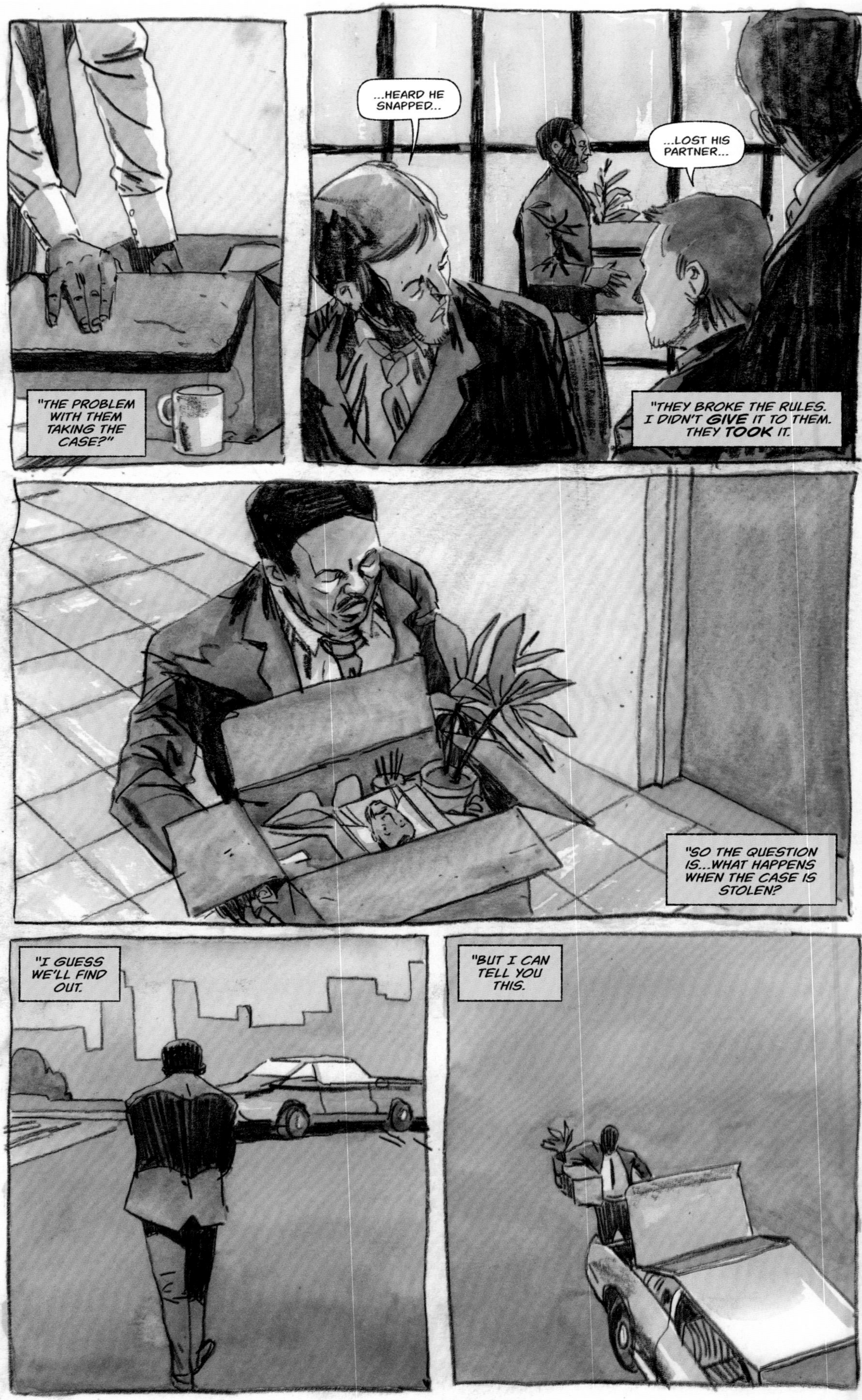
"THE PROBLEM WITH THEM TAKING THE CASE?"
...HEARD HE SNAPPED...
...LOST HIS PARTNER...
"THEY BROKE THE RULES. I DIDN'T GIVE IT TO THEM. THEY TOOK IT.
"SO THE QUESTION IS...WHAT HAPPENS WHEN THE CASE IS STOLEN?
"I GUESS WE'LL FIND OUT.
"BUT I CAN TELL YOU THIS.

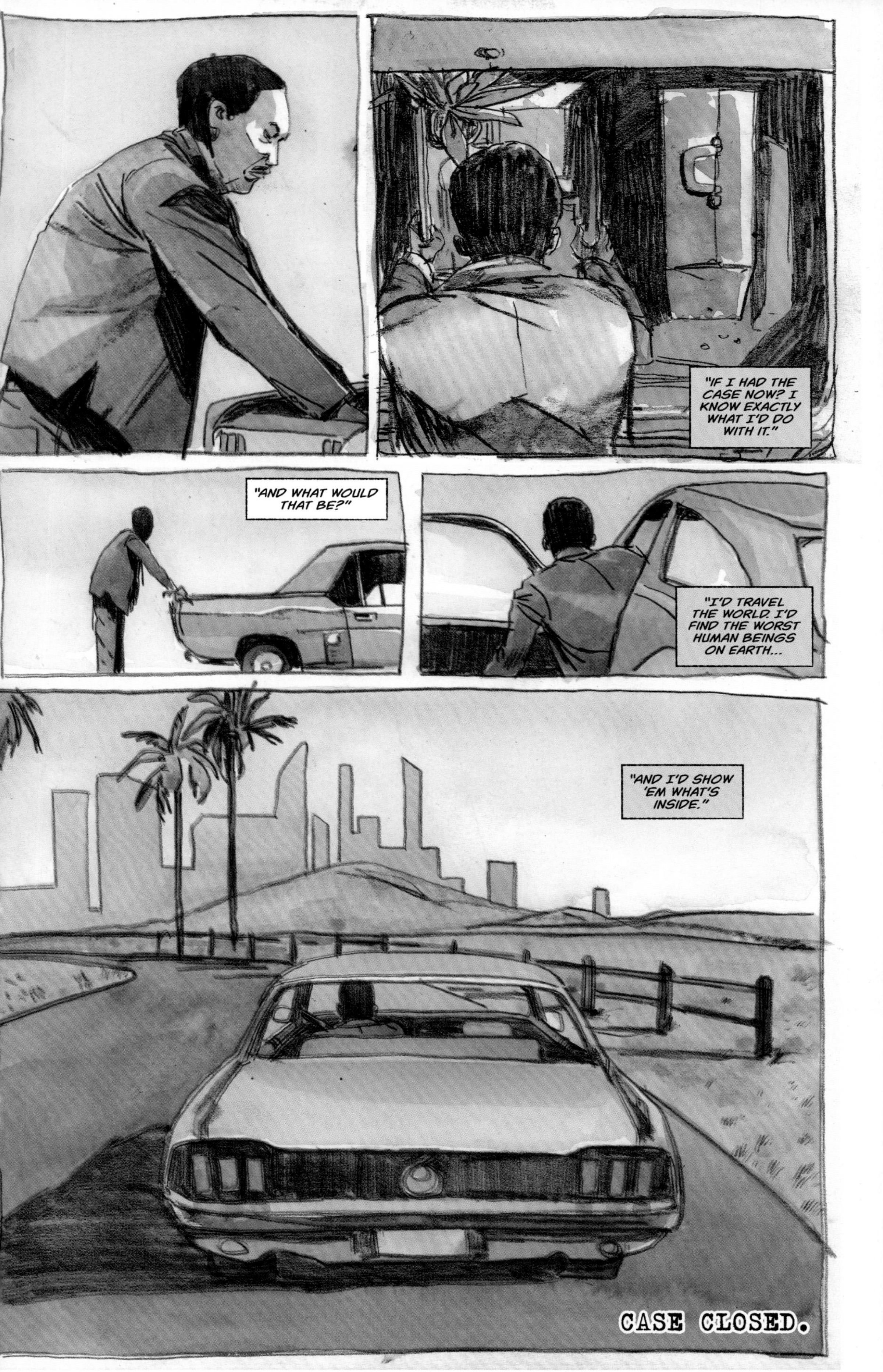
"IF I HAD THE CASE NOW? I KNOW EXACTLY WHAT I'D DO WITH IT."
"AND WHAT WOULD THAT BE?"
"I'D TRAVEL THE WORLD. I'D FIND THE WORST HUMAN BEINGS ON EARTH...
"AND I'D SHOW 'EM WHAT'S INSIDE."
CASE CLOSED.

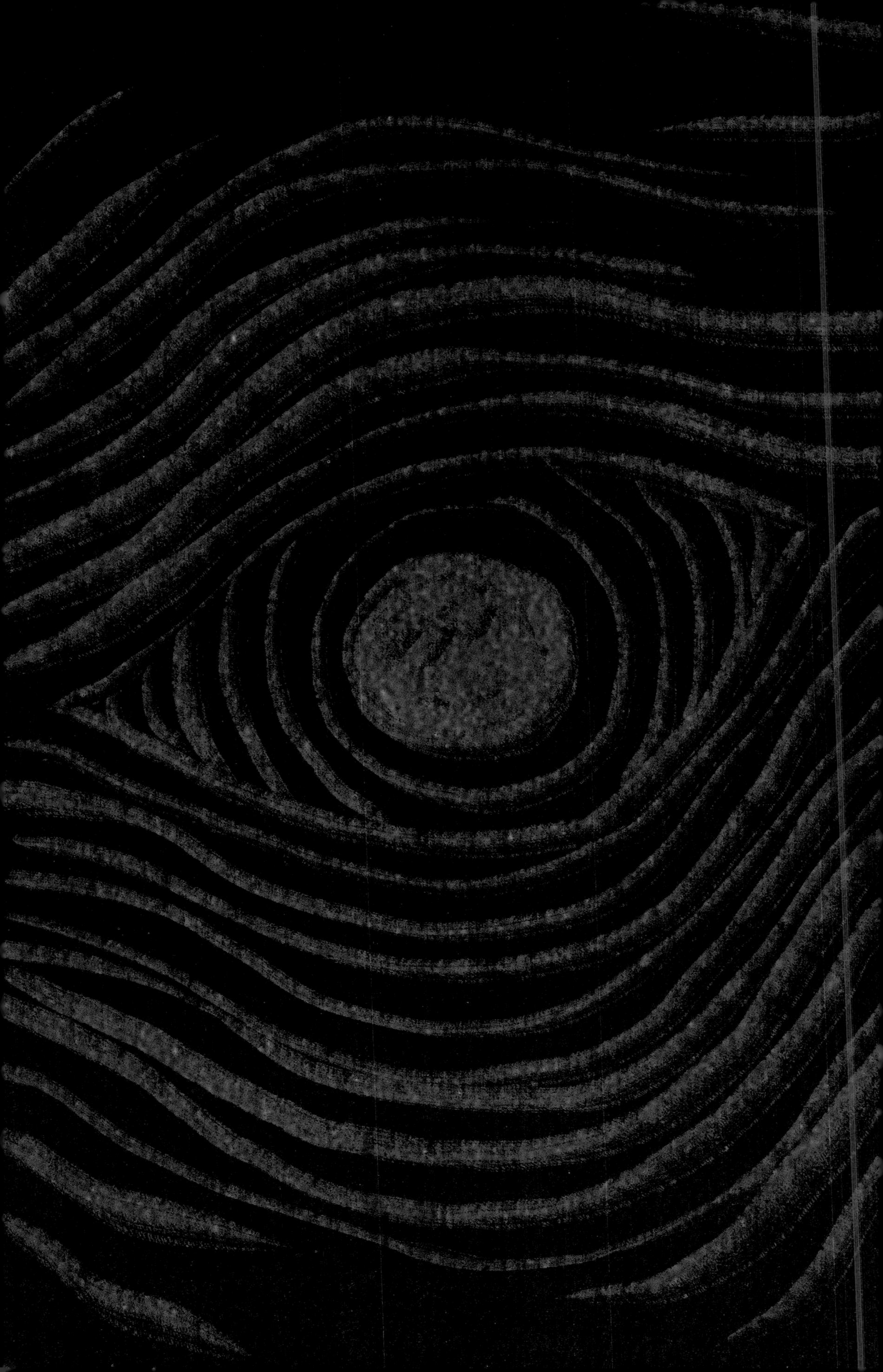

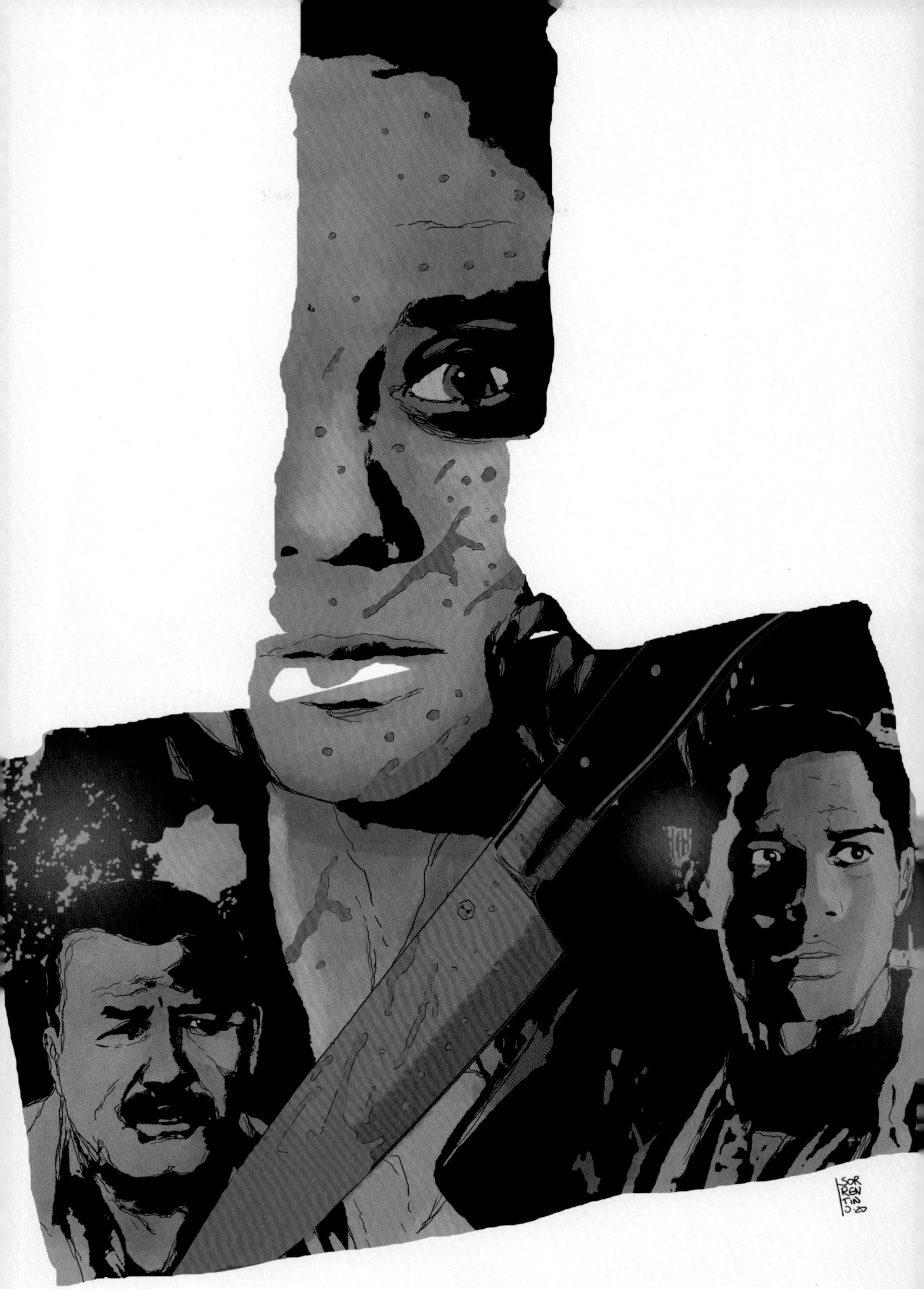
SOR
REN
TIN
O '20

FEAR CASE #1 SECOND EDITION COVER BY
ANDREA SORRENTINO

FEAR CASE #1 COVER B BY
DUNCAN FEGREDO

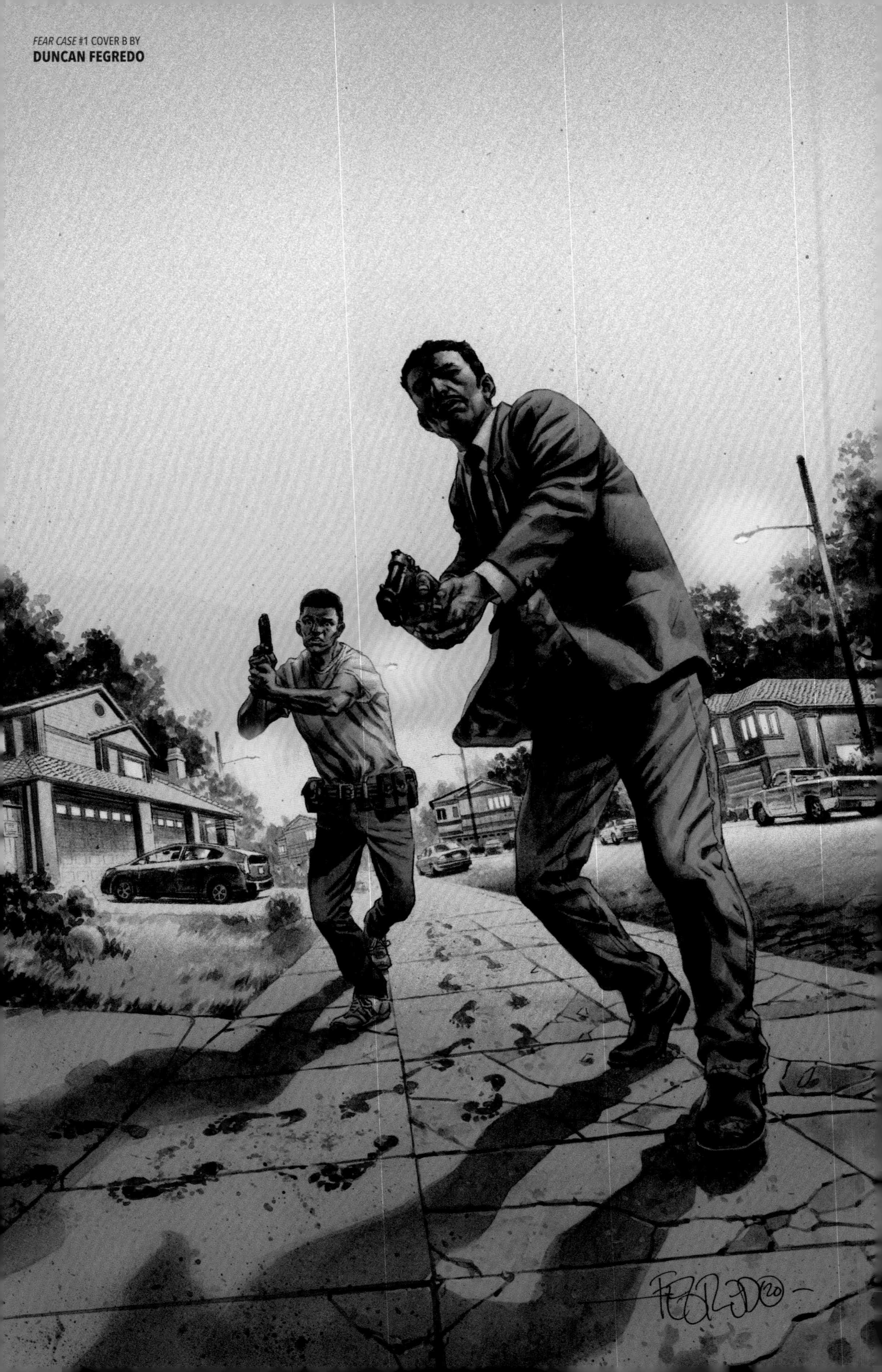
FEGREDO '20

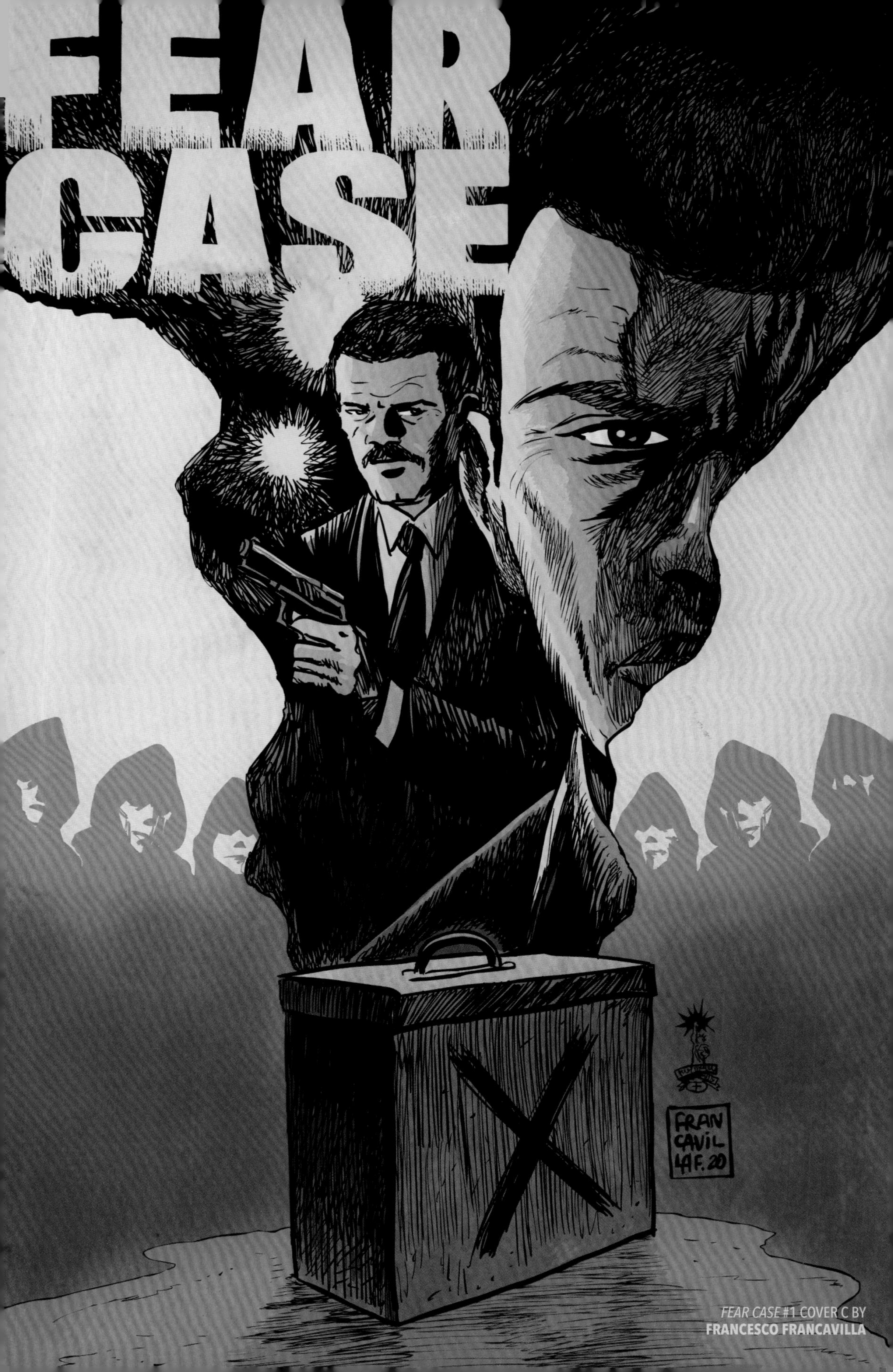
FEAR
CASE
FRAN
CAVIL
LA F. 20

FEAR CASE #1 COVER C BY
FRANCESCO FRANCAVILLA

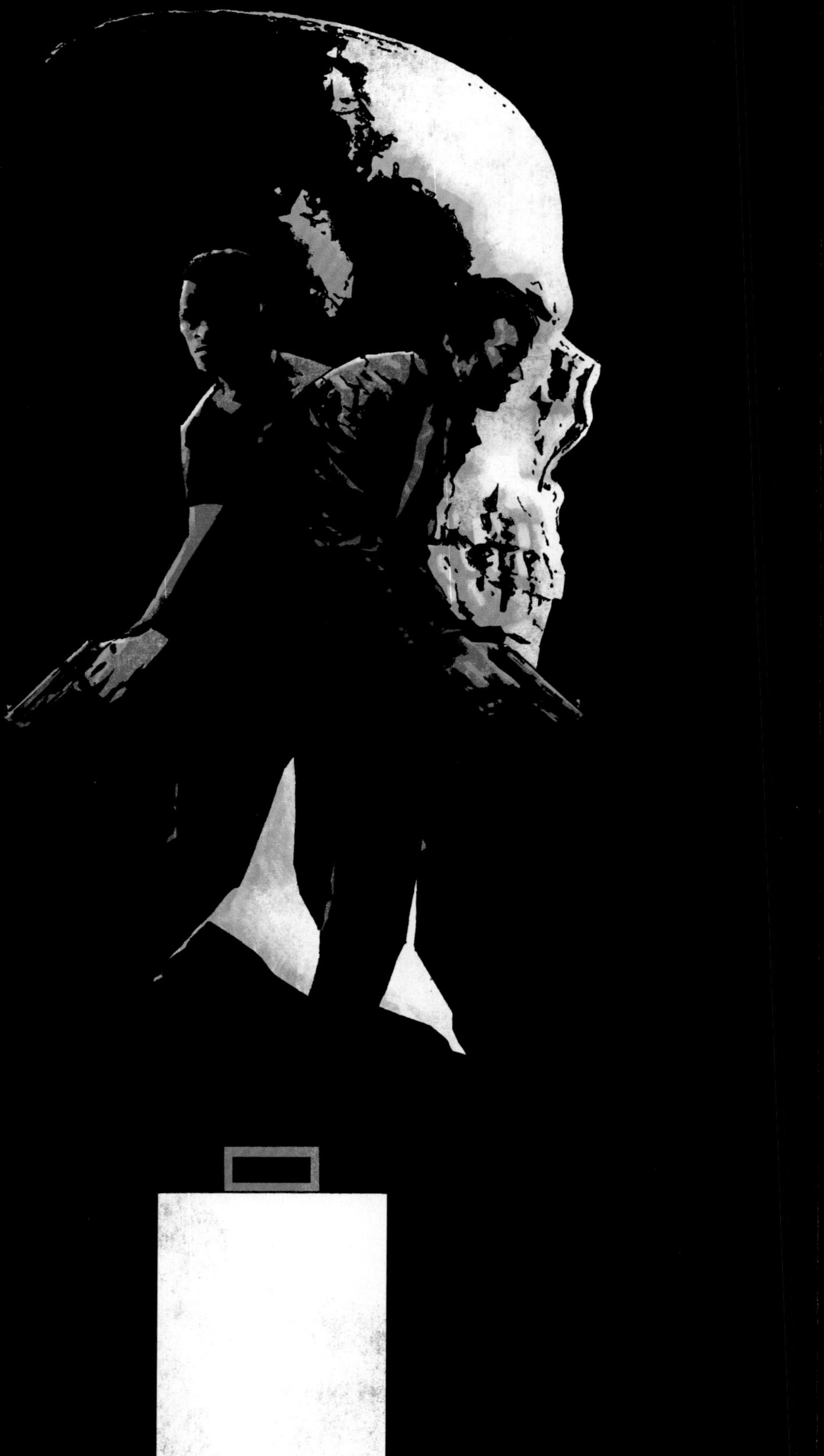

STEWART

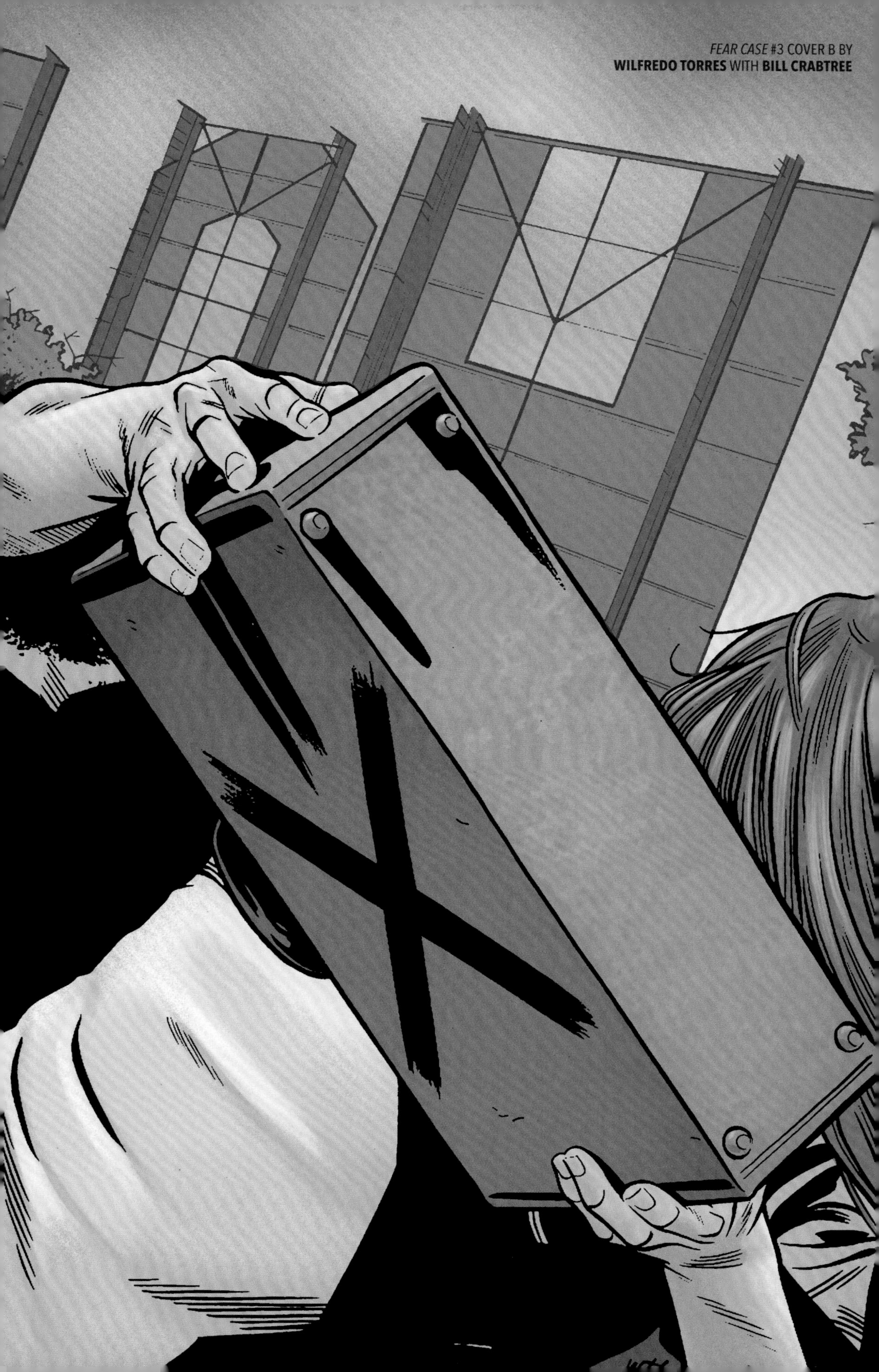

FEAR CASE #3 COVER B BY
WILFREDO TORRES WITH **BILL CRABTREE**

FEAR CASE #4 COVER B BY
LAURA PEREZ

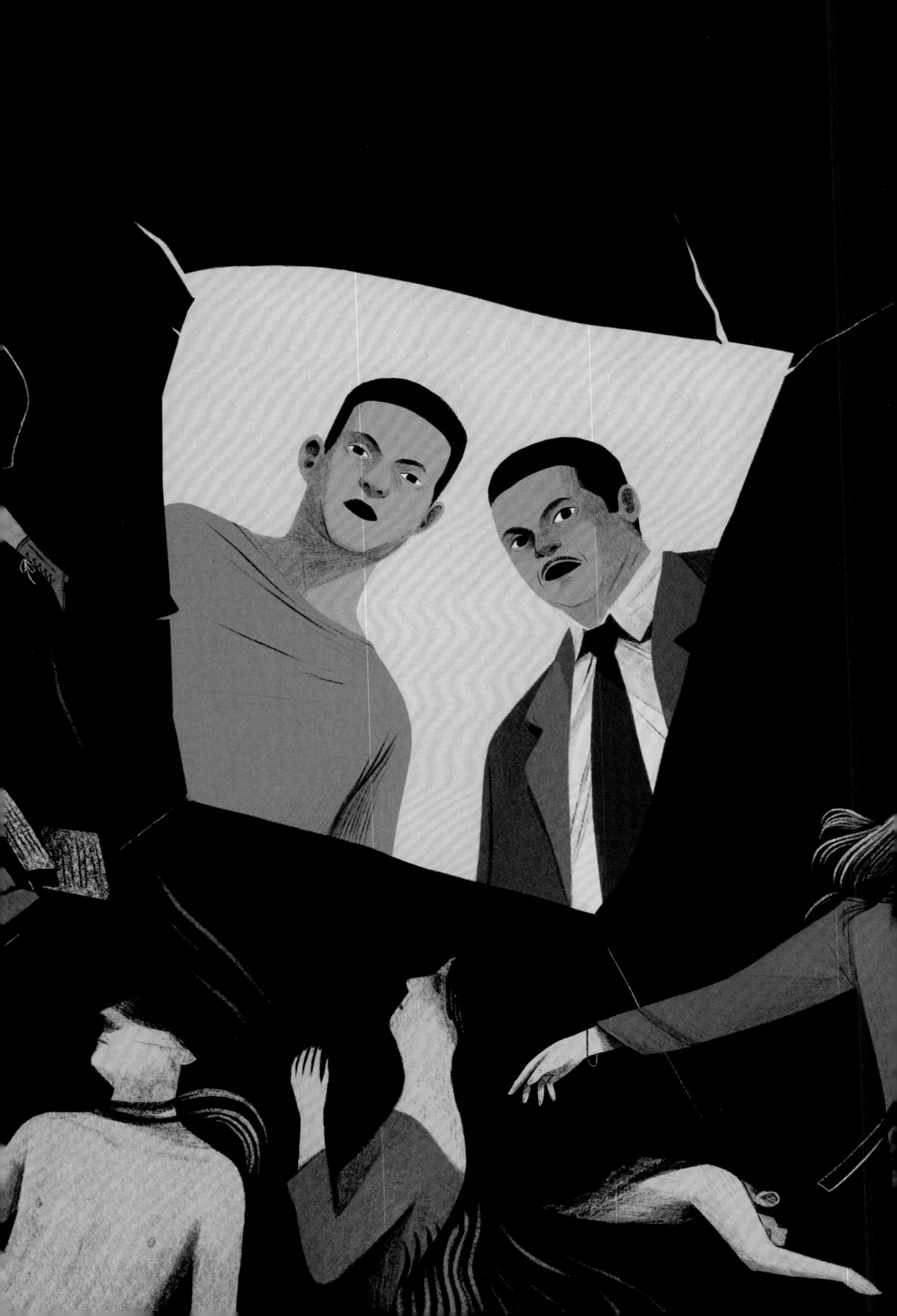

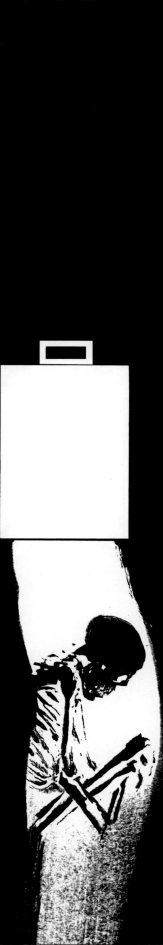

FEAR CASE #2 BACK COVER BY
LAURENCE CAMPBELL

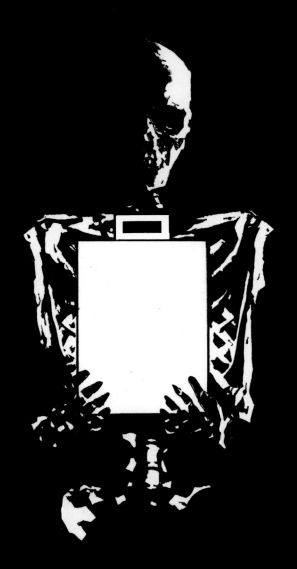

FEAR CASE

SKETCHBOOK

Notes by **TYLER JENKINS**

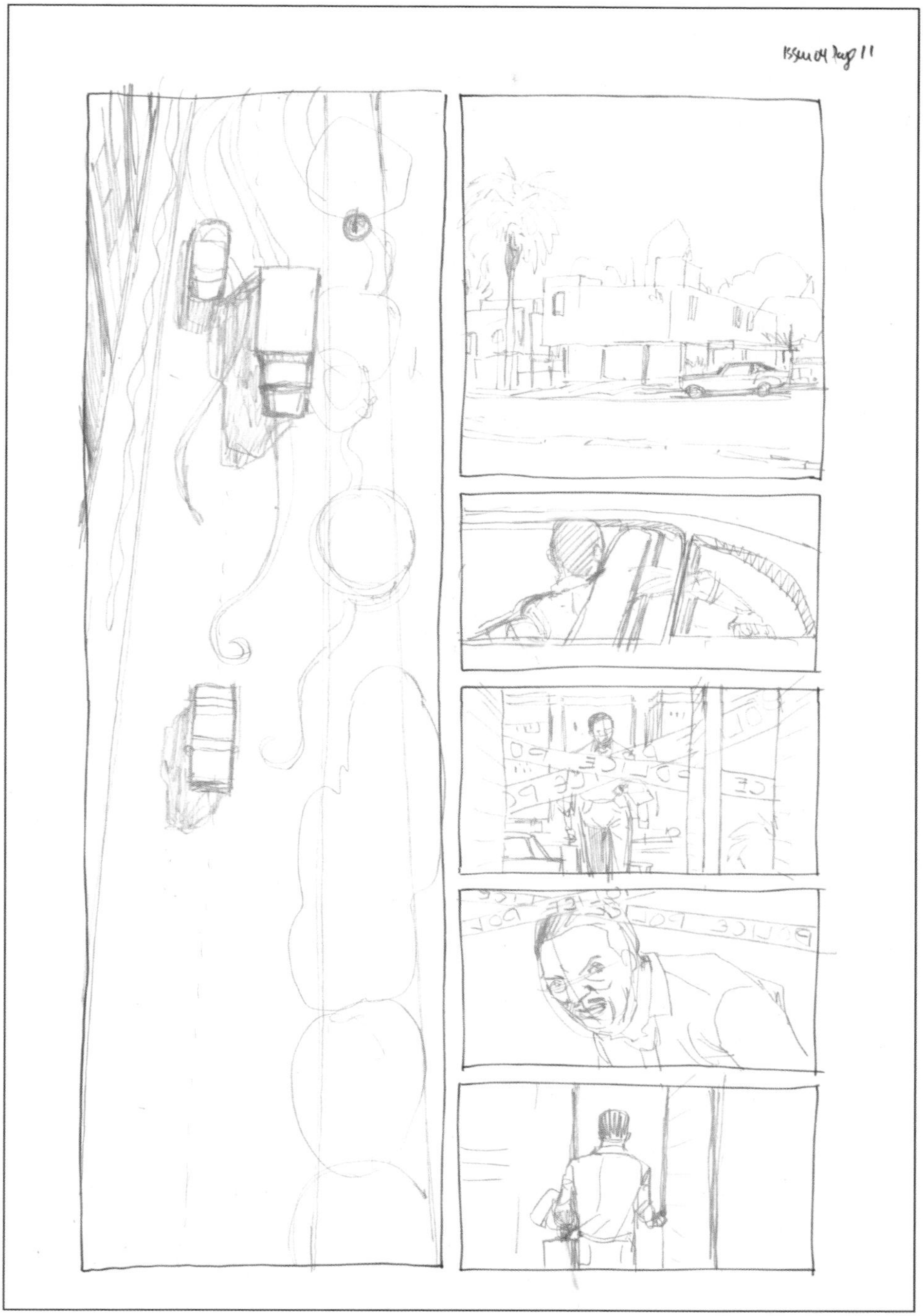
Issue 04 Page 11
POLICE

Pencils for page 11, issue 4. Typically, as in all of my projects, I attempt to put "just enough" detail into the pencils. This allows life and vibrancy to remain in the ink stage. Also, it's more fun, since the ink drawing is the only actual piece of finished art. The roughs and pencils are very clearly stepping stones.

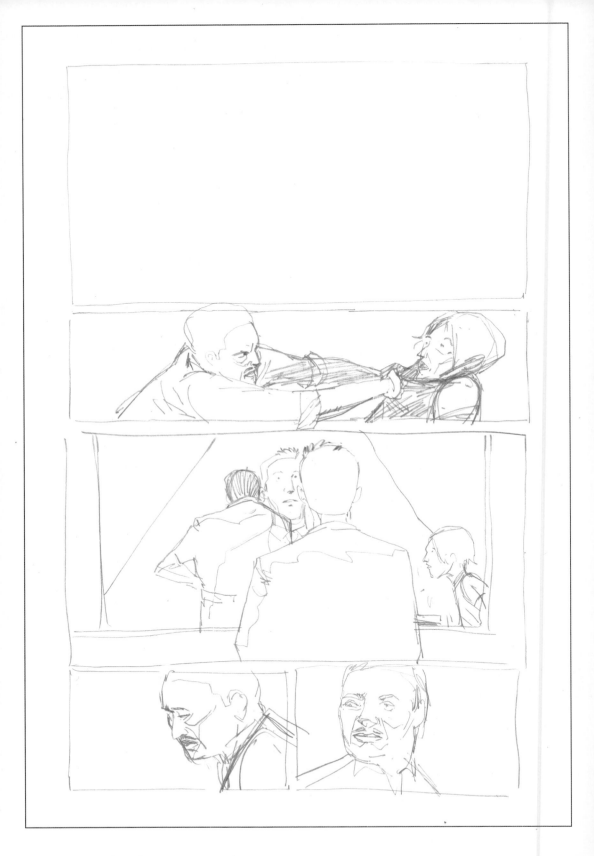

And back to drawing in pencil.

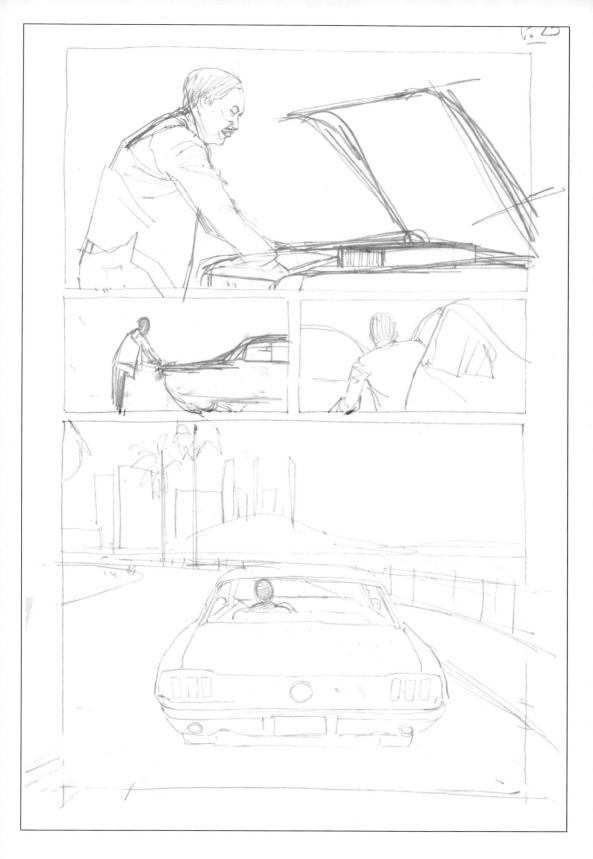

My lord, that suit in panel 1 is way too short. Also, I can't use the actual car logo, but it's not like those taillights aren't a dead giveaway!

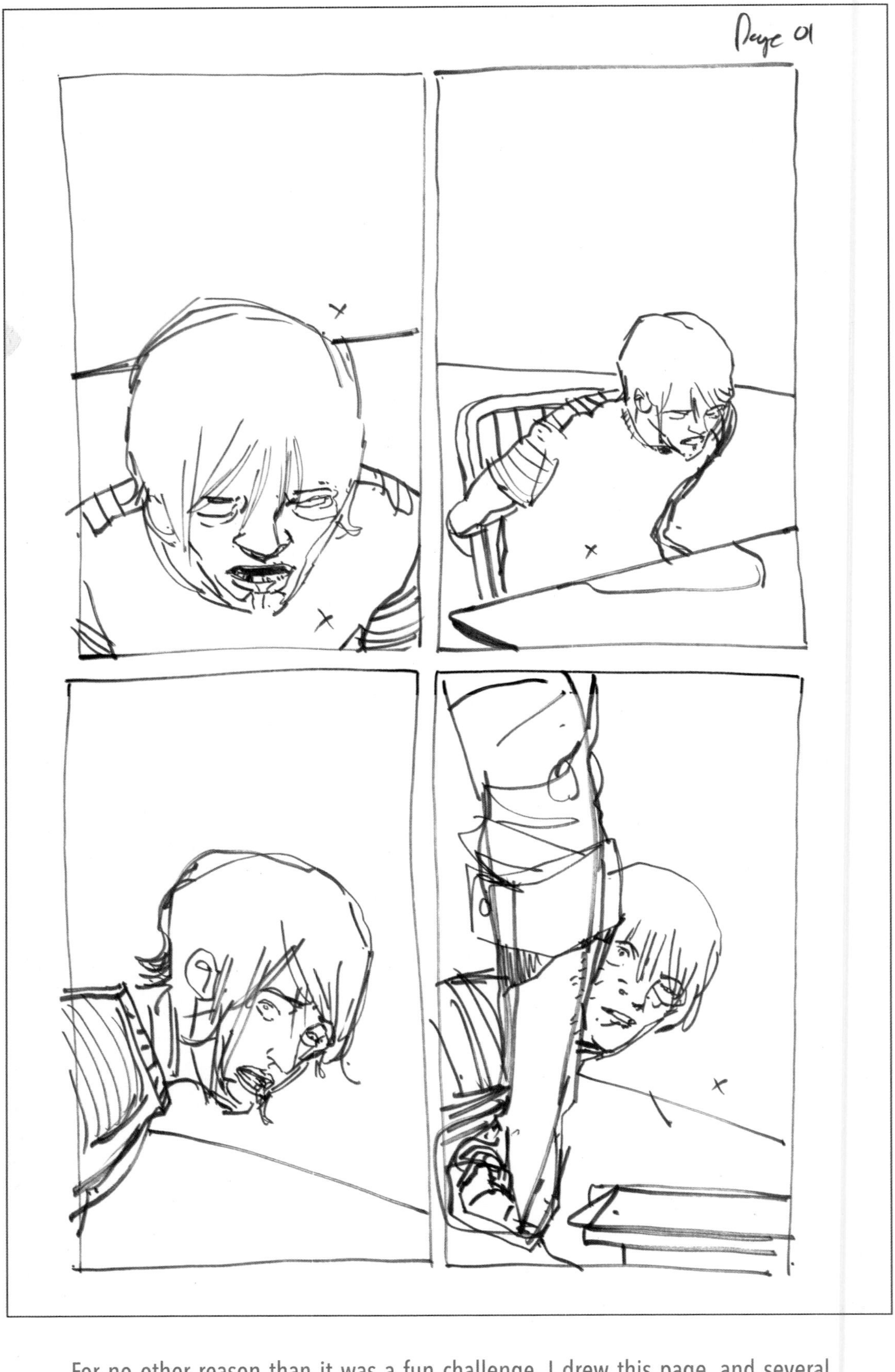
Page 01

For no other reason than it was a fun challenge, I drew this page, and several others, in marker only. No erasing. If I messed it up . . . redraw. I like when I nail it in almost one take.

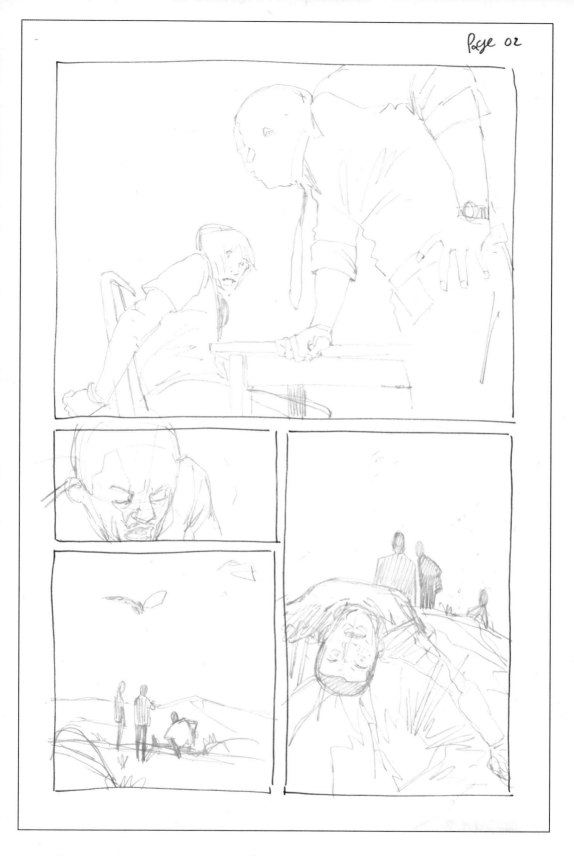

This was clearly a very emotional page to draw. I don't feel I did the death of our hero justice. And yet, maybe that's the point, a quiet death of no universal significance. A metaphor for the crushing power of evil.

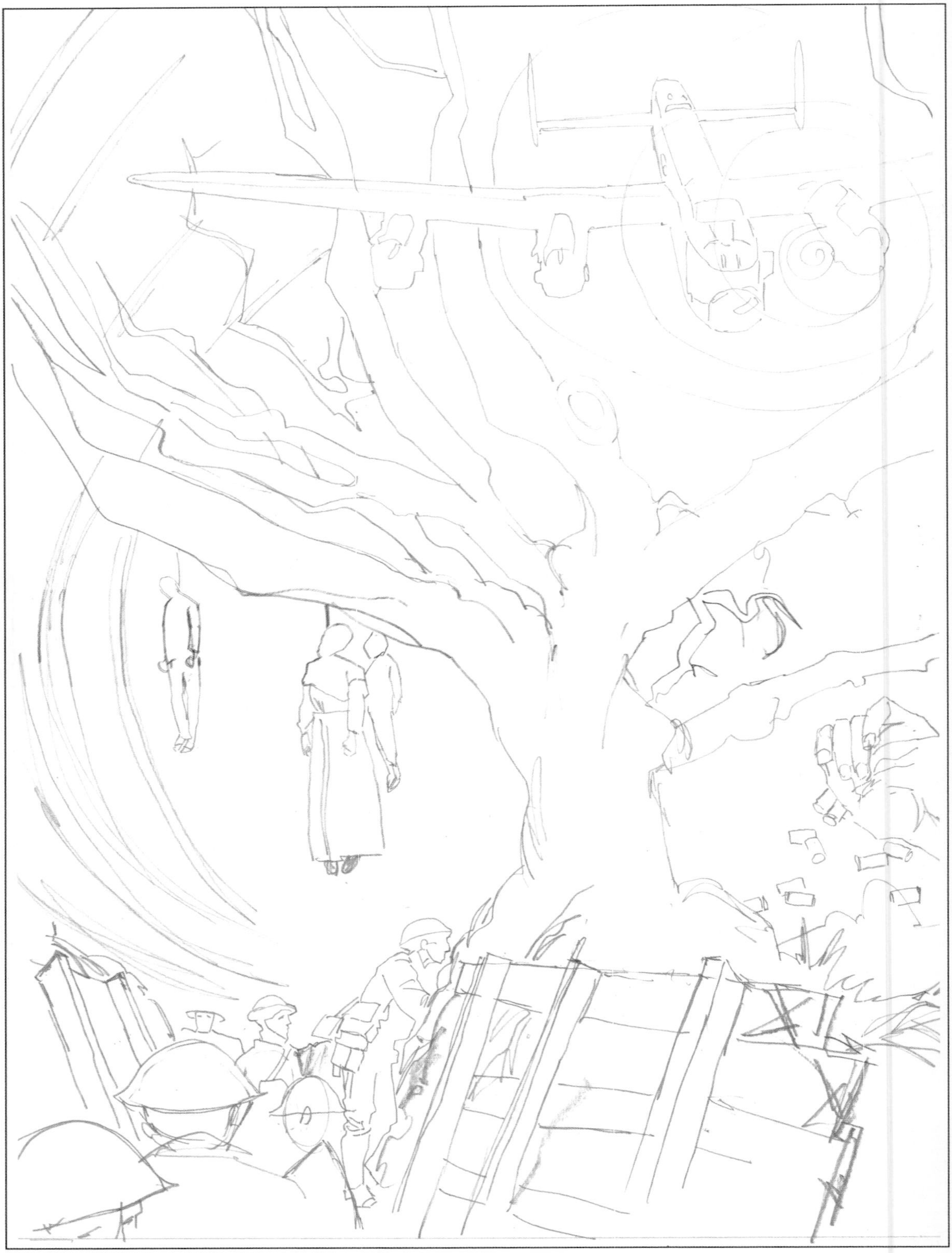

This double-page spread was so very much fun to create. I am a huge fan, and always have been, of montage-style illustrations. It goes hand in hand with growing up on a complete diet of Drew Struzan art.

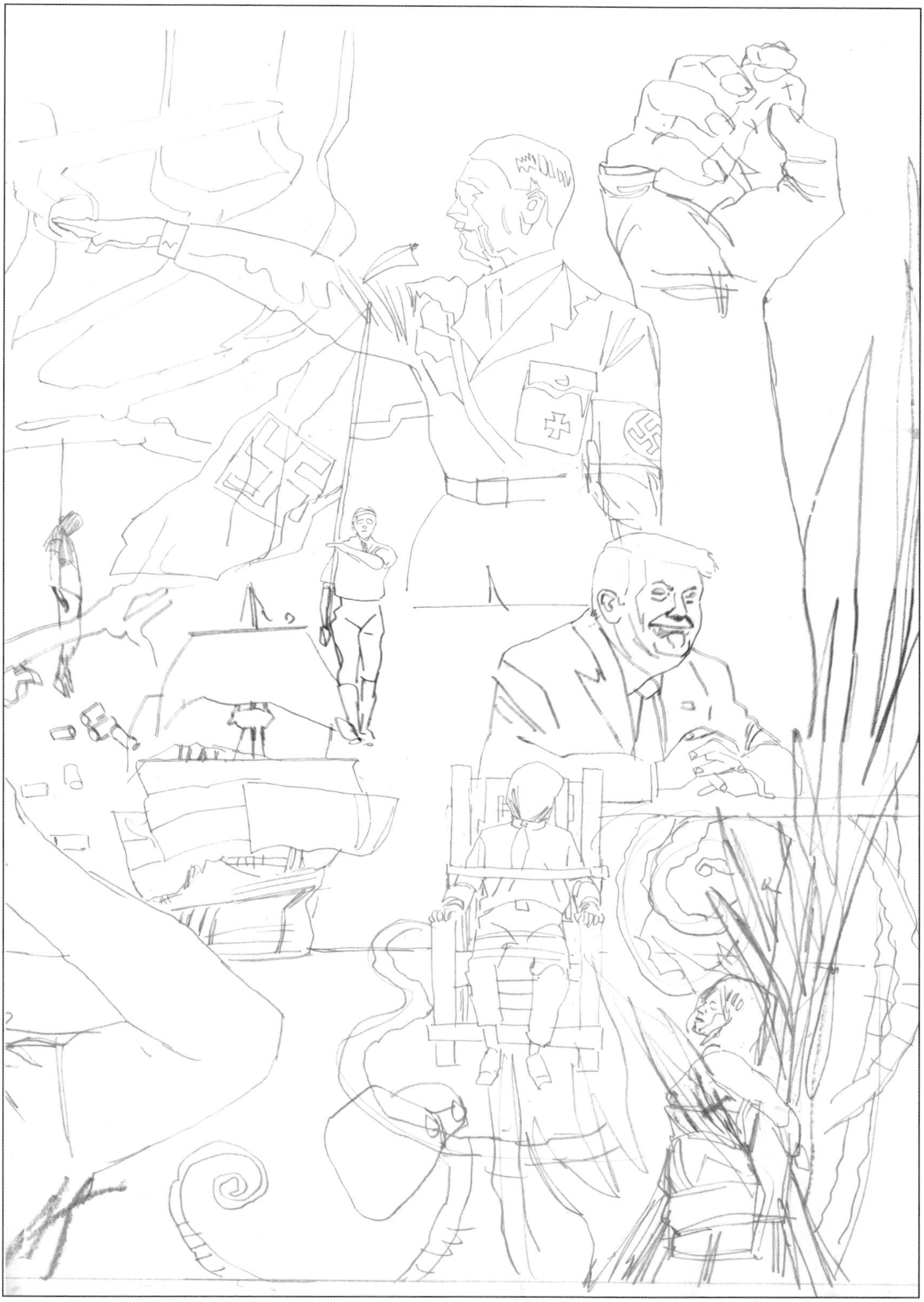

Trump is such an ass. Its hard to capture such dense, idiotic, criminal, and commonplace ignorance. Such an unbelievably uninspiring villian. Regardless, as I said, the montage is a wonderful design challenge.

matt kindt

"I'll read anything Kindt does." —Douglas Wolk, author of *Reading Comics*

MIND MGMT OMNIBUS
VOLUME 1: THE MANAGER
AND THE FUTURIST
ISBN 978-1-50670-460-9
$24.99

VOLUME 2: THE HOME
MAKER AND THE MAGICIAN
ISBN 978-1-50670-461-6
$24.99

VOLUME 3: THE ERASER
AND THE IMMORTALS
ISBN 978-1-50670-462-3
$24.99

DEPT. H OMNIBUS
VOLUME 1
ISBN 978-1-50671-093-8
$24.99

VOLUME 2
ISBN 978-1-50671-094-5
$24.99

**POPPY! AND THE
LOST LAGOON**
With Brian Hurtt
ISBN 978-1-61655-943-4
$14.99

PAST AWAYS
With Scott Kolins
ISBN 978-1-61655-792-8
$19.99

**THE COMPLETE
PISTOLWHIP**
With Jason Hall
ISBN 978-1-61655-720-1
$27.99

**3 STORY: THE SECRET
HISTORY OF THE
GIANT MAN NEW
EXPANDED EDITION**
ISBN 978-1-50670-622-1
$19.99

2 SISTERS
ISBN 978-1-61655-721-8
$27.99

BANG!
ISBN 978-1-50671-616-9
$19.99

ETHER
With David Rubín

VOLUME 1: DEATH OF THE LAST
GOLDEN BLAZE
ISBN 978-1-50670-174-5
$14.99

VOLUME 2: COPPER GOLEMS
ISBN 978-1-61655-991-5
$19.99

VOLUME 3: THE
DISAPPEARANCE OF
VIOLET BELL
ISBN 978-1-50671-151-5
$19.99

ETHER LIBRARY EDITION
ISBN 978-1-50671-152-2
$59.99

FEAR CASE
With Tyler and Hilary Jenkins
ISBN 978-1-50672-123-1
$19.99

CRIMSON FLOWER
With Matt Lesniewski
and Bill Crabtree
ISBN 978-1-50672-197-2
$19.99

**BLACK HAMMER '45:
FROM THE WORLD OF
BLACK HAMMER**
With Jeff Lemire, Ray Fawkes,
and Sharlene Kindt
ISBN 978-1-50670-850-8
$17.99

**BLACK HAMMER:
STREETS OF SPIRAL**
With Jeff Lemire, Dean Ormston,
Emi Lenox, and others
ISBN 978-1-50670-941-3
$19.99

**THE WORLD OF BLACK
HAMMER LIBRARY
EDITION VOLUME 2**
ISBN 978-1-50671-996-2
$49.99